SHAKESPEARE'S
ENGLISH
KINGS

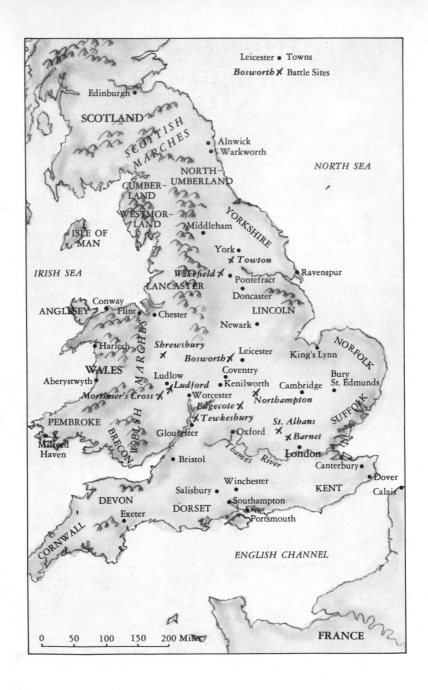

Leicester ● Towns
Bosworth ✗ Battle Sites

Edinburgh ●

SCOTLAND

*SCOTTISH
MARCHES*

● Alnwick
● Warkworth

NORTH SEA

NORTH–
UMBERLAND

CUMBER–
LAND

WESTMOR–
LAND

YORKSHIRE

ISLE OF
MAN

● Middleham

IRISH SEA

York ●
✗ *Towton*

Wakefield ✗
● Pontefract
● Ravenspur

LANCASTER

Doncaster ●

Conway
ANGLESEY ● Flint ●
● Chester

LINCOLN

● Harlech

Newark ●

Shrewsbury
✗

Bosworth ✗
Leicester ●

King's Lynn ●

NORFOLK

WALES

WELSH MARCHES

Ludlow
● *Ludford*

Coventry ●
● Kenilworth

Cambridge ●

Bury
St. Edmunds ●

Aberystwyth ●

Mortimer's Cross ✗
● Worcester

Northampton ✗

SUFFOLK

Edgecote ✗
✗ *Tewkesbury*

St. Albans
✗
✗ *Barnet*

PEMBROKE

BRECON

Gloucester ●

● Oxford

Milford
Haven

Thames River

London

● Bristol

Canterbury ●

Winchester ●

● Dover

DEVON

Salisbury ●
● Southampton

KENT

Calais

CORNWALL

Exeter ●

DORSET

● Portsmouth

ENGLISH CHANNEL

0   50   100   150   200 Miles

FRANCE

SHAKESPEARE'S ENGLISH KINGS

history, chronicle, and drama

PETER SACCIO

NEW YORK
OXFORD UNIVERSITY PRESS
1977

Maps drawn by David Lindroth

Copyright © 1977 by Peter Saccio
Library of Congress Catalogue Card Number: 76-42676
Printed in the United States of America

pRefatoRy note

This book recounts English history during the reigns of eight Plantagenet kings and one Tudor. That is, it concerns the people and events that Shakespeare put on stage in his ten history plays. I have written with an eye on the differences between medieval history as we now understand it and Shakespeare's version of that history. I hope that the book will be useful to students of Shakespeare, theatergoers, and general readers interested in these kings and these plays. My precise scope and purposes are more fully described in the first chapter.

Since childhood I have found the Plantagenets to be highly enjoyable, if occasionally disconcerting, company. Although some of them behaved like gangsters, they were at least high-minded and gorgeous gangsters, and they ruled England—often well—for three centuries. Shakespeare lavished ten years of his art upon them. Englishmen of their own and succeeding times held strong views about them; they inspire controversy still among modern historians; and I have some definite opinions about them, opinions that I have occasionally let creep into these pages. But I have no thesis to argue: I wish chiefly to provide information. My work is based largely on secondary sources, as acknowledged in the bibliography.

I am glad to thank a number of persons who have aided me

greatly in my work. James Steffensen first suggested that such a book would be useful and urged me to write it. Andrew Schuller and John Wright, with a patience unusual even in editors, slowly wrested the manuscript out of me, and Ellen Royer energetically coped with its peculiarities. Robert Grams Hunter, James A. Epperson, David Scott Kastan, and Colcord Frerichs have good-naturedly read various chapters and made many helpful comments and corrections. Professor Hunter has been particularly gracious in allowing me to use several of his own delicious phrases. I am especially grateful to Charles T. Wood, who has generously shared with me his detailed and extensive knowledge, and to Noel Perrin, who has been a considerate and encouraging departmental chairman as well as a keen-eyed and kindly critic.

None of these persons should be held responsible for any errors of fact or judgment that appear here. There are bound to be some. Aside from the ordinary fallibility of human nature, I am a literary scholar, not a professional historian. The need this book serves is adequately filled by no short, easily available work that I know of. That, together with the fun of writing about these old kings, must be my excuse for entering a marsh where better-trained historians than I have sought firm footing and often found it not.

My deepest debt is to my mother, who, by giving me a novel about Catherine Swynford when I was eleven, addicted me to the Plantagenets for life.

Sanborn House   Peter Saccio
Dartmouth College
April 1976

contents

Contents

SHAKESPEARE'S
ENGLISH
KINGS

hιstoRy and hιstoRy plays

Methinks the truth should live from age to age.

Late in Shakespeare's *Richard III,* three royal ladies, the dowager queens Margaret and Elizabeth and the dowager duchess of York, sit upon the ground to catalogue their losses:

> Margaret. I had an Edward, till a Richard killed him;
> I had a Harry, till a Richard killed him.
> [*to Elizabeth:*]
> Thou hadst an Edward, till a Richard killed him;
> Thou hadst a Richard, till a Richard killed him.
> Duchess [*to Margaret*].
> I had a Richard too, and thou didst kill him;
> I had a Rutland too, thou holpst to kill him.
> Margaret [*to Duchess*].
> Thou hadst a Clarence too, and Richard killed him.
> From forth the kennel of thy womb hath crept
> A hellhound that doth hunt us all to death.

This passage of mingled mourning and rebuke is a fitting summary of the self-destructiveness of the royal house of Plantagenet. Margaret and the duchess, ancient enemies, lament their dead and savagely point out each other's guilt for the deaths. But *who* are all these people? Some the playgoer or play-reader knows: the murderous Richard is the hero-villain of the piece, and several scenes have been devoted to his killing Clarence and the Edward and Richard of lines three and four. But Harry has appeared in this play only as a corpse, while the Edward of line one and the duchess's Richard and Rutland perished in an earlier play much less familiar to modern audiences. All these persons, moreover, are not only intricately related to each other in a prolific royal house, but also surrounded by a gallery of Norfolks, Suffolks, Warwicks, and Northumberlands connected to them by blood, marriage, alliance, or common interests, a throng confusing to a modern reader who tries to keep track of the large casts.

Shakespeare wrote eight plays on the later Plantagenets. Oddly, he did not write them in chronological order. He started with a tetralogy on the events from 1422 to 1485—the three parts of *Henry VI, Richard III*—and then, dovetailing into the previous work, composed a tetralogy whose story runs from 1398 to 1422—*Richard II,* the two parts of *Henry IV, Henry V.* Although the plays vary in quality, the first set being prentice work compared to the second, and although the reverse-chronological order of writing suggests that he started with an incomplete vision of the whole, the series of eight has high coherence as a history of fifteenth-century England. Indeed, far more than any professional historian, and despite the fact that the professionals have improved upon him in historical accuracy, Shakespeare is responsible for whatever notions most of us possess about the period and its political leaders. It is he who has etched upon the common memory the graceful fecklessness of Richard II, the exuberant heroism of Henry V, the dazzling villainy of Richard III.

Unfortunately, such central characterizations are often all that we retain from Shakespeare's history plays. Sometimes they are all a reader or playgoer ever firmly grasps. Not that Shakespeare neglected the exposition of surrounding circumstances: the problem lies in us. The characteristic complexity of Elizabethan plays suggests that Elizabethan audiences were more accustomed to comprehending a large cast and an intricate plot than modern drama has trained us to be. In the history plays, moreover, Shakespeare could rely upon a measure of prior knowledge in his audience. For example, *Richard II* opens with (among other things) the dramatic question, "Who killed the duke of Gloucester?" Many Elizabethan theatergoers would have known who this duke was and why his death provoked a political crisis. The Elizabethans frequently derived from the reign of Richard II analogies to their own political problems. To a modern audience the question seems less than pressing. Editors of Shakespeare, of course, write explanatory introductions and footnotes. Introductions, however, are usually brief, and footnotes, by nature fragmentary, are awkward vehicles for conveying any quantity of historical information as well as distracting interruptions for a reader concerned with the dramatic values of a scene. As a teacher of Shakespeare and an inveterate eavesdropper on lobby conversation at the various Stratfords, I find that many people let most of the history slip, consigning much of the dialogue about past relationships, present claims, and future intentions to a dimly perceived penumbra uneasily labelled "political complication." The process is understandable but unfortunate: it robs the playgoer of a good deal of the theatrical experience, and it places in the way of the student a considerable barrier to intelligent criticism of the plays.

Aside from the double tetralogy, Shakespeare wrote two other plays on English history, one on King John (reigned 1199–1216) and one on Henry VIII (reigned 1509–1547). These are also fairly intricate works, and about these kings as well Shakespeare could expect at least some of his audience to be knowledgeable. Since both of these plays are entirely self-contained works, not part of a series employing cross-reference between plays, their potential for confusing the reader is somewhat smaller. They present a different version of the problem: moderns are surprised by the contents of the plays. Nowadays if ordinary readers know anything at all about John before they take up the play, they know that his barons forced him to seal Magna Carta, an event that is held to be of great constitutional significance in the history of English-speaking peoples. Shakespeare does not even allude to Magna Carta, although the play dramatizes the baronial revolt that led to it. If ordinary readers know anything about Henry VIII, they know that he married six wives and brought about the English Reformation. There may also leap to mind the image of a cruel and gross king, handy with the chopping block and boorish in his table manners. Shakespeare's play, however, includes only two of the wives, deals scantily with the Reformation, and generally portrays the king with the greatest respect. With these two kings, Shakespeare has had little influence upon the common memory. Constitutional struggles after Shakespeare's time endowed Magna Carta with its present nearly sacred character, and the popular notion of Henry VIII owes a great deal to Holbein's paintings, a television series, movies, and historical romances.

This book is intended as background reading for Shakespeare's ten history plays. Only incidentally does it touch upon criticism or the more specialized problems of Shakespearean source-study: many excellent books are available on the artistry and the significance of these plays. I aim to provide a brief coherent account of English history in the reigns concerned, concentrating on the persons and the issues that Shakespeare dramatized. I hope that it will serve as a clear introduction and a useful work of reference for the complicated story told by the plays, so that the reader and playgoer may enjoy Shakespeare more fully and more swiftly. I have composed the narrative so that those pressed for time and interested only in certain plays may, after reading this introductory chapter, turn immediately to sections that concern them. I hope that others will wish, with Shakespeare, to grasp the whole saga.

Since students and playgoers may be thrust into the double tetralogy at any number of different points, it would be well, before plunging into detailed narration, to sketch the main lines of fifteenth-century English history. (Save insofar as this chapter will close with a few generalizations about Shakespeare's handling of history, the following remarks will not concern the two independent plays, *King John* and *Henry VIII.*) Different accounts and interpretations of the fifteenth century have of course prevailed at different times. Distinguishing them is one of the tasks of this book. Since Shakespeare's version is dominated by a struggle within the royal house, the following summary stresses the dynastic issue.

We must begin with Edward III, seventh of the Plantagenet kings and ruler of England for the middle half of the fourteenth century (1327–1377). This monarch's extraordinary capacity for begetting offspring lies at the root of subsequent internecine strife. Of his twelve legitimate children, five sons grew up, were endowed with extensive powers and possessions within the kingdom, and passed these on to their issue. As long as the royal family itself remained united, Edward's generosity to his sons constituted an effective policy for governing England. In the absence of family harmony, the kingdom was almost sure to follow the Plantagenets into disorder.

Family harmony hinged largely upon the strength of the king. Unfortunately, Edward III's eldest son and heir, Edward the Black Prince, predeceased his father. Consequently, upon Edward III's death the crown went to a boy ten years old, the Black Prince's son Richard II. Although Richard stayed on the throne for twenty-two years, distinguishing himself in several crises by great personal courage, his reign never fully recovered from the circumstances of its inception. Surrounded as he was by powerful, not to say greedy, uncles and cousins, Richard the child was perforce submissive and Richard the adult tyrannically vengeful. Finally, in 1399, he overreached himself. After the death of his most powerful uncle, John of Gaunt duke of Lancaster, he seized the Lancastrian estates. Gaunt's son Henry of Bolingbroke, exiled in Paris, returned to England and gathered an army. Although

Bolingbroke's professed aim was merely the recovery of his inheritance, he soon pushed Richard off the throne, into prison, and (some months later) into his grave, there being little else to do with a deposed medieval king.

As Henry IV, first king of the Lancaster branch, Bolingbroke was a ruler with obvious liabilities: a flawed title to his crown, blood on his hands, and debts in his pocket. Of the three, the debts were the most immediately important. Various noblemen had helped him to his precarious height. As soon as he displeased them (and no king can afford continual complaisance), it occurred to them to help him down again. For most of his reign, Henry's energies were consumed in meeting rebellions. As he was a shrewd politician and a competent soldier, he contrived to defeat the dissidents and die in his bed (1413). The record of his son was more spectacular. Henry V was another shrewd politician and probably the best general ever to sit on the English throne. Reviving an old claim of the English kings to the crown of France, he united his nobles by leading an expeditionary army across the Channel. At the end of two campaigns he was the acknowledged master of both kingdoms.

At this climactic moment history began to repeat itself. In 1422 Henry V died of dysentery at the age of thirty-five. The heir to two crowns, his son Henry VI, was nine months old. The house of Lancaster, having won its throne out of the turmoils of a royal minority, came to grief two generations later by producing a similar vacuum at the center of power.

Henry VI remained king of England for nearly forty years, but only nominally. The royal child became an adult saintly in personal character, incompetent in politics, and subject to occasional mental derangement. The royal uncles and cousins, in concert and in rivalry, asserted themselves. Driven out of France, which had been reinvigorated by Joan of Arc, they retired to England to bicker with each other. By the 1450s, their quarrelling had become armed conflict. In 1460, one of the royal cousins went so far as to claim superior right to Henry's crown. This was Richard duke of York, descended on both sides from sons of Edward III. Since his mother was heiress of the Mortimer family, the line springing from John of Gaunt's elder brother Lionel, Richard did indeed have a powerful claim, although it depended upon the principle that the royal succession could pass through a female—a controversial notion. The civil war thereupon became the dynastic struggle conventionally known as the Wars of the Roses: the Yorkists (white rose), led by Richard, versus the Lancastrians (red rose), led nominally by Henry but actually by his remarkable wife, the energetic Margaret of Anjou. When the dust finally settled, Richard, Henry, and Henry's son Edward were all dead, and occupying the throne was the house of York in the person of Richard's eldest son, Edward IV.

Except for a brief Lancastrian restoration in 1470–1471, Edward ruled competently for twenty-two years. Indeed, according to the arguments of recent historians, the reorganization of government that created the strong monarchy of the next century was in good part Edward's work. Dynastically, however, he created two serious difficulties for his house. First, instead of marrying the usual foreign princess, he wed an English widow named Elizabeth Woodville, a lady with an extraordinary quantity of relatives who promptly took advantage of their new royal connection by securing for themselves an abundance of titles, posts, and wealthy spouses. The inevitable quarrels between the older nobility and the upstart Woodvilles boded ill for the house of York. All might have been well but for the other dynastic difficulty: Edward died at the age of forty, when his two sons, Edward V and Richard, were but twelve and nine years old.

The familiar script was acted out once more, but this time at top speed. When Edward died in April 1483, the Woodvilles had custody of the young princes, whereas by the king's will authority was to reside in his brother Richard duke of Gloucester, who had no use at all for Woodvilles. Within three months and without a battle, the Woodvilles were out, the princes had disappeared forever, and Gloucester was crowned Richard III.

Richard's bold stroke, however, gave him only a two-year reign. In August 1485, one Henry Tudor invaded England from France, and the treachery of some of Richard's followers cost the last Plantagenet king his life at the battle of Bosworth. Henry claimed the crown by right of conquest and by Lancastrian inheritance: his mother was descended from the Beaufort family, John of Gaunt's bastard offspring who had been legitimated when Gaunt made his mistress his third wife. This rather feeble dynastic claim was strengthened by parliamentary confirmation and by Henry's subsequent marriage to Elizabeth of York, eldest daughter to Edward IV and sister to the missing princes. York and Lancaster were united in the new house of Tudor. The claim was made impregnable by Henry's efficiency as a king and by his and his son Henry VIII's thoroughness in disposing of the remaining Plantagenet heirs. The dynastic quarrel was over.

The preceding summary of fifteenth-century English history makes the dynastic issue paramount. Royal persons argue over who has the right to the crown; laws of inheritance and precise family relationships appear to control events altogether. To rest there, however, would be to falsify the picture. For example, given female succession, Richard duke of York did have a better claim than his cousin Henry VI. He refrained, however, from pressing that claim for many years; even after he asserted it, he was content at one point to be declared Henry's heir rather than his replacement. The original usurpation, that of Henry IV in 1399, was accomplished without much thought being given to the superior rights of the Mortimer line that was later to prove so troublesome. There was in the fifteenth century no written law governing inheritance of the crown, not even any established practice beyond the first principle that the eldest son of a king should succeed. Even the case of a grandson, as with Richard II, could raise some question, let alone circumstances involving more than two generations or descent through a woman. The various acts of parliament confirming monarchical titles in this period did little more than ratify accomplished fact, producing the genealogical justification appropriate to the case at hand and conveniently omitting whatever else might be said about the family tree. Whether parliament even had the right to declare who was king was a very delicate matter, debated then, and still under discussion by constitutional historians. This does not mean that anybody with sufficient influence, military capacity, and luck could have secured the crown for himself. The blood royal was necessary. Henry Tudor's promise to join his Lancastrian claim to the Yorkist claim by marrying a Yorkist princess brought him significant support. Given *some* dynastic justification, however, other factors determined the outcome.

Of other factors there was an abundance. International politics played a role. Edward IV's recovery from the brief Lancastrian restoration of 1470–1471 was made possible by the assistance of the duke of Burgundy. Henry Tudor's attack on Richard III received aid from the king of France. Needless to say, these continental rulers were not acting out of disinterested charity. England, France, and Burgundy were engaged in ceaseless diplomatic maneuvering, each power fearful of alliance between the other two.

Probably more important than external pressures were social and economic conditions within England. The original Lancastrian usurpation was for many people vindicated by the success of the first two Lancastrian kings. Only in the social chaos of Henry VI's time, when the incompetence and the injustice of Henry's government were exacerbated by chagrin at the loss of France, did the York-Mortimer claim receive significant support. Edward IV's hold on the crown was in turn made acceptable to most people by his strenuous effort to correct local abuses and stabilize the royal finances. The usurpation of his brother Richard III was welcomed by some who feared another prolonged royal minority and who respected Richard as an energetic administrator.

Possibly even more important influences upon events—at least at any given moment—were the ambitions of individual noblemen outside the royal family. The immediate success of a royal claimant depended very largely upon his ability to attract support from nobles who could call up a fighting force, and these nobles were not driven by abstract passions for the rights of Lancaster or York. They aimed to secure properties or protect rights of their own; an alliance with a Henry or an Edward arose from temporarily congruent interests. Much betrayal and side-switching resulted. In 1455–1461, for example, the house of York had no greater ally than the earl of Warwick, who was the duchess of York's nephew; yet in 1470 Warwick betrothed his daughter to the Lancastrian heir and drove Edward IV temporarily from the throne. Perhaps influenced by modern civil wars fought on fundamental ideological issues, we are likely to imagine the York-Lancaster strife as an affair of more massive, coherent, and irreconcilable parties than was the case. Our inclination is reinforced by the romantic label, the Wars of the Roses, evoking as it does a vision of England divided into two camps whose members proudly flourished their red or white badges. In fact, there was almost no ideology involved, the armies were very small, and England went unscathed by any general destruction of life or property. As for the roses, they were made prominent by the Tudor historians rather than the Plantagenet combatants, popularized by Shakespeare, and turned into the standard formal name for the war only in the nineteenth century.*

* As S. B. Chrimes has pointed out, the Plantagenets had many heraldic badges. A red rose was only one of those used by the dukes of Lancaster and their descendants Henry IV and Henry V, and it was not employed by Henry VI, the Lancastrian king under whom the wars were fought. Richard duke of York inherited a white rose from the Mortimers, but it was seldom used by Edward IV and never by Richard III. Henry VII revived the Lancastrian red rose and, to emphasize his union of the rival houses, invented the Tudor double rose, white superimposed upon red. Some recent historians have eschewed the term "Wars of the Roses": they consider it anachronistic (which doesn't matter: many

Just what did happen in the fifteenth century remains in many respects a puzzle. Vital documentary evidence has survived incompletely. Contemporary accounts are few in number, written by less talented chroniclers than those of the earlier Middle Ages, infected by rumor, and occasionally disfigured by prejudice in favor of one king or another. Modern historians have treated the period as something of a stepchild, a disorderly interlude between the achievements of the early Plantagenets and those of the Tudor Renaissance. Although much sound research has been done recently and many good books are available, there is little agreement on a number of issues and no authoritative history of the century. The relevant volume of the Oxford History of England, for example, is valuably detailed and instructive, but, significantly, it was the last (aside from the twentieth-century volume) of this standard series to appear, and the author is said to have revised repeatedly without feeling that he had achieved the desired synthesis.

In the following chapters, therefore, I shall be distinguishing among various perspectives. First, there is a modern understanding of what happened in the fifteenth century, incomplete and full of questions though it be, built up by research historians. Secondly, there is a Tudor understanding. Henry VII commissioned an Italian humanist, Polydore Vergil, to write an official history of England. Vergil's book is the foundation of a lively tradition of Tudor historiography, culminating in two works that were Shakespeare's principal sources of information: Edward Hall's *The Union of the Two Noble and Illustre Families of Lancaster and York* (1548) and Raphael Holinshed's *The Chronicles of England, Ireland, and Scotland* (1578; Shakespeare used the second edition, 1587). Basic to these Tudor accounts is a belief in

---

events have been named long after they occurred) and falsifying (this does matter: the phrase directs too much attention to the dynastic issue). I shall use the phrase: the roses can scarcely be avoided in discussing Shakespeare's version of the wars.

Henry VII as the savior of England. In part this belief sprang from the necessity to justify the Tudor acquisition of the throne: Richard III, for example, is made more spectacularly villainous than any man could possibly be, so that Tudor monarchy may appear the more desirable. In part the belief arose from the widespread sixteenth-century conviction that secular history displays patterns reflecting God's providential guidance of human affairs. Thus the deposition of Richard II is seen as a sacrilegious act interrupting the succession of God's anointed kings, a kind of original sin for which England and her rulers must suffer. The Lancastrians are then punished for their usurpation by the Yorkists, and the Yorkists by their own last king, until, England having atoned in blood, redemption may come in the form of Henry Tudor and his union of the rival houses. Thirdly, there is a Shakespearean perspective. This is, of course, still largely Tudor, since Shakespeare is writing during the reign of Henry's granddaughter, Queen Elizabeth, and drawing his material from Hall and Holinshed. Nonetheless, despite their large areas of agreement, the Tudor chroniclers, poets, and playwrights who dealt with historical matters (there were many) were certainly capable of individual interpretations of men and events. Shakespeare especially deviates from the received accounts because he is translating relatively formless chronicles into drama, taking historical liberties out of artistic necessity. Although there are limits on the liberties he can take—there is no point at all in writing a history play about Richard III if you have him *win* at Bosworth—he can, and does, change the personalities of historical figures, invent characters, compress the chronology, alter the geography, devise confrontations that never took place, commit anachronisms, and so forth. Margaret of Anjou, whose savage lamentations were quoted at the beginning of this chapter, had in fact been dead for a year at the time the scene is supposed to occur. Above all, Shakespeare personalizes. Whether or not history is really governed by the characters and the choices of individual men and women, the dramatist can only write as if it were. Social conditions, cultural habits, economic forces, justice and the lack of it, all that we mean by "the times," must be translated into persons and passions if they are to hold the stage.

Artist Unknown: *Richard II* (National Portrait Gallery).

҂ II ҂

RICHARD II
the fall of the king

More are men's ends marked than their lives before.

1. RICHARD'S REIGN TO 1397

Richard II reigned over England for slightly more than twenty-two years, from June 1377 to September 1399. For Englishmen of the succeeding two centuries, however, all that Richard did and suffered in his first twenty-one years of rule seemed insignificant beside his final loss of the crown to his cousin Henry of Bolingbroke. Modern scholars have protested against the distortion that arises from viewing a sequence of events solely through the glass of its final outcome. Social historians now rightly dwell upon the Peasants' Revolt, which occurred in 1381, and the influential proto-Protestantism of John Wyclif, who died in 1384. Constitutional historians properly investigate parliament's discovery and development of the powers of impeachment in 1376 and 1386. Literary historians naturally stress the works of Chaucer, who was writing throughout the reign. Biographers of the king himself fairly suggest that overemphasis on his final failure obscures his earlier achievements and the personal qualities that made them possible. But for most of those who lived under the

17

sway of the later Plantagenets and the Tudors, Richard was chiefly a king who fell. So much did his deposition dwarf his reign that two of the most important sixteenth-century writers concerned with him, the historian Edward Hall and the playwright William Shakespeare, began their accounts of him with the events of 1398, with the quarrel between Henry of Bolingbroke and Thomas Mowbray that precipitated Richard's downfall.

This quarrel, however, arose out of earlier conflicts to which Shakespeare alludes sparsely and unclearly. His original audience may have known enough about them not to have been puzzled. Some would have read Shakespeare's principal source, Holinshed's *Chronicles,* which gives a full account of the reign. More may have known a popular Elizabethan collection of verse-chronicles, *The Mirror for Magistrates,* which contains biographies of Richard and of several other persons important in the play. Habitual theatergoers might have known another Elizabethan play, the anonymous *Woodstock* (probably written shortly before Shakespeare's *Richard II* and sometimes called by modern scholars *Richard II Part 1*), which dramatizes major events between 1382 and 1397. But Holinshed, the *Mirror,* and *Woodstock* are now read only by specialists. Modern audiences and students may find a summary of events prior to the quarrel useful.

The quarrel was in fact the penultimate phase of a political struggle that recurred throughout Richard's reign. All political struggles, I suppose, involve the simple question, who is to rule? In late fourteenth-century England, the question took the form: who was to rule, given that the king was a minor? Even after the king grew up, the question altered only slightly: who was to advise, assist, and influence the king, given the factions, disputes, and attitudes that had developed during the king's minority? Indeed, the lines of conflict became clearer after Richard turned twenty: who was to wield power with and through the king, the king's personal favorites or those nobles (especially including the king's relatives) whose high position gave them a claim on public power?

Of relatives Richard had an ample supply. His grandfather, Edward III, had begotten, among other children, five sons who survived the perils of the fourteenth-century infancy, became figures of significance in the realm, and begot issue of their own. These were, in order of age, Edward prince of Wales (remembered by later generations as the Black Prince, presumably because of his black armor); Lionel duke of Clarence; John of Gaunt duke of Lancaster; Edmund duke of York; and Thomas of Woodstock duke of Gloucester (the protagonist of the anonymous Elizabethan play mentioned above). Of these five, Lionel does not figure in Richard's story: he died when Richard was a baby, and his descendants did not actively complicate the Plantagenet dynastic struggle until the next century. Edmund of York was apparently a person of mild temperament, certainly a political nonentity, who came into prominence only as an occasional council member or figurehead. The Black Prince, John of Gaunt, and Thomas of Woodstock, however, were energetic and ambitious men. The Black Prince had won great military renown in the Hundred Years War, the long conflict with France started in 1337 by Edward III. The prince's untimely death in 1376 left his only surviving son Richard heir to the throne. At that time, however, Edward III being sunk in senility, royal affairs were dominated by John of Gaunt. An action of parliament taken immediately after the Black Prince's death reveals a significant anxiety: the commons asked the king to send young Richard before them so that they might formally honor him as heir apparent. Evidently some feared that Gaunt was scheming to usurp the throne from his nine-year-old nephew as soon as the old king died. When Richard did succeed the next year, the council that was appointed to rule for him included none of the royal uncles.

In the ensuing struggle three groups of persons converging

upon the king stand out. John of Gaunt and his Lancastrian supporters comprise the first. Besides being the senior surviving uncle of the king, Gaunt was the greatest magnate in England, the possessor of castles, forests, manors, and other estates scattered throughout the realm. As Lancaster was a county palatine, a semiautonomous political entity, Gaunt had nearly regal powers within it: the duke's writ ran to the exclusion of the king's. These extensive properties brought him a host of supporters and agents: retainers, county officials, feudal tenants, and representatives of allied interests (e.g., London merchants). Shakespeare makes of this enormously powerful and wealthy man a patriotic and patriarchal figure of great probity and dignity: he is "old John of Gaunt, time-honored Lancaster." In this the playwright departs from his source Holinshed, who, with far greater historical accuracy, depicts Gaunt as a contentious and ambitious baron. Gaunt, in fact, spent three years of his nephew's reign (1386–1389) fighting unsuccessfully in Spain to enforce his own dubious claim to the crown of Castile. The commons disliked him and were suspicious of him, and the Kentish peasants gleefully sacked his great London palace in the Revolt of 1381. He was, however, fundamentally loyal to his nephew, and remained Richard's faithful advisor throughout the 1390s.

Gaunt's temporary withdrawal from English affairs may have been prompted not only by his desire to win a kingdom of his own but also by the growing importance of rivals for the king's ear. After the Peasants' Revolt, in which Richard displayed remarkable courage in winning the allegiance of an inflamed and hostile mob, Richard began choosing his own friends. Chief among these were Michael de la Pole, whom Richard made earl of Suffolk, and Edward de Vere, to whom Richard gave successively the exalted titles of marquess of Dublin and duke of Ireland. This court party, largely dependent upon his personal favor, encouraged him to break free of tutelage. Apparently Richard took their advice. From 1383 on, parliament frequently complained of the extravagance and instability of Richard's behavior and the evil counsel of the favorites who encouraged it. In 1386, after Gaunt's departure, a deputation of lords led by Richard's youngest uncle, Gloucester, rebuked Richard severely for misgovernment, parliament impeached de la Pole, and the entire charge of affairs was put into the hands of a new council. Richard responded the next year. During a long trip through the north and west, he consolidated a royalist following and arranged for a group of judges led by Sir Robert Tresilian to condemn the impeachment of de la Pole and the imposition of the new council as treasonable acts violating the royal prerogative.

At this point the third faction clearly emerged. The royal duke of Gloucester, together with two earls of long eminent family and some military fame, Warwick and Arundel, lodged in parliament an appeal (accusation) of treason against the favorites, and gathered an army of their own. In these actions they were later joined by two younger men, Gaunt's son Henry of Bolingbroke earl of Derby, and Thomas Mowbray earl of Nottingham. These five Lords Appellant, two from the royal family and all related to each other by marriage, represented the established nobility opposed to the king's new friends. They defeated the king's army (led by de Vere: Richard was no soldier) at Radcot Bridge in Oxfordshire. Then, in the so-called Merciless Parliament of 1388, they won their case against the favorites. Those royalists who had stayed in England, such as Tresilian, were executed; those who had fled abroad, such as de Vere and de la Pole, died in exile. Having carried out a massive purge, the Lords Appellant ruled for a year.

There is some evidence that Richard was very briefly deposed between the battle of Radcot Bridge and the trial of the favorites. If such an attempt was made, it foundered upon the Appellants' own failure to agree upon a successor. The king was carefully kept in the background during the parliamentary proceedings, and remained quiet during the Appellants' ascendancy. In 1389, now twenty-two years old, he announced his intention to rule on his own. The coalition of Appellants broke up, Gaunt returned from Spain, and a reasonable harmony prevailed for seven years, the brightest stretch of the reign. Richard carried out worthwhile projects with the help of a royal council that included Gaunt, friends of the king, and some of the former Appellants. In 1394 he achieved a pacification of Ireland that ranked as his most notable accomplishment since the Peasants' Revolt. Pursuing a peaceful foreign policy, he arranged in 1396 a long truce with France and cemented it dynastically by marrying the French king's daughter Isabel, then a child of seven. (Shakespeare's mature queen and her moving farewell to Richard in Act V of the play are unhistorical inventions.)

In 1397, however, the struggle between the king's friends and the nobles broke out again. This time the king played a larger role, and the personnel of the parties was slightly rearranged. The king's friends now included the duke of York's son Edward earl of Rutland, soon to be made duke of Albemarle (Shakespeare's Aumerle); Thomas Mowbray, reconciled with Richard since the Appellants crisis and soon to be made duke of Norfolk; and two of Richard's maternal relatives, his half-brother John Holland duke of Exeter and his nephew Thomas Holland duke of Surrey. (Richard's fondness for giving his friends ducal titles excited some ridicule: these four men became known as the *duketti,* or dukelings.) Also close to him were three members of parliament, Sir John Bushy, Sir William Bagot, and Sir Henry Greene, and the subchamberlain of the royal household, Sir William Scrope. (Bushy and Greene were Lancastrian officials, Bagot a dependent of Norfolk's. All three were respectable knights, but they received a bad press from subsequent chroniclers. By the time they reached Shakespeare, they had already been turned into what the playwright calls "the caterpillars of the commonwealth." Scrope, under his later title of earl of Wiltshire, is frequently mentioned but never appears in Shakespeare's play.) Bolingbroke's position at this time was vague. He had been pardoned by Richard, had sat briefly on the king's council, and would soon be given the duchy of Hereford, but he had had little to do with political affairs since his father's return, spending much time on crusade in Lithuania and on pilgrimage to Jerusalem. The senior Appellants, Gloucester, Arundel, and Warwick, were still hostile to the king.

The immediate cause of the crisis of 1397 is obscure. By some means Gloucester, Arundel, and Warwick once again offended the king: tales are told of refused royal summonses, of speeches disparaging Richard's foreign policy, and even of renewed plotting by the three lords. However incited, Richard suddenly arrested all three. Richard's motives at this point are also disputed. The occasion may have provided him with an opportunity for a thorough, if belated, revenge upon the Appellants. One of Richard's recent biographers has argued that the king, somewhat unbalanced by his previous misfortunes, had long been revolving plans of vengeance. On the other hand, he may have been moved by a larger, less personal motive: the desire to establish beyond question the indefeasibility of the royal sovereignty. Richard certainly held a theory of the kingly dignity and power more exalted than that of his predecessors. Shakespeare picks this up from Holinshed and has his Richard express a grandiose notion of monarchy, although it is couched of course in language and concepts developed by Elizabethan political theorists rather than in medieval terms. Whether historically Richard desired revenge or vindication of his prerogative, he certainly got both. His friends (Aumerle, Norfolk, Exeter, Surrey, and Wiltshire among others) lodged in parliament a bill of appeal against the three senior Appellants in a careful legal parody of the latters' appeal nine years earlier. In a well-planned procedure, with Gaunt as hereditary lord high steward prominent in the accusations and Bushy as speaker of the commons, the three lords were convicted. Warwick, breaking down and confessing, was exiled, and Arundel, defiant, was beheaded. A more mysterious fate befell Gloucester. In the middle of the trial Norfolk, who had been assigned to guard Gloucester in the fortress at Calais, announced that his prisoner had died there. Almost certainly he was murdered. Whether he was murdered at Richard's orders, and if so whether Norfolk was the agent, and if so whether Norfolk obeyed the command willingly or complied with it only after conscience-stricken delay, are questions that have never been satisfactorily settled.

Shakespeare's source, Holinshed, describes Gloucester as "fierce of nature, hasty, wilful . . . and in this greatly to be discommended, that he was ever repining against the king in all things." Although Gloucester had a popular following in the 1390s, and was certainly justified in some of his complaints against the king, Holinshed's judgment is reasonable in light of the historical facts as we presently know them. As the protagonist of the Elizabethan play *Woodstock,* however, he is a plain-spoken, well-intentioned, patriotic counsellor to a wayward young king. This latter conception lies behind all three of the royal uncles in Shakespeare's *Richard II.* In Gaunt such a figure is exalted with passionate eloquence. In York the type has been weakened with indecisiveness and semicomic confusion. Gloucester is of course dead at the curtain's rise, but his ghost, which haunts the opening scenes, is just such a "plain well-meaning soul." Richard's murder of him, suggested obliquely but never doubted, creates the moral weakness of the king's position in Acts I and II. A youthful, headstrong Richard resists the wisdom of his royal uncles, and his hands are stained with the royal blood.

2. THE BOLINGBROKE-NORFOLK QUARREL

Richard's destruction of the three senior Lords Appellant naturally alarmed the remaining two. Norfolk apparently warned Bolingbroke that the king might rescind the pardons they had received and "undo" them because of "the deed of Radcot Bridge." At any rate, Bolingbroke reported such a conversation to his father Gaunt. If this conversation actually occurred, it had an effect opposite to what Norfolk presumably intended. Warning Bolingbroke that Richard was not to be trusted, he failed to consider that Bolingbroke might not be any more reliable. And indeed he was not. Upon Gaunt's advice, Bolingbroke charged Norfolk with treason before parliament in January 1398. Parliament, then near the end of its session, set up a committee of lords and knights to deal with the charge. The second meeting of this committee, in April, provided Shakespeare with the opening scene of *Richard II*. Bolingbroke elaborated his accusation to include misappropriation of money and complicity in the death of Gloucester, while Norfolk denied all the charges and asked for trial by combat. Since no evidence appeared to support either duke, and since they refused reconciliation, Richard ordered such a trial to take place at Coventry in September. At Coventry, however, Richard stopped the proceedings immediately before battle was joined, conferred with the parliamentary committee for two hours (Shakespeare telescopes this conference into a bit of pantomime covered by "a long flourish"), and issued sentences of banishment: ten years for Bolingbroke, life for Norfolk.

The rights and wrongs of this episode are difficult to disentangle. If the dukes genuinely feared revenge from Richard—a reasonable apprehension—it is hard to understand why they allowed a quarrel between themselves to place them at the king's mercy. Perhaps Bolingbroke was acting as straightforwardly and loyally as he claimed, merely reporting a possible treason. Perhaps he wanted to avenge his uncle upon a man implicated in his uncle's murder, although there is no particular evidence of close affection between Bolingbroke and Gloucester. Perhaps he wished to strengthen his own relationship with Richard. Norfolk, on the other hand, may have counted upon Richard's indebtedness to him (both in the murder and in the appeal against Arundel and Warwick) for protection against Bolingbroke's charges. Yet he may have felt his position to be weak: some accounts report that his hesitation over Richard's order to murder Gloucester caused him to fear Richard's displeasure. Here we enter a realm of pure speculation: Norfolk and Richard both presumably knew exactly how Gloucester had died, but, since we do not, we can only guess at their motives for their subsequent behavior to each other. That the quarrel furnished Richard with an excellent opportunity to rid himself of both junior Appellants is obvious. That he allowed the affair to drag on for nine months only to abort the duel at the last moment looks like a fondness for theatrical gestures on his part.

Norfolk left England and died at Venice within a year. Bolingbroke, his exile reduced to six years just before his departure, took up residence at the French court. During the time of the quarrel and for six months after its conclusion at Coventry, Richard embarked upon a series of financial exactions. He secured from parliament an unprecedented lifetime grant of the customs on wool and leather. He required men and even counties associated with the Appellants' rising to buy costly pardons. He forced prominent persons to affix their seals to blank charters whose contents he evidently intended to fill in when it suited him. Much of the money thus gained he spent on magnificent living. By way of Holinshed, these activities become the "farming of the realm" and the ostentatious vanities for which York and the dying Gaunt rebuke Richard in Shakespeare's play. Upon Gaunt's death in February 1399, the king made his greatest mistake: illegally extending the authority of the parliamentary committee set up to deal with the Bolingbroke-Norfolk quarrel, he had them revoke the license enabling Bolingbroke's attorneys to claim the Lancastrian inheritance on behalf of the exiled heir. Since in default of heirs property reverted to the crown, Richard had, in one stroke, seized for himself the greatest patrimony in the kingdom, turned Bolingbroke into an irreconcilable enemy, and profoundly alarmed every other magnate in England. If Richard could thus contrive to steal Lancaster, he could steal any inheritance in the land.

Shakespeare dramatizes the response of the magnates to this confiscation in the conversation of three lords, Northumberland, Willoughby, and Ross, at the end of II.i. (Again, and more drastically, Shakespeare accelerates the time sequence: the scene begins with Gaunt still alive and ends, impossibly, with the news that Bolingbroke is already returning in quest of his stolen estates. In my experience, however, very few readers, let alone playgoers, notice the sleight-of-hand.) The three lords Shakespeare selects for this conversation are drawn from Holinshed's list of those who flocked to Bolingbroke shortly after his landing in the north of England; all three belonged to prominent northern families. The most distinguished of them, Henry Percy earl of Northumberland, was head of the greatest of the noble families of the north, an indefatigable warrior against the Scots and a former supporter of Gaunt. (Although he was Gaunt's contemporary, he appears in Shakespeare to belong to Bolingbroke's generation. His son, also named Henry, who is introduced two scenes later, is thereby made into a youth and thus prepared for his important role as Hotspur in *1 Henry IV*.) A chief agent of the usurpation, Northumberland later rebelled against the king he had made, a betrayal predicted by Shakespeare's Richard in Act V.

Richard's subsequent departure for Ireland, although not as radical a misstep as his appropriation of the Lancastrian estates, certainly entailed an error of timing. To leave England after so thoroughly antagonizing the magnates was foolish. Yet Ireland required attention. Dominion over Ireland had brought the English a host of problems ever since Henry II conquered the western island in the twelfth century. In 1394, by quelling revolt and reorganizing the relationship between the English overlords and the Irish chiefs, Richard had strengthened English rule there. A new outbreak of rebellion in 1398–1399 threatened to shatter his previous gains. His second Irish expedition constituted reasonable policy, fatally timed.

3. *THE USURPATION*

In July 1399 Bolingbroke landed near Ravenspur on the Yorkshire coast, an area of strong Lancastrian influence. Servants and retainers of his late father were there to meet him, and as he moved south his following swelled. The alarmed councillors in London sent word to Richard and then travelled west themselves, aiming to join the king upon his return from Ireland. Wiltshire, Bushy, and Greene took refuge at Bristol, the duke of York and others at Berkeley castle in Gloucestershire. Bagot parted company from his fellow caterpillars and apparently joined Richard, either immediately in Ireland or a little later in Wales. Informed of their moves, Bolingbroke also diverted his march to the west, evidently hoping to prevent Richard from meeting his friends. In this he was successful: at Berkeley he secured the submission of the spineless York, and at Bristol he forced the surrender of the caterpillars and had them executed.

We do not know what Bolingbroke's real plans were when he returned from exile. That is, we do not know when he decided to reach for the crown itself. While in Yorkshire, he appears to have proclaimed that he sought merely the restoration of his inheritance (incuding the post of lord high steward) and the reformation of Richard's government. Yet the executions, and certain appointments that he made, were acts of quasi-regal authority. Possibly he did not know his own purposes for a time: he was testing out a difficult situation with a caution and a reserve ingrained in him by his earlier unhappy experiences. In Shakespeare's play, Bolingroke is likewise noncommittal about his intentions, veiling anything beyond the claim for the duchy of Lancaster in ambiguity and silence until the crown is actually handed him in Act IV. Since the playwright does not reveal to us the usurper's mind, the psychological interest of Act III lies in Richard's responses.

Word of Bolingbroke's actions reached Richard late, delayed by adverse winds on the Irish Sea. His measures to meet the crisis were ill judged. He sent some of his soldiers, with orders for further recruitment, to the north of Wales under the leadership of John Montague earl of Salisbury, an experienced commander and faithful royalist. He himself hesitated for a time in Ireland and then crossed to southwest Wales, probably hoping to join his councillors at Bristol. Then, deciding to rely upon Salisbury's men, he disbanded his own tired troops and travelled north. Salisbury's army, however, believing a rumor that Richard was dead, melted away into the Welsh mountains. Thus Richard and Salisbury were eventually left in the castle at Conway with about a hundred men. There Northumberland found them. Swearing upon the sacrament, he promised Richard that, were Richard to restore the duchy of Lancaster and surrender certain advisors for trial, Bolingbroke would allow him to retain his crown and power. Thus lured from Conway (whence he could have escaped by sea to find help elsewhere), Richard was ambushed by Northumberland's troops, and taken first to Flint castle and then to Bolingbroke's headquarters at Chester. From here Bolingbroke issued writs for a parliament in Richard's name and then escorted Richard across England to the Tower of London.

Richard himself was not wholly responsible for the mismanaged response to the threat of Bolingbroke. It was his cousin Aumerle, his chief companion in Ireland, who caused him to delay his return and who advised the splitting of the army and the dismissal of the southern troops in Wales. After delivering this disastrous counsel, Aumerle went over to Bolingbroke. Holinshed, however, does not report Aumerle's role here. If, as is unlikely, Shakespeare learned of it from the French chronicle of

Jean Créton (whence we know of it), he decided not to use it: his Aumerle is a loyal friend trying to support Richard's spirits and urging him to decisive action. Deserting Richard at about the same time as Aumerle was another trusted man, Northumberland's brother Thomas Percy, steward of the king's household and recently the recipient of the earldom of Worcester. Holinshed and Shakespeare do mention Worcester's desertion, but Shakespeare moves it to a less crucial time: his Worcester never goes to Ireland or Wales, but deserts Richard's household in London upon the first news of Bolingbroke's arrival (this is reported in II.ii). Finally, Shakespeare altogether omits Northumberland's perjured promise and the ambush, although Holinshed includes both. Historically, then, Richard was the victim of multiple treacheries in Wales, whereas Shakespeare's Richard, although in a difficult position, is challenged by more honorable opponents and accompanied by more faithful supporters. These supporters (Aumerle, the bishop of Carlisle, Wiltshire's brother Sir Stephen Scrope) exhort him to resourceful action, but he ignores or resists their advice. First placing an unrealistic faith in the divinity that doth hedge a king, and then despairing prematurely, Shakespeare's Richard falls, almost of his own choice, into the hands of his enemies.

Bolingbroke brought Richard to London in August, and was himself crowned Henry IV on 13 October. In the intervening two months he had to devise a generally acceptable means for Richard's deposition and his own accession. The second part of this task was more difficult than the first. A precedent existed for deposition in the case of Edward II seventy years earlier, but there the successor was Edward's son. Although a reign was artificially terminated, the natural inheritance of the crown was not tampered with. By contrast, Henry was merely Richard's first cousin, and a closer heir by blood existed in the person of Lionel of Clarence's great-grandson, the seven-year-old earl of March.

Commissions of lawyers and officials were set to work to formulate a justification for Henry's accession. For their consideration Henry first advanced a claim to the crown on grounds of lineal descent (through his mother) from Edmund Crouchback, the first earl of Lancaster and younger brother of Edward I. The pertinence of this claim, however, rested entirely upon the fantastic story that Crouchback was really the elder brother, unfairly passed over in the succession. Henry next attempted a claim by conquest, but the implications of this horrified the commissioners. Such a precedent could justify future seizure of the crown by anybody who had the strength to take it. He finally "challenged" the crown "through the right that God of his grace hath sent me, with the help of my kin and friends to recover it," a magnificently ambiguous formula.

The formulation of the claim, however, was only half the matter; the claim also had to be generally acknowledged as persuasive. For this action the best instrument was parliament. But the parliament called by Richard's writs in August technically ceased to exist the moment that Richard ceased to be king. The lords and commons who met on 30 September 1399 to hear the formal charges against Richard, to approve of Richard's deposition, and to accept Henry's "challenge" were in fact the people called by Richard's writs who would normally constitute a parliament, and who under fresh writs did constitute Henry's first parliament a week later, but they were not a parliament on that day. Further, it is questionable how far Henry wished to rely on a title granted by parliament, since what a parliament had enacted it could presumably later reverse.

Henry had to be speedy, had to get the crown securely on his head before the momentum of his success slackened, before significant opposition formed or other candidates put themselves forward, and before the French king intervened on behalf of his son-in-law Richard. He was successful, of course, and the ground and validity of his claim have remained stubbornly ambiguous, a fruitful subject for controversy among his own lords within a few years and among constitutional historians ever since. The official account of the proceedings in the Parliamentary Roll, supplemented by chroniclers who favored the Lancastrian claim, attempted to seal his success by omitting to report dissident voices. In particular, these accounts pretended that at Conway Richard had promised Northumberland to abdicate, and that in the Tower he cheerfully carried out his promise, naming Henry as his heir. Coerced in the Tower, Richard in fact finally set his crown upon the floor and resigned it to God, a striking and characteristic last gesture.

Two centuries later Holinshed, more sympathetic to Richard than the Lancastrian chroniclers had been, judged him to be "a prince the most unthankfully used of his subjects, of any one of whom you shall lightly read." Holinshed also had access to more than the official account. He stresses, for example, the protest of the bishop of Carlisle. This was Thomas Merke, a Benedictine monk who had received his bishopric in reward for long and faithful administrative service in Richard's reign. During the proceedings of September and October 1399, Carlisle argued stoutly in defense of Richard that subjects had no right to judge their king. From Holinshed's long account of the transfer of power, rich in incidents such as this of Carlisle, Shakespeare creates the splendid and quite unhistorical scene of Richard's public deposition before parliament, complete with Carlisle's protest, York's assent (York clearly standing here for the lords as a body), and Northumberland's attempt to make Richard read aloud a formal list of his misdeeds. Henry obviously could not have permitted Richard a public hearing of this or any other kind. Indeed, Shakespeare's theatrical scene, composed two centuries after the event, was thought so inflammatory that it was censored out of the earliest editions of *Richard II.*

4. THE EARLS' REBELLION

Despite the legal difficulties discussed above, Henry's determination, together with Richard's unpopularity, ensured a fairly smooth transfer of power in 1399. Later generations looking back upon Richard's deposition saw the event as more catastrophic than did most of those who actually lived through it. Yet even with Henry acclaimed and enthroned, ticklish matters remained to be settled. What was to be done with Richard's evil advisors? What was to be done with Richard himself?

Settling the fate of Richard's friends once again brought up that thorny issue, the responsibility for Gloucester's death. Bagot, when brought before parliament as the only surviving caterpillar, accused Aumerle of arranging Gloucester's murder. Aumerle angrily denied the charge. A rash of accusations and challenges broke out as the dispute entangled other lords, most of whom had helped Richard in the appeal against Gloucester, Arundel, and Warwick. Shakespeare dramatizes this dispute at the beginning of the deposition scene, climaxing the episode with Carlisle's announcement of Norfolk's death in Venice. At this point Shakespeare breaks off, satisfied with demonstrating that Henry is in firm control. Historically, Henry allowed the issue of Gloucester's death to lapse and behaved mercifully to the favorites. Only an unfortunate yeoman of Norfolk's, who claimed to have guarded the door during Gloucester's murder, was executed. Bagot was allowed to retire to the country, and the lords concerned suffered only a removal of the titles Richard had given them. Aumerle, Exeter, and Surrey lost their duchies and had to console themselves with their former rank as earls of Rutland, Huntingdon, and Kent respectively.

Henry's mercy was ill rewarded. In December 1399, the degraded earls, together with Richard's much tried commander Salisbury, the bishop of Carlisle, and other friends of Richard, meeting in the house of the abbot of Westminster, hatched a plot to murder Henry and his sons and to restore the deposed king. In January the rebellion took place, and failed completely. Henry was warned in time, and his armies easily scattered the conspirators, some of whom were lynched by mobs. Most of the rest received trial, condemnation, and execution. The position of Carlisle and the abbot, complicated by their ecclesiastical status, was later resolved by pardons.

A greatly compressed account of the earls' rising occurs in Shakespeare's fifth act. The reportage consists largely of rather meaningless lists of names and obscure epithets applied to persons who do not actually appear on stage. Henry's sarcastic phrase, "our trusty brother-in-law," for example, refers to Huntingdon, who was married to Henry's sister Elizabeth. Some stress is laid on the abbot. With him, Shakespeare follows Holinshed in a picturesque historical error: he is made the chief architect of the plot and, upon its failure, he dies of sheer conscience and melancholy. Historically, it is not at all clear how deeply involved in the plot the abbot was, and he certainly did not perish immediately afterwards, of low spirits or anything else. In handling the earls' rebellion, however, Shakespeare is principally concerned with the ironies produced when family feelings conflict with political obedience. He places the chief dramatic emphasis upon Rutland (Aumerle). This feckless young man revealed the plot to his father York and thereby eventually to Henry, thus gaining the king's pardon. Rutland was certainly an outstanding knave, betraying first Richard in Wales, then Henry in London, and finally his fellow earls. That he eventually died fifteen years later fighting heroically for Henry V at Agincourt is the only action of his known to history that casts any favorable light upon his character. Since Shakespeare has omitted his betrayal of Richard, however, making Rutland a staunch supporter of the deposed king, his initial participation in the earls' plot looks like devoted loyalty to his old friend. His betrayal of the earls is made to result from parental pressure that Shakespeare heightens—quite without warrant from history or Holinshed—by stressing the duchess of York's maternal concern for her only son. In fact, the duchess in 1400 was York's second wife, a stepmother merely, and Rutland had a younger brother, later distinguished for treachery in his own right.

During the month after the rebellion Richard died, exactly when or how we do not know. Held secretly in the castle of Pontefract in Yorkshire, he may have starved himself or been starved to death. Rumor maintained that he died by violence. As the earls' conspiracy had shown, a surviving deposed king constituted a continual threat to his successor's security; he may have been killed at Henry's orders or by persons seeking to gain Henry's favor. Whether Henry directly commanded Richard's death or not, he was certainly responsible for it indirectly. As English history repeatedly demonstrates down to the time of Charles I, deposition is but a first step that makes the second step obvious. Shakespeare, adopting one of several accounts that Holinshed proffers, has Richard assassinated by an otherwise unknown person, Sir Piers of Exton, in response to Henry's oblique suggestion. Although the play clearly shows Henry to be a more competent ruler than his cousin, it closes, as it had opened, on a king whose hands are stained with royal blood.

Artist Unknown: *Henry IV* (The painting's source, The National Portrait Gallery, has called into question the identity of the sitter).

ꝭ III ꝭ

HENRY IV
the king embattled

All my reign hath been but as a scene
Acting that argument.

1. THE USURPER AND HIS CHALLENGERS

The reign of Henry IV came to Shakespeare's hand already possessed of a dramatic shape, a perceived pattern of historical cause and effect. In 1399, at about the age of thirty-three, Henry of Lancaster usurped the crown of his first cousin Richard II, retaining it until his own death of natural causes in 1413. Shakespeare's Henry, on his deathbed, attributes all the troubles of his reign to his having "snatched" the crown. Henry's overthrow of Richard had implicitly invited others, when they became discontented with his rule, to attempt another deposition. Shakespeare's king exaggerates slightly: the last five years of Henry's reign were in fact free of major domestic upheaval. For the first eight years or so, however, he may have felt like the captain of an undermanned and badly caulked ship, plugging leaks that refused to stay plugged and continually having to move the pumps about. Wales was in revolt every summer from 1400 to 1408. During the same period a variety of English rebels beset him as well, hatching minor plots from time to time and causing major crises in 1403 and 1405. Until 1409, the best efforts of Henry himself and of his eldest son (whom I, to avoid confusion, will call by his Shakespearean nickname Hal) were devoted to keeping the house of Lancaster on the throne it had seized.

Henry IV was born Henry of Bolingbroke, only surviving son of the first marriage of John of Gaunt duke of Lancaster, who was in turn the third surviving son of Edward III. By his early thirties he had acquired a distinguished international reputation. He was famous as a jouster in tournaments; he had become an experienced campaigner while on crusade in Lithuania; he was noted for courtesy and generosity in the European courts that he had visited when returning from a pilgrimage to the Holy Land. He was energetic, learned, pious in an orthodox way, and popular among his own people. He was also a widower and the father of four sons. From time to time he had played a significant role in English politics.

Since the circumstances of Bolingbroke's usurpation provide some of the issues over which the characters of *Henry IV* wrangle, they must be related briefly here. In 1398, as readers of the previous chapter will recall, mutual accusations of treason brought Bolingbroke and Thomas Mowbray duke of Norfolk to the point of trial by combat. The duel, however, never took place. King Richard, presiding over the ceremony, threw down his staff of office to interrupt the proceedings, and, after consultation with his council, exiled both men. Early in the following year, when Bolingbroke's father died, Richard seized the Lancastrian estates. Bolingbroke thereupon broke exile, returning from France in July to regain his inheritance. Landing in the north, he was joined by various powerful noblemen who volunteered their assistance in the recovery of his rights and the reform of Richard's erratic behavior and financially exacting government. He proceeded to secure the capitulation of Richard's officials and to execute some who were held particularly responsible for misleading the king (the so-called caterpillars of the commonwealth). Richard himself, meanwhile, was in Ireland, attempting to crush rebellion there, and thus found himself badly placed to deal with the threat of Bolingbroke. He was, moreover, held there for some time by contrary winds and poor communications. Upon his return to Wales, his mismanagement of his troops, the treachery of some of his supporters, and the stratagems of Bolingbroke's friends resulted in his capture. Although Bolingbroke originally appeared to be seeking only the duchy of Lancaster, the unpopularity and collapse of the king allowed him to seize the throne of England as well. Richard was deposed and Henry crowned. After certain earls loyal to Richard attempted to restore him in January 1400, Richard himself died a mysterious death in prison. It was widely thought that he was murdered on Henry's orders, or at least by Henry's friends on his behalf.

The subsequent challenges to Henry's rule came both from persons who had assisted him and from those he had offended by taking the throne. Chief among his assistants was a family of border lords, the house of Percy. The Percies were the most powerful magnates in the northern counties of England, holding important castles and tracts of land in Yorkshire, Cumberland, and Northumberland. At the time of the usurpation, thanks in part to Richard's recent destruction of various other nobles, they were probably the most powerful subjects in the realm after Henry himself. They had repeatedly held the wardenships of the east and west marches (the areas on the Scottish border), thus directing border policies and receiving crown revenue to guard against Scottish invasion. In the raids and skirmishes common to the region, they gained much military experience and earned the intense loyalty of the people of the north. The head of the family was Henry Percy, upon whom Richard had bestowed the earldom of Northumberland in 1377. (Born in 1341, Northumberland was a generation older than Henry IV; in Shakespeare, however, the king and the earl appear to be about the same age, and their sons are rivals in youthful chivalry.) Active in most of the political and military affairs of his time, Northumberland raised his family from the position of merely local northern influence it had enjoyed since the Norman Conquest, and from the barony it had held since 1314, into an earldom of national importance. His son, also named Henry Percy but known in his own time and ever since by the nickname Hotspur, was born in 1364. A soldier from his early teens, he led a distinguished career in the border warfare of the last decades of the fourteenth century. There was also a third significant Percy, Thomas, younger brother to Northumberland and uncle to Hotspur. Thomas eschewed the northern raids for service in the French wars under Edward III and in John of Gaunt's attempt to win the crown of Castile. Subsequently he rose in royal service at the court of Richard II, becoming steward of the household in 1393 and earl of Worcester in 1397.

Northumberland and Hotspur had been foremost among the nobles who flocked to Bolingbroke upon the latter's return to England in July 1399. They gave him valuable military support, and Northumberland carried out the essential maneuver of that summer, the capture of Richard himself in Wales. Worcester, having gone with Richard to Ireland, played a less central role. Nonetheless he significantly weakened Richard's position by deserting him, breaking his steward's staff and dismissing the royal household. One chronicler further reports Worcester to have been the first to acclaim Bolingbroke as king during the parliament that deposed Richard. If any besides Bolingbroke himself acted as kingmaker in the events of 1399, it was the house of Percy. By way of reward, the new king increased the Percies' already extensive power by granting them additional offices, revenues, and lands. Northumberland himself was made constable of England.

In 1403 this dangerous trio revolted against the king they had made. The causes moving them to insurrection are somewhat obscured by the biases of later chroniclers. Writers favoring the

Lancastrians present the revolt as a proud and ambitious outbreak on the part of turbulent and ungrateful lords. Writers favoring Richard or the later Yorkist kings, committed to the belief that Henry's usurpation was unjust and disastrous in itself, see the Percies as rightfully opposing an unlawful king whom they had never intended to crown: they had willingly helped Henry when they believed that he sought only his stolen inheritance, after which events and Henry's cunning outstripped them. The heart of the matter is still a historical question: did Henry swear to the Percies, when he was gathering troops at Doncaster for his march south in July 1399, that he had no designs upon the throne? In 1403 the Percies claimed that he had so sworn, and that now they intended to rectify a wrong they had been tricked into abetting. Lancastrian chronicles either make no mention of such a vow or palliate its terms. To most modern historians it appears that no one as capable and experienced as the Percies undoubtedly were could have helped Henry to the extent they undoubtedly did without some perception of what the outcome might be; and that if they protested against that outcome when, with Richard locked up, Henry was openly arranging his own accession in September 1399, it is certainly strange that he should have loaded them with honors and powers once the crown was on his head. That is, if Henry did perjure himself at Doncaster, the Percies do not seem to have minded nearly so much in 1399 as they claimed they did four years later.

Money also caused trouble between Henry and the Percies. The latter were subject to heavy expenses as wardens of the marches, and the crown revenues assigned to them to meet these expenses were slow in coming. Here the Percies undoubtedly had a point. Henry IV had financial trouble throughout his reign; anxiety over money probably contributed to his premature aging and comparatively early death. As the heir of Lancaster, he had been a very rich young man who could and did spend lavishly and give generously. As king he had an even larger income, but far greater responsibilities. At one point his treasurer anxiously reported that, far from being able to obey Henry's orders to pay certain lords, he had no money in the coffers to pay even the messengers who were to bear summonses to members of the council. A particular difficulty lay in the late medieval system of royal finance, which was poorly designed for military expenditure. The regular crown revenue from crown lands, prerogatives, customs, and levies was barely sufficient to meet the king's ordinary expenses. Military campaigns were considered extraordinary expenses, requiring taxation in the form of subsidies voted by parliament. (There was no standing army.) Such subsidies entailed bargaining with parliament over each instance, and were moreover subject to long delays in collection and disbursement. Unfortunately for Henry, military campaigns were not in the least extraordinary in themselves. He was continually faced with border warfare in Scotland and Wales, and skirmishes with the French, as well as civil uprisings. The Percies had a just complaint, but it seems only fair to add that their financial arrears did not result from malicious or personally abusive designs on Henry's part. Hal, the king's own son, trying to govern Wales, and his brother Thomas, posted in Ireland, similarly complained about their inability to pay their garrisons. Everyone dependent upon crown funds, most of all the king himself, had the same problem.

Henry and the Percies were also at odds over the ransom of prisoners. In September 1402, at Homildon Hill in Yorkshire, Northumberland and Hotspur met a Scottish army led by their counterpart the Scottish warden of the marches, Archibald earl of Douglas. The Percies inflicted a crushing defeat, capturing Douglas and a large number of other Scottish nobles. (A short list is given when the victory is reported in the first scene of Shakespeare's *1 Henry IV*.) As was customary with high-ranking captives, the king claimed the prisoners for himself, and Northumberland accordingly surrendered some. Hotspur, however, refused to surrender his (they included Douglas), arguing that their ransoms were due him in place of the crown revenues Henry had not paid him. The subsequent quarrel was entangled by another matter of ransom. Three months earlier Hotspur's brother-in-law, Sir Edmund Mortimer, had been captured by rebels in central Wales. The king refused to ransom Mortimer, a refusal that outraged Hotspur and hardened him in his resolution to keep his Scots.

The argument about the usurpation, the money problem, and the quarrel over ransoms all contributed to the worsening relationship between the king and his former allies. To what extent the Percies' grievances were just is still debatable. As a dramatist with an extraordinary ability to balance his characters against each other, Shakespeare does not decide which party has the better case: in *1 Henry IV* each side is allowed occasionally to make sound points, occasionally to bluster, and occasionally to fall victim to undermining ironies.

Perhaps the most significant cause of the Percy rebellion was a dynastic matter not yet mentioned: the rebels had a rival candidate, the earl of March, to place on Henry's throne. Henry IV's father, John of Gaunt, was the third son of Edward III. In seizing the crown after the deposition of Richard II, Henry had bypassed the issue of Edward's second son, Lionel duke of Clarence. This prince had died in 1368, leaving only a daughter, Philippa, wife to Edmund Mortimer third earl of March. (The Mortimer lands lay in the Welsh marches, that is, the border areas of western England and eastern Wales: hence the name of the earldom.) Both Philippa and her husband were dead by 1381, so that for the bulk of his reign Richard II's heir presumptive (formally so designated by the king) was their son Roger Mortimer, the fourth earl. His murder by the Irish in 1398 was the immediate cause of Richard's ill-timed trip to Ireland the next year. He in turn left a son, Edmund Mortimer the fifth earl, aged six at the time of his father's death. He was also survived by a brother, Sir Edmund Mortimer, a man in his twenties, and a sister Elizabeth, wife to

Hotspur. (Holinshed calls her Elianor; Shakespeare changes the name to Kate.) If inheritance of the crown could pass through a female, Edmund the fifth earl of March, was, strictly speaking, the right inheritor of Richard's crown. Bolingbroke's swiftness in arranging his own accession and March's tender years prevented any significant claim being made on March's behalf in September 1399, but the existence of the Mortimers constituted an obvious threat to Henry thereafter. Accordingly, Henry kept young March in semicaptivity at Windsor from the beginning of his reign and, when Sir Edmund fell into Welsh hands in 1402, Henry was only too delighted to leave him there.

In the rebellion of 1403 the Percies aimed to put young March, now aged eleven, on the throne. From him they could expect greater power and less frustration than from Henry. Indeed, with Hotspur as his uncle by marriage, they must have expected to control the government altogether. Unfortunately, some confusion attends this dynastic issue for readers of Shakespeare. Shakespeare's sources (the historians Hall and Holinshed, the poet Daniel) mixed up the Mortimers, conflating into one person the youthful earl who was heir to the throne with his adult uncle who was Hotspur's brother-in-law and a Welsh captive. Shakespeare follows in this confusion: his "Mortimer" is an adult, Hotspur's brother-in-law, and a prisoner of the Welsh, and he is also the earl of March whom Henry's usurpation has deprived of his royal rights. (It is possible that, even if Shakespeare's authorities had not misled him, he would have conflated the Mortimers anyway, simply out of dramatic expediency. But it must be admitted that Shakespeare is not entirely consistent in the conflation: his Lady Percy at one point refers to "my brother Mortimer," and yet elsewhere she is called by him "aunt Percy.")

Discontent with Henry's rule sprang, not only from the houses of Percy and Mortimer, but also from Wales. During the late Middle Ages the English dominion over Wales, like the attempt to rule Ireland and the occasional assertions of overlordship in Scotland, inspired from time to time the actively expressed resentment of the local population. Throughout Henry IV's reign flourished Owen Glendower, the most pertinacious Welsh rebel since Edward I's thirteenth-century conquest of Wales. Glendower was a landowner of considerable position in north Wales, holding properties that his ancestors had ruled as independent Welsh princes. About forty at the time of Henry's coronation, he was a polished and educated gentleman. In his youth he had been an apprentice-at-law in one of the London Inns of Court and had married the daughter of a justice of the King's Bench. (Shakespeare combines this educated background with an expansion of Holinshed's hint that supernatural portents occurred at Glendower's birth: thus his Glendower becomes a remarkable union of English civilization and Welsh mysticism.) Glendower was not at first a revolutionary starry-eyed with the prospect of Welsh independence: only after several years of fighting did he pursue such goals. Initially he merely sought recognition of his rights as a landowner.

The Welsh revolt originated in a petty quarrel between Glendower and a neighboring English magnate, Reginald Lord Grey of Ruthin. In the summer of 1400, Grey occupied some property whose ownership both men claimed. Shortly after, when Henry led an army into Scotland to demand the homage of Robert III, Grey may also have prevented Glendower from receiving the king's call to military duty, thus making Glendower look like a traitor. In September Glendower retaliated by burning Ruthin. He also sacked other English settlements in north Wales, his relatives (including the powerful family of Tudor in Anglesey) joining the outbreak. Responding upon his return from Scotland, Henry marched through north Wales, confiscating property and receiving submissions from some of the Welsh. There was no pitched battle, however, and Glendower himself eluded capture. Plagued by supply problems and unable to cope with guerilla warfare in a difficult and unfamiliar landscape, Henry withdrew.

Every summer for the next eight years Glendower was on the

attack. By the end of 1401 he was master of much of north Wales. In 1402 he captured Grey (who was ransomed) and Mortimer (who was not). That fall Mortimer threw in his lot with the Welsh, marrying Glendower's daughter and urging his friends by letter to join the Welsh cause. Thus Henry lost the allegiance of the Mortimer districts in the Welsh marches. Risings on Glendower's behalf also occurred that year in south Wales, and the royal armies were again prevented by difficulties of supply and by bad weather from coming to grips with him. In 1403, although he could not get to Shrewsbury in time to aid the Percy revolt, Glendower's successes continued in the same pattern. During the first half of 1404 he took the fortresses of Harlech and Aberystwyth in western Wales, part of the great chain of castles Edward I had built to secure his conquest. By this time he was leading a full-fledged national revolution: a Welsh parliament declared him prince of Wales and he concluded a treaty for assistance with the French. Although Glendower's aims concerned Welsh independence, not Henry's crown, a curious episode in this year reveals the direct threat Glendower posed to the new dynasty. The sister of the duke of York (Richard II's Aumerle), Lady Despenser, whose husband had been beheaded for his participation in the earls' plot of 1400, kidnapped young March and attempted to deliver him to Glendower. (The fugitives were overtaken before reaching Wales; York himself was probably privy to the conspiracy.)

The year 1405 marked the high point of Glendower's efforts. With French reinforcements, he invaded the west of England as far as Worcester. Here he in his turn experienced the difficulty of maintaining supply lines, and Henry, always at his best when speed was requisite, prevented him from getting to the city gates. The failure of two English rebellions, and the withdrawal of his French allies in 1406, severely damaged Glendower's cause. He lost Aberystwyth in 1408 and Harlech in early 1409. In the fall of Harlech to the English, Sir Edmund Mortimer was killed and most of Glendower's family, including Mortimer's children, were captured. Glendower himself seems to have returned to north Wales. He tried once again in 1410 and then disappeared into the Welsh mists. He probably died around 1415. Holinshed, however, reports that he perished of starvation in 1409, information that Shakespeare uses in *2 Henry IV*.

English control over Wales was largely the responsibility of the king's eldest son. The title "prince of Wales," bestowed upon the English heir apparent since Edward I's conquest, was no idle decoration. Those portions of Wales not held by marcher lords like Grey and Mortimer were ruled as a principality from Chester, albeit under the close supervision of the king at Westminster. Hal, aged twelve in 1399, could at first only be the nominal head of the governing council. As part of his reward for his assistance in crowning Henry, Hotspur was given chief authority. Hotspur resigned his post in 1401, complaining of the administrative difficulties and wishing to pursue his northern interests. His successor died not long after taking on the responsibility, and by 1403 Hal himself, at the age of sixteen, was king's lieutenant for Wales. Until the fall of Harlech he was principally occupied with the Welsh rebellion. If there is any truth behind the stories of his youthful profligacy in London that Shakespeare inherited from late Plantagenet and Tudor legend and used in *Henry IV,* Hal must have squeezed a great deal of self-indulgence into his winter trips to the capital. During campaign season he was otherwise occupied.

2. THE BATTLE OF SHREWSBURY

1 Henry IV actually begins in 1402, with Mortimer's capture by Glendower (June) and Hotspur's victory at Homildon (September) as the latest news. The triple threat of Glendower, Percy, and the Mortimer claim, bound together by the Percy-Mortimer and Mortimer-Glendower marriages and by their common enmity to the new Lancastrian king, is emerging into the open. Neither in history nor in Shakespeare, however, does Henry lack support against the threat. Many lords remained loyal. Among them three require mention here.

The young earl of Arundel was son to the Arundel whom Richard II had executed in 1397 and nephew to Henry's archbishop of Canterbury. He had fled England after the execution of his father, returned with Bolingbroke in 1399, and regained his confiscated estates in 1400. Since these estates included extensive lands in the north of Wales, he was active in the conflict with Glendower and became friendly with Hal. In Shakespeare he is much less important than he was historically, appearing briefly and wordlessly in 2 *Henry IV* under his other title as earl of Surrey.

Henry was also helped by a renegade Scotsman, George Dunbar the Scottish earl of March. In Shakespeare Dunbar receives only a single confusing allusion as having sent Henry a message about the rebels' movements. (The allusion—to "Lord Mortimer of Scotland"—is confusing because Shakespeare was confused. He refers to the Scottish earl of March as "Mortimer" because that was the family name of the English earls of March. The families had nothing to do with each other, and Dunbar's "march" was of course the northern border, not the Welsh.) Historically, however, he played a much larger role. After a quarrel with Robert III and the earl of Douglas, Dunbar had thrown his allegiance to the English crown and had helped the Percies at Homildon. Despite this comradeship in arms, his relationship with the Percies was fragile. Seeking under his new king control over border areas that he had held or threatened when loyal to the Scottish crown, he naturally came into competition with their territorial ambitions. Apparently it was he who first alerted Henry to the Percy conspiracy; certainly he urged Henry to deal with it swiftly and forcefully.

Another territorial rival to the Percies, and one who appears frequently in both parts of *Henry IV*, was Ralph Neville earl of Westmorland. In many respects Westmorland resembled Northumberland. Each was descended of a distinguished baronial family with northern properties; each had served as warden on the Scottish marches; each raised his family to an earldom; each was among the lords who first supported Bolingbroke in 1399. Unlike Northumberland, however, Westmorland remained loyal to the Lancastrian king, thus earning from Henry extensive gifts of land, offices, wardships, and pensions. Westmorland further married two heiresses, the second of whom was no less a person than Henry's half-sister, Joan Beaufort, John of Gaunt's daughter by Catherine Swynford. With the assistance of these wives he managed to rival Edward III's record for begetting influential offspring: of his sixteen children surviving infancy, four of the sons became peers, another became a bishop, and seven of the daughters married into noble families. The dynastic connections of the Nevilles made them one of the most powerful forces in fifteenth-century politics. Over half the people to be mentioned later in this book were the issue of or otherwise related to the first earl of Westmorland.

Shakespeare depicts the Percy rebellion as occurring swiftly but not so unexpectedly that the king lacks contingency plans or the time to send three armies out of London, led respectively by Westmorland, Hal, and himself. Actually, it occurred much more suddenly than that, and the royal family was not in London. The king was taken quite by surprise, and indeed the pace of events proved fatal to the rebels who initiated them. In the early summer of 1403, Hotspur raised an army in Cheshire. With him were three major confederates: his uncle Worcester, who had brought money from Hal's treasury in London to pay the rebel troops (he was officially Hal's governor); the earl of Douglas, who, like Mortimer, had become his captor's ally; and Sir Richard Vernon, a major Cheshire landowner. Hotspur had further concerted plans with Glendower and Mortimer in Wales. (Hotspur seems to have been on good terms with Glendower for some time: in 1401, when he was charged with the English defense in Wales, he had endeavored to secure a pardon for Glendower.) Northumberland, meanwhile, was still writing Henry letters from the north demanding money and reinforcements to meet the threat of a Scottish invasion. He told the king he feared revenge for the victory at Homildon. Henry started north, having decided first to aid his warden and then to move against the Welsh. On 13 July, while in Nottingham, he received news of the Percy revolt: Hotspur had issued proclamations renouncing his allegiance to Henry and was marching upon Shrewsbury, where Hal and his army were quartered. Persuaded by Dunbar not to return to London, Henry got to Shrewbury with remarkable speed, not only reaching the town before Hotspur but arriving well before Hotspur could expect reinforcement from his father in the north or from Glendower.

Battle was joined on 21 July two miles north of Shrewsbury. A parley preceded the battle, but the rebels rejected Henry's offers of reconciliation. According to one chronicle, Worcester, who served as the rebels' spokesman, deliberately misrepresented Henry's mercy when reporting back to Hotspur, thus causing Hotspur indignantly to refuse it. It is not certain that this was so: Worcester and Hotspur may genuinely have disagreed about the value of Henry's promises. That Worcester was treacherous even to his own nephew, however, was the tradition that came down to Shakespeare. In Holinshed, Worcester's aim "was ever (as some write) to procure malice and set things in a broil." That is, he was a born agent of chaos, something like a witch out of *Macbeth.* Shakespeare's Worcester is similarly malign, "malevolent to [the king] in all respects"; he is the evil genius of rebellion who, fearing that the king may later secure revenge upon him while forgiving Hotspur, deliberately suppresses the king's offers.

The battle itself was long and unusually bloody. Some combatants were still struggling at nightfall and casualties were very high. The earl of Stafford, who commanded one wing of the royal army, was killed; Hal, commanding the other in his first full-scale engagement, was shot in the face with an arrow but continued fighting. Inability to distinguish friend from foe led to much confused slaughter. Douglas and Hotspur made determined attempts to kill the king, during which many about him were cut down, including his standard-bearer Sir Walter Blunt. (Blunt, or Blount, had long been a retainer to John of Gaunt. After serving as Gaunt's executor, he naturally transferred his loyalty to Gaunt's son; he died at Shrewsbury at least partly because his armor greatly resembled that of his master.) Dunbar eventually withdrew the king from the forefront of the melee. Finally Worcester, Douglas, and Vernon were captured, and Hotspur perished, it is not known by whose hand. (Students of Shakespeare's sources have rightly pointed out that an ambiguous sentence in Holinshed makes it possible to suppose that Hal killed Hotspur. Hall's chronicle, however, which was Holinshed's own source at this point and was possibly consulted by Shakespeare, does not convey this false suggestion, and surely Shakespeare, having arranged Hotspur's age, the king's anxieties about his son, and many passages of dialogue to bring Hal and Hotspur into competing contrast, could have invented the climactic duel of *1 Henry IV* without the aid of stray ambiguities.) Much of the rebel army then fled. After the battle, Douglas was kept in captivity, from which he was not finally released until 1408. Worcester and Vernon, however, were immediately executed for treason. Portions of their bodies and of Hotspur's were then placed on public display in various cities, the customary manner of advertising the fate of rebels.

3. *GAULTREE FOREST AND BRAMHAM MOOR*

At the end of *1 Henry IV,* after the battle of Shrewsbury, Shakespeare's efficient king orders the remaining rebels to be mopped up. In *2 Henry IV* this takes place without much sense of time-lapse, after which Henry soon dies. In fact a decade of rule remained to Henry after Shrewsbury, half of which had passed before the Percy threat was terminated.

The defeat of the rebels at Shrewsbury left Glendower and Mortimer untouched in Wales, and Northumberland still at large in the north. Against the latter Henry immediately moved. At York in August, under the pressure of armies led by the king and by Westmorland, Northumberland was obliged to capitulate. His castles and offices were taken from him and distributed among the loyalists: Hal and Westmorland assumed the Percy posts as wardens of the east and west marches respectively, and Henry's third son John became constable of England. The house of lords, however, decided that Northumberland's offense had been merely trespass rather than treason. His life was spared and he swore new fealty to the king. He also contrived to retain the old Percy strongholds of Alnwick and Warkworth in the county of Northumberland itself.

The enmity between Percy and Lancaster did not disappear. Indeed, in February 1405, the triple alliance of Percy, Mortimer, and Glendower resurfaced in an astonishing document, a tripartite indenture signed by their agents under the supervision of Welsh ecclesiastics in Bangor. In this compact, the three principals swore mutual loyalty in defense of England. The remarkable part of the agreement lay in what they proposed to do to England themselves. Once they were rid of Henry of Lancaster, they planned to slice the country into petty kingdoms. Glendower was to have Wales, the Welsh marches, and chunks of the western counties; Northumberland the north, the midlands, and Norfolk; and Mortimer the south and east. (In Shakespeare, this agreement occurs earlier in the story. Following Holinshed, he places the tripartite indenture prior to the battle of Shrewsbury. He thus creates a fine scene in *1 Henry IV* for Hotspur, Glendower, and Mortimer as they argue over the terms of division, but *2 Henry IV* is thereby left a little thin in political substance. The characters of the latter play repeatedly speak of maneuvers, imminent confrontations, and the general sickness of the realm, but they seldom get down to specific issues and alliances. *Part 2,* however, does reflect some of the destructive spirit of the indenture in Northumberland's rage to bring chaos to the land, his desire to loose "the wild flood" and "let order die.")

The revival of the Percy-Glendower-Mortimer combination was only half the threat to Henry IV in 1405. Uncertainly connected with it was a second conspiracy, led by Richard Scrope archbishop of York, Thomas Mowbray earl of Norfolk and Nottingham and hereditary earl marshal, and Thomas Lord Bardolf. Mowbray, not yet twenty years old, was son and heir to the Norfolk whose quarrel with Bolingbroke had initiated the fall of Richard II. Bardolf was an obscurer person, married to a Lincolnshire heiress. The dominating figure of this faction was the archbishop. Scrope was a relative of the William Scrope whom Richard II had made earl of Wiltshire and whom Bolingbroke had executed in 1399 as one of the caterpillars of the commonwealth. Indeed, resentment over his cousin's death is said by both Holinshed and Shakespeare to have motivated his rebellion. Historically, however, he appears to have favored Lancaster over Richard II and to have rebelled for larger motives. Although given his archbishopric by Richard, he served on the parliamentary commission that received Richard's forced abdication in the Tower. Further, he assisted Thomas Arundel, the archbishop of Canterbury, in enthroning the new king, and lent Henry money for his 1400 expedition into Scotland. But he was also closely connected with the Percies, his brother having married the widow of Hotspur's brother, and his cathedral having benefited from the Percies' generosity. Although remaining behind the scenes, he counselled the Percies in the rebellion that ended at Shrewsbury. The formal statement of grievances against the Lancastrian regime that he issued in spring 1405, however, stressed general rather than personal loyalties. Posted around the city of

York, this document charged Henry with bad government, specifically with indignities inflicted upon the clergy, destruction visited upon the secular lords, and unbearable taxes imposed upon the commons. The vicious financial circle in which Henry was caught is here apparent: some of his subjects rebelled in protest against the taxation he required to defeat rebellion. The authority which the archbishop wielded in York and the respect in which he was held there caused other northern lords and the citizens of York itself to join his banner.

Again the anti-Lancastrian cause suffered from poor coordination and the speed of the royalists. In 1405 Glendower, with French aid, invaded England nearly to the gates of Worcester. He did so only in August, however; the archbishop initiated his rising in late May. Westmorland, as swift as his master, defeated a group of Percy retainers before they could join the archbishop and then met Scrope's army near Gaultree Forest in Yorkshire. Here he worked by craft rather than force. Having confronted the archbishop's troops for three days, Westmorland offered to parley. By promising to settle the rebels' grievances in negotiation, Westmorland induced them to dismiss their men. Then, to their surprise, he arrested Scrope, Mowbray, and other leaders. Henry, arriving a few days later, appointed a judicial commission, headed by the chief justice of the King's Bench, to try them for treason, demanding conviction and the death penalty. Given Westmorland's rather shabby promise, this turn of events was sufficiently harsh for the secular lords concerned. It was worse for Scrope: by both precedent and canon law, a lay court could not order the execution of an archbishop, or of any cleric. (To be punished by the secular law, a cleric had first to be stripped of his clerical status by an ecclesiastical court, and then formally handed over to the secular arm.) His fellow archbishop, Arundel of Canterbury, protested. So did the chief justice, Sir William Gascoigne, who resigned from the tribunal. But Henry, fed up with rebels, was apparently determined to create a startling example.

He had his will. Together with his fellow conspirators, the arch-bishop was beheaded under the walls of York, reviling no one and claiming that he died for the laws and good governance of England. Henry then moved west to drive Glendower out of Worcestershire.

In later years popular opinion dated Henry's first attack of illness (said by some to be leprosy) immediately after Scrope's death. Divine wrath was supposedly visited upon the king for the sacrilege of executing an archbishop. Certainly Scrope was revered as a saint and martyr in York; certainly Henry did suffer recurrent illness (although not leprosy) during the latter half of his reign. Whatever we may think of the theory of divine retribution, Henry himself, always orthodox in religion, probably believed in it, and neurotic anxiety over his health and his deeds may have darkened his later years. Shakespeare, however, eliminates the king and the hasty trial altogether from his version of the Gaultree episode. His emphasis falls upon the trick by which Scrope was captured, and here he modifies history by reassigning the responsibility for it. Not Westmorland but Prince John promises redress of grievances to the rebels, a promise which they take to imply their own personal safety as well. After arresting them, he points out the distinction they have overlooked, and directly orders them borne "to the block of death." Thus the forthright virtues of Hal, heroic victor of Shrewsbury, are placed in relief against the clever calculation of his rather Machiavellian brother.

Meanwhile, the inglorious Northumberland had once again failed to arrive for the battle. In July 1405 he fled to Scotland with Bardolf. (Shakespeare, who frequently seeks scenes in which family loyalties cut athwart political alliances, has him persuaded into flight by Lady Northumberland *before* the archbishop meets the royal army. Actually, Northumberland was a widower, and his escape followed Scrope's execution by a month.) In the subsequent year and a half, Northumberland and Bardolf rather miserably travelled to Wales and France seeking aid for a further attempt against Henry. By the end of 1407 they were back in Scotland. In February 1408, they invaded the north of England once more. Encountering at Bramham Moor a hastily raised force led by no more exalted a person than the sheriff of Yorkshire, Northumberland perished in battle and Bardolf died of wounds shortly after. Although Hotspur's son survived to carry on the line, regaining the earldom of Northumberland in 1415, the Percies never again influenced the fate of England to the extent that they had when the first earl supported and then opposed Henry IV.

4. THE KING AND THE PRINCE

After the death of Northumberland in early 1408 and the collapse of the Welsh revolt a few months later, the Lancastrian grip on the throne was at last secure. It is the effort to make that grip secure, Henry's long struggle against the Percies, Glendower, Mortimer, and Scrope, that provides the political story of *1 and 2 Henry IV*. Immediately after receiving the news of Bramham Moor in *2 Henry IV*, Shakespeare's king suffers a fatal apoplexy. The remaining six scenes of the play present Hal's accession to power.

In the large-scale construction of the Henry IV plays, Shakespeare has wrought two major alterations on history. First, he has excised the last five years of Henry's reign: the king did not die until March 1413. To the historical events thus omitted we shall in a moment return. Second, he has intermingled the history of the rebellions with much nonhistorical matter. The political turmoil already related constitutes only about half of the material of *1 and 2 Henry IV*. A comparison with Shakespeare's earlier history, *Richard II*, clarifies the point. The dramatic action of *Richard II* consists almost wholly of a reasonably accurate account of the major political events during the period it covers. If newspapers had existed in medieval England, a collection of headlines for 1398–1400 would read much like a brief plot summary of the play. Furthermore, servants excepted, all the characters of *Richard II* are historical personages directly concerned with the high affairs of government. The Henry IV plays, on the other hand, interweave the political story with many private events, scenes in taverns and rural locations involving persons of little or no public note, many of whom Shakespeare has invented. Indeed, the protagonist of the plays is not the king but his son Prince Hal, and except for the final act of each play Hal engages, not in the military and administrative activities recorded of him by history, but in a series of private encounters with his personal friends and his father. The political story is but one thread of a saga whose central action is the growing up of the crown prince.

Shakespeare's desertion of strict chronicle history for the mixed historical mode of *Henry IV* can be accounted for on a number of grounds. The matter belongs in part under the heading of technical source study, in part in the domain of pure literary criticism, neither of which is the strict concern of this book. In connection with the real history of the fifteenth century, however, two points must be made. First, the natural dramatic shape that I have asserted Henry's reign to possess extends only to the death of Northumberland and the defeat of Glendower. The Elizabethan view of Henry's reign as a period of domestic turmoil, turmoil inevitably resulting from Bolingbroke's usurpation, is a perfectly justified interpretation, but it does not include the years 1408–1413. During this lustrum no dissident nobleman sought to unseat Henry. The government could turn more fully to matters of religious and foreign policy. These issues proved tangled and inconclusive, and their development took quite a new turn when Henry V came to the throne. For a dramatist, Henry's final years lack promising material. To his most recent biographer, indeed, Henry IV's life and reign look anticlimactic: an accomplished and capable prince seizes a crown, spends nearly a decade defending it, and then achieves nothing particularly significant in the years remaining to him. (It is possible that moderns, accustomed to large and legally omnicompetent governments, looking to them for "leadership" and a vast array of services, expect too much from medieval kings, whose more modest objectives were to uphold their dignity as hereditary lords and to protect their subjects' rights.) Second, the mixed historical character of the Henry IV plays can be attributed to a lively legendary tradition about Hal. On the strength of his spectacular victories in France, Henry V was regarded by later generations as an outstanding national hero. Stories about the youth of this hero, stories ignoring his official activity and concentrating on his private life, began accumulating shortly after he died. Some of these were accepted in Elizabethan times as history: they appear in Holinshed and other sober chroniclers. More remained in a realm of semihistorical, semilegendary anecdote, and can be traced through such popular works as the anonymous pre-Shakespearean play *The Famous Victories of Henry V.* Such legendary material, dismissed or at least regarded with skepticism by modern scholars, is as important to the making of Shakespeare's *Henry IV* as the history already recounted. Through the dextrous disposition and weaving together of these two threads, Shakespeare creates his tragical-comical-historical epic, mingling high politics and romantic legend to explore the nature of heroism, honor, justice, and good rule.

Since my purpose is the narration of the history, and since the final years of Henry IV afford some clue to the origin of the Hal legend, it will be appropriate to look briefly at the rest of the reign. Henry experienced frequent illness, occasionally being obliged to surrender affairs to the direction of his council. He did not become a mere figurehead, however; except for brief periods of really severe illness, he retained a large measure of personal control. Nonetheless, Hal began to move toward center stage. By

1406, when he was nineteen, Hal was immensely experienced. Having struggled with the Welsh since 1400 and having participated in most of the important battles fought by his father, he had learned much about warfare, siegecraft, strategy in hostile territory, and the difficulties of ruling a restive population. He also knew well the administrative and financial problems that lay behind the military activity. As the Welsh rebellion subsided, he took on responsibilities elsewhere. In 1409 he was made constable of Dover and warden of the Cinque Ports (the coastal cities in southeast England, on the narrows of the Channel). In 1410 he became captain of Calais, the English-held city on the opposite side of the Channel. Above all, from late 1406 to late 1411 he regularly attended the king's council and often dominated it.

As the government gained control of domestic discontent, foreign policy absorbed more of the council's attention. Scotland had become less of a problem. By sheer accident, the crown prince of Scotland had fallen into English hands shortly before the death of his father Robert III in 1406. After Robert's death, Scotland was ruled by the duke of Albany, whose son, Murdach earl of Fife, had been captured at Homildon and turned over to Henry. (Shakespeare, misled by Holinshed's punctuation, erroneously describes "Mordake" as son to Douglas.) With both the young king and the regent's son in his power, Henry feared little from the Scots. Rather it was France that concerned the council. By the treaty of Brétigny (1360), Edward III had surrendered his claim to the French crown in return for sovereignty over two parts of France that were all-important to the English: Calais, which was important militarily for its control over the Channel and economically as the market in wool, hides, and tin and as the nexus for England's trade with northern Europe; and Bordeaux, the port for the wine trade and the entrance to the Aquitaine, the great southwestern fief that Henry II's queen, Eleanor of Aquitaine, had brought to the English crown. Enforcement of the treaty had always been difficult. In the later years of Henry IV, the chaos of French royal politics offered a rare opportunity for the English to get what they had been promised.

Charles VI, king of France from 1380 to 1422, suffered periodic fits of madness. When the king was sane, he governed; when he was mad, France was divided into factions led by his brothers and uncles, chief among whom were the royal dukes of Burgundy and Orléans. After Louis of Orléans was assassinated in 1407, their strife reached the point of civil war. In these murky waters the English fished by offering their alliance to the rival parties. In July 1411 Hal, as head of the council, concluded an agreement to give Burgundy military aid in return for control of certain Flemish towns and assistance in an English conquest of Normandy. Hal had in mind the security of Calais. That fall an English expedition led by Hal's friend the young earl of Arundel marched with Burgundy's troops into Paris. In 1412, however, Henry accepted an alliance with the Orléanists that satisfied English interests in the Aquitaine, despatching his second son Thomas, now duke of Clarence, with a similar expeditionary force. This army marched across France to Bordeaux, but before it did any significant damage it was bought off (at a very high price) by the French: King Charles had come to his senses and forced a reconciliation of his hostile dukes.

This rather comic foreign policy resulted not only from the peculiarities of French politics but also from divisions on the English council. Hal had exerted much control over the council's decisions in 1410–1411. He was backed by a group of younger men, among them his uncle Henry Beaufort bishop of Winchester, Arundel, and Richard Beauchamp earl of Warwick. (Warwick appears in several court scenes in *2 Henry IV*, once being erroneously addressed by Westmorland's surname, Neville. He had fought in Wales and at Shrewsbury, and had served on the commission that convicted Archbishop Scrope. Later he performed distinguished diplomatic and military services in the French wars under Henry V and Henry VI.) Bishop Beaufort went so far as to suggest in 1411 that the king abdicate in Hal's favor. The suggestion did not please the king. He dismissed Hal and his party from the council, replacing them with Thomas of Clarence, Archbishop Arundel of Canterbury, and their followers. The change in French alliances more or less coincided with the change in council personnel. Although Hal did sign the treaty with the Orléanists, it constituted a rejection of his pro-Burgundian policy. Throughout 1412 a strained relationship prevailed between the prince and the king. Hal felt obliged to issue an open letter in June explaining why he was not leading Clarence's expedition to Bordeaux and denouncing rumor-mongers who whispered of dissension within the royal family and accused him of seeking to depose his father. Later he sought an interview with Henry at which they came to some degree of reconciliation.

These events appear to provide the historical basis for the later legend of the scapegrace Hal and his troubles with his father. That Henry suspected him of disloyalty and inordinate ambition, that he was once replaced on the council by his brother, and that he tried to clear himself of various charges, incidents that appear in Shakespeare albeit under different colors and circumstances, are true. Other episodes that Shakespeare draws from the legends are almost certainly not true. Few sober historians can believe that he opened his final interview with Henry by trying on the crown for size. Nor can they believe that he was ever arrested by the chief justice for obstreperous behavior in the court of the King's Bench, only to commend the judge and retain him in office after he became king. (Arrest of the heir apparent would certainly be recorded in contemporary documents, yet no mention of that story appears before the sixteenth century. Furthermore, the chief justice, the same Sir William Gascoigne who acted so conscientiously in the trial of Archbishop Scrope, was in fact not kept on by Henry V.) Obviously Hal, being human, must occasionally have sought diversion. There may be some truth behind the mid-fifteenth-century tales of highway robbery and riotous activity in

Eastcheap. On the other hand, these may be mere gossip, reinforced by Hal's unstinting devotion to duty after his coronation. Above all, the character of his chief crony in Shakespeare, Falstaff, is a dramatic invention. Falstaff has very indirect roots in two fifteenth-century persons. The first is Sir John Fastolfe, a soldier accused (wrongly) of cowardice in the French wars of Henry VI. He appears in *1 Henry VI*, and this seems to be the source of both the name and the association of that name with cowardice. But this man was Clarence's retainer, not Hal's. The second is Sir John Oldcastle: this was Falstaff's name in *1 Henry IV* until, apparently, Oldcastle's Elizabethan descendants requested a change. Oldcastle certainly was a friend of Hal's, but he was a man very different from Falstaff; he was a distinguished soldier and a dedicated Lollard to whose execution for heresy and treason the orthodox Hal consented in 1417. The real genesis of Shakespeare's fat knight lies in the theatrical traditions of the Vice of the morality plays, the braggart soldier of Roman and humanist comedy, and the comic buffoon. Above all, it lies in Shakespeare's genius.

Whatever strains and suspicions existed between the king and the prince, there was no open breach. As the king lay dying from December 1412 to March 1413, authority quietly passed from the elder Henry to the younger. Apart from hanging onto his dubiously won crown, Henry IV may not now appear to have accomplished anything significant. If so, the appearance is partly due to Shakespeare: his Henry, an embodiment of the cares of kingship who carries on with his difficult job while the more striking figures of Hal, Hotspur, and Falstaff enjoy the limelight, has heavily influenced the modern idea of this king. To say that Henry merely retained his crown, merely carried on, is to cover a complex enterprise in unnecessarily dismissive phrasing. The actions of Richard II in 1399 had presented Henry with a situation to which there was no wholly satisfactory solution. Henry took the route of usurpation, and was able to consolidate his questionable sovereignty over contentious nobles without turning outright tyrant. That is an achievement relatively rare among English kings. Leaving behind a thoroughly trained and accomplished heir is even rarer.

Artist Unknown: *Henry V* (National Portrait Gallery).

☙ IV ❧

ḢENRY V
the king victorious

No king of England, if not king of France.

1. THE ENGLISH THRONE

Henry V ruled England for nine and a half years, inheriting his father Henry IV's throne in March 1413 at the age of twenty-five, and dying in August 1422, just before his thirty-fifth birthday. His was thus the shortest of the three Lancastrian reigns. It was also the most conspicuously successful. Whereas his father before him and his son after frequently faced domestic rebellion, no one waged civil war against Henry. Indeed, he differs from all the rest of the kings treated in this book in that the most significant events of his reign concerned foreign policy. The other late Plantagenets, Lancastrian and Yorkist alike, were obliged to worry principally about retaining the English crown. Henry had little trouble in this regard. He easily crushed the one dynastic and the one religious plot against him. Never as king did he have to meet rebel Englishmen on the field of battle. Rather he gained a second kingdom for himself and his heirs.

65

Readers of Chapter III will recall Henry's career as prince of Wales. From his father's usurpation of Richard II's throne in 1399, when Henry was but twelve, he was active in the government of England. Until about 1408 he was chiefly occupied in combatting the rebel Owen Glendower in his own Welsh principality. From 1408 until a year before his accession, he was busy in the affairs of the king's council, wrestling with the difficult problems of royal finance and foreign policy. Henry V came to the throne extensively experienced in politics, administration, and warfare: few kings have been so well trained for their job. Popular legend, however, developing later in the fifteenth century and flourishing in Shakespeare's time and beyond, attributed an irresponsible youth to Henry. He was supposed to have been a madcap prince, indulging in adventurous and illegal exploits with a pack of rascally friends. This unstable and undignified conduct, moreover, was supposed to have brought him into frequent clashes with his father. The specific stories told of him probably contain little truth. They cannot be substantiated from contemporary evidence, and apocryphal anecdotes are only too likely to accumulate around the youth of glamorous national heroes. Truth may lie at some distance *behind* the tales. Even hardworking princes relax at times, and the relaxations of a young military veteran and his friends may occasionally take a rowdy form. Furthermore, the council politics of Henry IV's last years were marked by some rancor: in late 1411 the king removed the prince and his adherents from the council altogether, replacing them with other advisors and reversing their policy toward France. Suspicion and coolness prevailed for a time between the two Henrys, and the prince felt obliged publicly to contradict rumors that he aimed to thrust his father aside. It is almost inevitable that the relationship between an aging king (especially one whose possession of the crown has been repeatedly challenged) and an experienced, competent, and eager heir will have moments of strain. But Henry's long labors as prince contravene any notion of fundamental disloyalty, irresponsibility, or profligacy.

Henry's first actions as king may have given more impetus to the later stories than his career as prince did. The heart of the madcap legend is the contrast between Henry as heir and Henry as ruler. His contemporaries were struck with the energy and devotion with which he tackled his new responsibilities. Since, after his dismissal from the council over a year before, he had been in effect a prince without a job, his vigorous seizure of the reins of power could be seen (with the use of some imagination) as a sudden access of sobriety and dedication. His vigor, moreover, was touched with religious overtones. According to one chronicle, he spent the night after his father's death consulting an anchorite at Westminster Abbey, preparing himself for kingship. Throughout his reign he maintained an active piety, visiting shrines, founding new houses of religion, insisting on proper conduct in already established ones, personally attempting to convert heretics, and consistently attributing his military victories to God rather than his own prowess. Whatever his life as prince had been, there is material here that, taken together with the energy, directness, and success of his secular policies, would assist later generations to suppose that Henry underwent a decisive change at his coronation. He "put on him the shape of a new man," reports Shakespeare's authority Holinshed, echoing earlier chronicles and perhaps more importantly echoing St. Paul's notion of the regenerate "new man" who is born out of the sinful "old man." Thus given the clue, Shakespeare has the archbishop of Canterbury, in the first scene of *Henry V,* describe the new king in extravagant terms appropriate only for a full-scale religious conversion. (Of course, Shakespeare also has Prince Hal plan the creation of exactly this effect years earlier.)

The energy of Henry's kingship was immediately apparent in his effort to harmonize the mighty in his kingdom. In various ways he tried to win the allegiance of his magnates and bury the quarrels that had resulted from his father's usurpation. His chief act was a literal burial. The corpse of Richard II had lain at King's Langley since his (probable) murder in 1400: Henry had it disinterred and ceremoniously reburied at Westminster Abbey, in the tomb that Richard had built for himself during his own lifetime. This was a gesture of piety. It was also probably a gesture of friendship, as the young Henry had once served as page to the king his father deposed. Politically, it was a gesture indicating that the past was past: the usurpation was to be considered a closed issue. Further, he released and restored to his noble position Edmund Mortimer the young earl of March, who, as great-grandson of Edward III's second surviving son Lionel, had a better claim than the Lancastrians to be Richard II's heir, and who on that account had been kept under house arrest by Henry IV. Another member of the royal house whom he sought to conciliate was Edward duke of York, son to Edward III's fourth surviving son Edmund. (Edward appears as the duke of Aumerle in *Richard II;* he succeeded to the York title when his father died in 1402.) York had twice participated in plots against Henry IV, the earls' rebellion to restore Richard II in 1400 and a later attempt to kidnap young March and carry him off to Wales. Henry V quashed the legal proceedings still on record against him. He also elevated York's younger brother Richard to the earldom of Cambridge. Henry's efforts to heal these old wounds also extended beyond the royal family. Thomas Montague earl of Salisbury and John Holland earl of Huntingdon, both sons of other conspirators in the earls' rebellion of 1400, became distinguished commanders and diplomats for Henry. Above all, he sought to conciliate the great aristocratic house of Percy and the northern lords loyal to that house. Two generations of Percies had perished in repeated attempts to unseat Henry IV. The Percy heir, aged fifteen at the time, had been left in Scotland when his grandfather, the first earl of Northumberland, died in the battle of Bramham Moor. Shortly after his accession, Henry initiated negotiations to have young Percy returned and the earldom restored to him.

Henry's consolidation of his court further entailed the creation of new dignities. His brother Thomas, who had served during their father's reign as governor of Ireland and had replaced Henry on the council in 1411, had already been made duke of Clarence. Henry proceeded to raise his two younger brothers to ducal rank: John, who had been constable of England, became duke of Bedford, and Humphrey, whose youth had prevented him from playing any major role during the previous reign, became duke of Gloucester. According to Holinshed, Henry at the same time granted his half-uncle Thomas Beaufort the dukedom of Exeter. This Thomas was one of the sons of John of Gaunt by his mistress (eventually his third wife) Catherine Swynford. He had held a variety of important military posts under his half-brother Henry IV, had served for two years as chancellor of England, and had been created earl of Dorset. Actually, Henry did not elevate Thomas to the Exeter title until 1416, a year after the battle of Agincourt, but Shakespeare follows Holinshed in consistently calling him Exeter. A year after Henry's accession, the death of Archbishop Arundel of Canterbury provided him with the opportunity to appoint an old friend to the chief English ecclesiastical post. He gave the archbishopric to Henry Chichele, formerly bishop of St. Davids, a distinguished ecclesiastical lawyer, diplomat, and university man who had served with Henry on the council in the old king's time.

These men formed a united court with the old Lancastrian standbys. Henry IV had relied much upon knightly retainers inherited from his father John of Gaunt. Some of these were still flourishing, notably Sir Thomas Erpingham, Henry IV's chamberlain. The earls of Warwick and Westmorland, whose connections and service to Henry IV were mentioned in the previous chapter, were given important diplomatic and military assignments under the new king.

Except for March and the Percy heir, all the men mentioned above appear in Shakespeare's *Henry V*. Except for Richard of Cambridge (who figured in a conspiracy to be discussed below) and the archbishop, they appear with undifferentiated personalities. So unified is the English court that its lords are almost a Greek chorus; so loyal are they all that it scarcely matters which of them speaks which lines. It therefore scarcely matters that Shakespeare occasionally makes minor historical errors about them: Warwick and Westmorland, for example, were in fact not present at the battle of Agincourt, but busy elsewhere on the king's business. No matter: other lords were at Agincourt, and Shakespear's Warwick and Westmorland are hardly specific persons—just *lords*. And there is historical truth in this dramatic method. Although no group of real human beings could ever achieve such unanimity and uniformity as the magnates do in Shakespeare's version of Henry's court and Henry's camp, the dramatic effect constitutes, in its way, a reasonably accurate depiction of Henry's achievement in England. During the reign of Henry V, with the exception of two minor episodes, England was wholly loyal to her king for the first time since the palmy days of Edward III. Shakespeare's genius for individual characterization, thus excluded from the lords, is visited instead upon the fictional officers and footsoldiers of Henry's army: Fluellen, Pistol, Michael Williams, and their like. But even here the theme of national unity crops up. Although the English, Welsh, Scots, and Irish captains of Act III mock each other's regional peculiarities, all are united in the king's army.

The first minor exception to English loyalty in this period is neither dramatized nor mentioned by Shakespeare. A Lollard uprising occurred in January 1414, shortly before the first anniversary of Henry's accession. Henry, warned in advance, had soldiers ready at the Lollards' rendezvous. The subsequent encounter was scarcely a skirmish; executions for heresy and treason followed. Sparks of Lollard rebellion continued to flicker for the next three years chiefly because the Lollard leader, Sir John Oldcastle, had eluded capture. He was finally run to earth and executed in 1417.

The Lollard grievances were principally religious, political only by implication. As spiritual heirs of the fourteenth-century proto-Protestant John Wyclif, the Lollards rejected the authority of the Church Temporal. They believed that the true church was the fellowship of the elect, which did not necessarily correspond to the church of the priests. They also believed that the route to religious truth was private perusal of the scriptures by the humble spirit. That is, they were fundamentalists who dismissed centuries of theological elaboration. These heresies, which entailed the rejection of certain doctrines about the sacraments as well as the authority and wealth of the ecclesiastical establishment, spread to Oxford dons, country knights, and various humbler folk. The church hierarchy vigorously opposed them. The Lollards' views eventually led them to a rejection of secular lordship, which they saw as the product, not of God's ordinance for the government of his people, but of the accidents of history. The Lollard uprising, then, was not the usual fifteenth-century dispute over who should be king, but a genuine (though ill planned and quite abortive) revolution against all established earthly authority. It arose from religious zealots, not from that usual source of medieval rebellion, the aristocracy. Only one peer figured in the revolt: Oldcastle himself, who, having married an heiress, held the title of Lord Cobham in his wife's right. He was a distinguished veteran of the wars against Glendower, during which he had gained Henry's friendship. Indeed, only his friendship with Henry allowed him to engineer the uprising. He had been convicted of heresy in 1413, several months before the revolt; execution was stayed at the behest of the king, who endeavored personally to reconvert his friend to orthodoxy. While the unsuccessful persuasion was in progress, Oldcastle escaped from the Tower to organize the revolt. It is easy to see why Shakespeare omits all this. Not only is religious revolution irrelevant to his play about the conquest of France, but also English attitudes toward the Lollards had changed by his time. To Protestant Englishmen after the Reformation, Oldcastle died a martyr. Shakespeare cannot present his king as the agent of Papist persecution.

The single plot in Henry's reign of the usual aristocratic and dynastic sort, a plot that does appear in Shakespeare's play, was equally a fiasco. This occurred in the summer of 1415, as Henry assembled his army at Southampton for the invasion of France. Richard the new earl of Cambridge, Sir Thomas Grey of Northumberland, and Thomas Lord Scrope of Masham (who, as treasurer, was one of the three principal officers of government and a member of the king's council) conspired to assassinate the king and replace him with the earl of March. The plot was revealed to Henry by none other than March himself, who, having been brought up under close royal supervision, had become a friend of Henry's. Among the many episodes of betrayal in the history of the later Plantagenets, March provides a stunning counterexample of cousinly loyalty. Although possessing a good claim to the crown, and urged by the conspirators to take advantage of that claim, he remained Henry's trusted and trustworthy vassal. Upon March's revelation, Henry crushed the plot. The three confederates were immediately arrested, tried, and executed. Discreetly, Henry omitted to inquire about other persons on the fringe of the conspiracy.

Some historians have seen this episode as the final spasm of the turmoil of Henry IV's time. The Percy plots of 1403–1408 had been hatched in favor of the March heir. Because the younger Percy (Hotspur) was married to March's aunt, the Percies hoped to dominate the government if March were made king. A similar ambition moved Cambridge in 1415. He had been married to March's sister, Anne Mortimer, although the lady had died by the time of Cambridge's plot. As both kingmaker and brother-in-law, he would have exerted extraordinary leverage over a crowned March. The other two conspirators, Grey and Scrope, both had Percy connections. Scrope, moreover, trusted friend and servant of Henry V though he was, was also the nephew of that Richard Scrope archbishop of York whom Henry IV, in defiance of the precedents and the canon law against the execution of ecclesiastics, had beheaded for treason in 1405. The conspirators also had connections with the surviving followers of the Welshman Owen Glendower. The Cambridge plot, in sum, revived the repeated Wales-Mortimer-Percy-Scrope alliances that had given Henry IV sleepless nights for much of his reign. It was the epilogue to an old struggle.

It is also possible to see the Cambridge plot as a prologue to later contention. March eventually died childless in 1425. His claim to the throne thereby passed to Richard of York, his sister Anne's son by Cambridge. This Richard was only three at the time of his father's execution. Forty years later, however, during the chaotic reign of Henry V's incompetent son, Richard of York's ancestry became a most powerful dynastic fact. It provided the dynastic justification for the Wars of the Roses and ultimately for the displacement of the Lancastrian line in favor of Richard of York's son Edward IV. In a sense Cambridge finally triumphed: in 1461, when he had been mouldering in his grave for forty-six years, his grandson, as king, had parliament reverse the judgment on the dead traitor.

That we may see the Cambridge plot both as the epilogue to the reign of Henry IV and as the distant prologue to the reign of Henry VI isolates the unique characteristic of Henry V's rule that we have been discussing. Whereas all the other kings of England from the late fourteenth to the early sixteenth centuries had to struggle repeatedly with threats to their dynasty, Henry V hardly had to worry about such things at all. He swiftly dealt with one feeble conspiracy and thereafter could rest secure in his lords' loyalty. So strong was his influence that Lancastrian dynastic security lasted for three-quarters of his son's long riegn. Although Henry VI was but an infant upon his accession in 1422, no one, not even his York or Mortimer cousins, tried to unseat him until a complication of disorders in England, and the loss of the conquered territories in France, brought matters to a crisis decades later.

So great was Henry V's success, indeed, that Shakespeare omits to point out that the conspiracy even had a dynastic motive. In the abbreviated dramatization given the Cambridge plot in *Henry V*, II.ii, the king has already taken steps to deal with the conspirators. Their personalities and connections are not developed, and the charge against them is simply that they have been suborned by the French to murder the king. At the end of the scene, Cambridge mutters that he had another motive for the plot besides French gold, but he does not reveal what the other motive was. The earl of March is never mentioned, here or elsewhere in the play. The dynastic issue is altogether obliterated. Now to some extent, Shakespeare is merely following his sources Hall and Holinshed, both of whom introduce the Cambridge plot as inspired by French bribery. But both immediately go on to discuss the dynastic motive and to indicate its ramifications later in the century. Furthermore, although both chroniclers mention that Cambridge, in an effort to avoid endangering March and his own infant son, suppressed the dynastic motive when making his confession, Holinshed adds that Cambridge's formal indictment certainly included the charge of conspiring to crown March. (Both Hall and Holinshed say that Cambridge knew that March was unable to beget heirs, and thus that Cambridge's ultimate goal was the diversion of the royal succession to his own son. I find this rather odd: why, one wonders, did the Tudor chroniclers think Cambridge could be so certain about the reproductive shortcomings of a man of twenty-four?) In other words, Shakespeare here consciously modified his sources by deciding to omit the dynastic motive from the episode. His Henry merely meets a generalized threat of largely foreign origin. He is not the wearer of a disputed crown but an unquestioned king administering justice and a man deeply wounded by his friend Lord Scrope's betrayal. But although he thus mutes and blurs the facts of the Cambridge plot, Shakespeare is thereby truer to something more important. Had he made the dynastic implications of this one episode clear, he might have upset his depiction of the general state of affairs in Henry's reign. England at large was loyal to her hero-king. Exceptions to that generalization could be treated as insignificant, and saddled on the French.

2. THE FRENCH THRONE

Henry V's major achievement was the conquest of France. This began with a diplomatic offensive shortly after Henry's accession in 1413. It was carried out by three military ventures: an expedition in 1415 that took Harfleur and ended with the victory at Agincourt; a sustained campaign in 1417–1420 to reduce Normandy that concluded with the treaty of Troyes; and a final series of sieges in 1421–1422 that was cut short by Henry's death. Shakespeare represents some of the diplomacy and most of the Harfleur-Agincourt expedition. He hastily summarizes the events between Agincourt and Troyes in the choral narrative preceding Act V, and altogether eclipses the final campaign, barely mentioning Henry's death in the epilogue to the play. To understand the genesis and the significance of this conquest, we must look at dynastic entanglements on both sides of the Channel.

Henry claimed France on two grounds, by treaty and by inheritance. In invading France he was renewing the Hundred Years War initiated by his great-grandfather Edward III in 1337. (The conventional time span of the Hundred Years War is 1337–1453, but it would be clumsy to speak of a Hundred and Sixteen Years War.) The first phase of the war had concluded in the treaty of Brétigny (1360), which granted Edward sovereignty over Calais and surrounding areas on the Channel coast in northeast France, and over Bordeaux and surrounding Gascony on the Atlantic coast in southwest France. The signing of a treaty, however, does not automatically entail the fulfillment of its provisions. Edward had grasped Calais firmly, expelling the French inhabitants and repopulating it with Englishmen, making it an English garrison and the nexus of English commerce with northern Europe. The rest of his French territories presented more problems. Anglo-French relations after 1360 were marked by sporadic fighting over the lands Edward had been promised. The negotiations and expeditions late in Henry IV's reign, described in the previous chapter, were part of that struggle.

A larger claim lay in the background, however, an English claim to the crown of France itself. To grasp this, we must turn to the French royal genealogy. Philip IV of France ("Philip the Fair"), who died in 1314, begot three sons, each of whom ruled France in his turn without begetting a surviving son of his own: Louis X ("Louis the Quarreller," died 1316), Philip V ("Philip the Tall," died 1322), and Charles IV ("Charles the Fair," died 1328). He also begot a daughter, Isabella, who married Edward II of England (died 1327) and bore him Edward III. Upon the death of Charles the Fair, the French throne was claimed for Edward III in his mother's right. The lords of France, however, understandably not wanting an English king, decided that no woman could transmit a claim to the French crown. (They had previously decided, with reference to Louis the Quarreller's daughter, that no woman could herself wear the crown.) The

76

Capetian dynasty thereby came to an end, and the French crown went to Charles the Fair's cousin Philip of Valois, who became Philip VI. (This Philip acquired no lasting nickname.) Edward III was not immediately in a position to do anything about the matter. A dozen years later, however, when he had already gone to war in support of certain feudal rights he held in France, he chose to dispute the ruling: the English, after all, had no prohibition barring a brotherless woman from succeeding to the throne or passing on succession to her offspring. Edward proclaimed himself king of France and quartered the fleurs-de-lys on his coat of arms. Henry V, in his turn, could press the claim for Gascony and the environs of Calais based on the treaty of Brétigny, or the claim for all of France based on his descent from Philip the Fair through Isabella and Edward. As a matter of fact, his byzantine diplomacy featured a careful deployment of both claims, as well as the use of several pretensions derived from other treaties and inheritances. The ancient duchy of Aquitaine, for example, of which Gascony was but a part, had been brought to the English crown in 1154, when Henry II and his wife Eleanor of Aquitaine became king and queen of England; and Normandy could be claimed as his inheritance from William the Conqueror, although King John had lost it to the French two centuries before Henry V's time.

Henry's pretensions may look to us like an antiquarian and legalistic refusal to accept the verdicts of history. To a modern mind, claiming foreign territories on the basis of genealogical facts buried a century or more in the past appears to be not only a ridiculous move in itself but also a frivolous reason for starting a war. Consequently, the complicated harangue of the archbishop of Canterbury in the first act of *Henry V,* whereby he proves to his own and Henry's satisfaction that there is no sound basis in French law for barring a woman and her issue from succession, is often read as and performed for comedy. Now it is true that

Henry had other motives for invading France. The territories promised by the treaty of Brétigny were commercially important to the English: the Bordeaux wine customs alone constituted a major source of income for the English crown. Further, the prosecution of a foreign war minimized the chances of domestic revolt by nobles who would necessarily take the field with the king. But these were not the determining issues either to Henry himself or to Shakespeare. The inheritance of property by the correct bloodlines was an extremely serious matter in the Middle Ages and long after. It was an elementary premise undergirding the whole social organization. That is why Henry IV had gained the support of the English nobility in deposing Richard II after Richard had confiscated his huge inheritance from John of Gaunt. Richard had committed other undesirable and alarming acts, but sequestering a magnate's inheritance (except in cases of treason) was lawless tyranny. The settlement of property disputes in this period involved the hauling forth of ancient genealogical rolls as characteristically as, in modern business transactions, it involves the searching of title deeds. The lively importance of such considerations was still felt in Shakespeare's time two centuries later. Four years after he had composed *Henry V,* the English crown passed to a foreign monarch, James of Scotland, because, as great-grandson of Elizabeth I's elder aunt, James was the late queen's nearest living relative. Naturally, a crown presented more problems than an ordinary piece of property would: the law was not clearcut as to how they differed, and mundane political considerations often interfered with the execution of pure theory. When the French finally did acknowledge Henry V as "heir of France" in the treaty of Troyes, he had solidified his position by a series of indisputable military victories and had agreed to marry the French king's daughter. Nevertheless, when Shakespeare's Henry asks the archbishop, "May I with right and conscience make this claim?," he is raising an honest and vital question, and the archbishop's lengthy exposition constitutes an appropriate legal case. The archbishop may make much of persons we now know to be mythical (King Pharamond, Blithild daughter to King Clothair); he may also fall into incidental ironies (after reciting much obscure history, he announces that the whole matter is "as clear as is the summer's sun"); but the speech as a whole is not comic. As a matter of fact, it is almost verbatim Holinshed, altered only insofar as it is versified. Holinshed was no disciple of the comic muse.

That much said, it must be admitted that the opening scenes of *Henry V* are fairly unhistorical. Henry did claim France on the grounds described above, and the claim immediately led to parliamentary discussions, the consultation of genealogical rolls, and negotiations with the French. Shakespeare's first act, however, which shows these things occurring, is based with great fidelity upon misinformation in Holinshed. There are three chief errors. First, Archbishop Chichele almost certainly never made the speech on the Salic law that is assigned to him. He was probably not present at the parliament upon which the scene is based.* Second, the motives attributed to the archbishop are unhistorical. Holinshed and Shakespeare show Chichele persuading Henry to war, and contributing an enormous sum to his war-chest, largely in order to win his favor. He wants Henry to quash

---

* A minor point might be made about the Salic law. Women were barred from the French crown by the specific fourteenth-century rulings mentioned above. Those rulings sought to deal with an unprecedented crisis in the French monarchy: since the establishment of the Capetian line in 987, no French king prior to Louis the Quarreller had failed to leave a son behind him. Some years after the rulings were made and the house of Valois took the throne, the Valois lawyers resurrected a penal code of the sixth century called the Salic law. In this ancient and neglected code, they pretended to find a precedent justifying the anti-feminist rulings. That is why the law governing succession to the French crown came to be falsely called the Salic law. (It is this sort of thing that leads anyone trying to explain the archbishop of Canterbury's speech into talking like the archbishop himself.)

a parliamentary bill that would strip the church of all its wealth. It is true, as the archbishop mentions to the bishop of Ely, that such a bill was advanced in Henry IV's time; but it is not true that the bill was revived in the new reign. Although the bishops did contribute substantial funds for the campaign, their donation was not the extraordinary amount described in the play. Finally, and unfortunately for lovers of the picturesque, it is not true that, during negotiations with the French, the dauphin Louis insulted Henry for his youth by sending him a packing-case of tennis balls. Such a story did circulate in England during Henry's time; doubtless it made good propaganda; but no French chronicler mentions it. One historian has supposed that it is based upon some verbal jest, but it too closely resembles a tale told of negotiations between King Darius of Persia and the young Alexander to be wholly credible. Louis, moreover, could hardly have sneered at Henry for his youthfulness: he was Henry's junior by nine years.

On the opposite side of the Channel there existed, not a dynastic, but a governmental tangle. As readers of the previous chapter will recall, Charles VI, great-grandson of that Philip of Valois who gained the throne through the French antifeminist ruling, suffered periodic fits of madness. When his mind wandered, his country was misruled by various royal dukes, each with portions of France loyal to him. Each tried to control Paris and govern in the name of the mad king. Each operated by a combination of intrigue, civil war, and occasional reconciliation with or assassination of his rivals. At the time of Henry's accession, the competing parties were the Burgundians, led by King Charles's first cousin John the Fearless duke of Burgundy, and the Armagnacs or Orléanists, led by Bernard count of Armagnac and his son-in-law, the king's nephew Charles duke of Orléans. John the Fearless ruled in the county and duchy of Burgundy in eastern France, and in Flanders. The Armagnacs were dominant at various places near Paris, on the River Loire, and in the south.

Among the Armagnacs were Charles d'Albret the constable of France, and the turbulent John duke of Bourbon. The heir to the French throne, the dauphin Louis, was also associated with the Armagnacs. Occupying a middle position was John duke of Berry, who is now best remembered for his Books of Hours, the splendid volumes of medieval illumination that he commissioned and that inspired the costumes and sets of Laurence Olivier's film version of *Henry V*. The master fence-straddler was young John of Brittany, whose duchy (like that of Burgundy) was a semi-independent fief of the French crown. Brittany was ostensibly an Armagnac, but he had arranged a secret treaty with Burgundy and was to do likewise with the invading Henry. He was also incidentally, Henry's stepbrother, his mother Joan of Navarre having been Henry IV's second wife. All these persons except for Count Bernard and John the Fearless appear in *Henry V*. (A duke of Burgundy appears in the last act, but this was John's son, as will be explained below.) Their characterization is handled nearly as lightly as that of the English lords. King Charles is not portrayed as lunatic, although Shakespeare's sources mention his "frenzy" and some actors have imported it into their performances of the role. The various princes exist largely as examples of French arrogance and boastfulness, the dauphin being distinguished only by the superlative degree of his fatuity.

During the first years of Henry's reign, the Armagnacs controlled Paris and the king, while Burgundy kept to his own dominions. Henry, however, negotiated with both factions, each of which sought his alliance against the other, and from each of which Henry sought the satisfaction of his claims. Marriageable princesses, dowries, and duchies glittered amid a jumble of words. While conducting this maze of diplomacy, Henry, fortified by parliamentary subsidies and loans, raised an army. After dealing with the Cambridge plot, he set sail across the Channel in August 1415, landed at the mouth of the Seine, and besieged

Harfleur. As the Armagnacs in Paris could send no significant aid to the city, and Burgundy stood aloof, Harfleur was forced to capitulate to cannonade and the threat of starvation on 22 September. Exeter was made governor of the town, high-ranking inhabitants were held for ransom, and many of the poorer folk were evacuated: Henry planned to repopulate Harfleur with English colonists as Edward III had done with Calais. His army, however, was forbidden to plunder. On this point Shakespeare is closer to historical accuracy than is Holinshed, who says the town was sacked. Shakespeare has Henry order Exeter to "use mercy to them all," and this indeed was Henry's consistent policy in the invasion of France. France, after all, was *his:* one does not loot one's own country, nor commit wanton depredations upon people whom one wants to rule as faithful subjects. The hanging of Shakespeare's fictional Bardolph for robbing a church is based upon a historical incident: a nameless soldier was in fact executed for such a theft.

This first victory was not painless. Casualties, desertions, and dysentery—the last a frequent affliction of medieval soldiers, especially those fighting in swampy areas in the summer heat—cost Henry a third of his army. The depletion of his forces and the lateness of the season prevented Henry from marching inland toward Paris. Determined, however, not to leave France after only one adventure, and anxious to see more of the country he claimed, he did not immediately reimbark. Instead he decided to march 150 miles along the coast to Calais and sail home from there. On 6 October he started on a trek supposed to take eight days, but it proved longer than that. To get to Calais his army had to cross the Somme. When the French broke the causeways over the marshy mouth of the river, he was forced to turn inland after all, marching upriver well beyond Amiens, passing other broken bridges and fords too strongly held against him, until he finally got his army across near Nesle, thirteen days after leaving

Harfleur. On the next day they crossed the tracks of a French host dispatched by Charles and the dauphin from Rouen. The two armies marched north, just out of sight of each other, until 24 October, when the French brought Henry to bay near the village of Agincourt. The English expeditionary force of possibly 6000 exhausted men faced an unwearied French army many times its size. Henry sent a message to the French leaders (the Constable d'Albret, Marshal Boucicaut, the dukes of Orléans and Bourbon) offering to reduce his claims to France and to pay for damage done, in exchange for unmolested passage to Calais. (In Shakespeare, this moment of attempted conciliation is blurred. Henry, although admitting to the French herald the sorry state of his troops, merely says that he will neither seek nor shun battle.) The offer, which he may have made only to secure a night's rest for his army, was refused. The English expected to be wiped out on the morrow, although Henry continued to affirm his faith that God could give them victory.

On the next day Henry did indeed gain one of the most astonishing victories in military history. Whether or not God intervened, Henry benefited greatly from the deadly power of his archers and from his shrewd placement of his troops where forests protected his flanks. On their side, the French were hideously encumbered by their extremely heavy armor, by the soft, newly ploughed, heavily rained-on field over which they attempted to charge, and by their very numbers. (So great was the press they could not use their lances.) The French commanders, who had confidently played dice for the English lords the night before and who eagerly sought places in the front line, fell in heaps. Over them the more lightly equipped English clambered, cutting their throats. Slaughter and the capture of prisoners went on for several hours, until Henry, alarmed at the apparent regrouping of the third French line for renewed assault, ordered the killing of all but the highest-ranking prisoners lest they impede further fight-

83

ing. This ruthless command was carried out by a special squad of 200 archers. (It was not the case, as Shakespeare's Gower and many historians have supposed, that Henry angrily ordered the prisoners slain when the French plundered his baggage. It has now been established that the plundering occurred before the battle.) In the event, the expected assault did not amount to much; the French dispersed, leaving Henry master of the field. The final miracle of Agincourt (from the English point of view) was the casualty ratio. Something in the range of 7000 Frenchmen died. Among the remarkable number of lords and princes of the blood who perished were Constable d'Albret, the admiral of France, the dukes of Bar, Brabant, and Alençon, and seven counts. Among the surviving prisoners were the Armagnac dukes of Orléans and Bourbon. (Burgundy, still at odds with the Armagnacs, took no part in the 1415 war, and neither the aged Berry nor the dauphin were present at Agincourt. The dauphin, indeed, died of natural causes two months later.) By contrast the English lost at most 500 men, including only two lords, the earl of Suffolk and the duke of York. Shakespeare's Exeter gives these two noblemen a brilliant chivalric epitaph; history, however, adds its usual sour note by pointing out that York perished, not by the sword, but by suffocation or a heart attack after falling off his horse. He was quite fat.

Readers of *Henry V* cannot be blamed for supposing that the Agincourt victory gained Henry the whole kingdom of France. In fact, Agincourt constituted no sort of conquest. It did, however, make the subsequent conquest possible. Agincourt badly demoralized the French. It also caused wild rejoicing among the English: they took it for granted that Henry would pursue his rights in France, and parliament voted the money for him to do so. In other words, Agincourt gave him the financial and patriotic backing to carry out the much more important Normandy campaign of 1417–1420, a campaign that Shakespeare does not dramatize.

The Normandy campaign, however, did not begin immediately. Agincourt was followed by twenty months of diplomacy. Henry engaged in his usual game of talking with both the Burgundians and the Armagnacs. The Holy Roman Emperor Sigismund intervened, trying to establish political peace in western Europe as a means of establishing religious peace at the Council of Constance, which was then meeting to resolve the Papal Schism. But plans for a summit conference among the three monarchs, Henry, Charles, and Sigismund, were blown up when the count of Armagnac, now constable of France, insisted upon a war policy and besieged Harfleur. Henry, pointing out to Sigismund the duplicity and insincerity of the French, signed a treaty of perpetual friendship with him on the same day that Bedford defeated the French fleet off Harfleur and revictualled the city. Henry then tried to encircle France by negotiating with John of Brittany and by inviting Burgundy into the Anglo-Imperial alliance. What exactly was agreed upon in these secret parleys is not known. Certainly Burgundy did not become an active ally of the English. By July 1417, however, Henry was ready to return to France and try once again the way of force. He made Caen, which fell to him in September, his headquarters. From there he proceeded to reduce the strongholds of Normandy one by one. The Armagnac government sent no army to oppose him, and each Norman city fell after siege had led the citizens to promise capitulation if no relief arrived within a stated time. In August 1418, with most of the duchy in his hands, he settled down to besiege its capital, Rouen.

Meanwhile the French continued divided among themselves. The Armagnac government could not oppose Henry significantly because they feared that Burgundy would take Paris if they marched out of it. If John the Fearless was not really an ally of Henry's, he was not an ally of theirs either. In this stalemate they continued until November 1417, when Charles's queen, the self-indulgent, licentious, and flighty Isabel of Bavaria, altered the balance of affairs by leaving the Armagnacs to join John. Claiming the regency of France, she and the duke organized a government at Troyes. The following spring, some months before Henry started the siege of Rouen, a popular rising in Paris opened the city gates to Burgundy and the queen. Those Armagnacs who did not escape the capital were rounded up, many of them (including the count himself) being lynched. Prince Charles, however, the younger brother to the late dauphin and now dauphin himself, escaped from the city, and around him an Armagnac government formed at Poitiers. Now Burgundy, although in control of Paris and the king, no more dared to leave the city and confront Henry than the Armagnacs had. The relationships had reversed but the position was the same. Henry proceeded to negotiate with both sides and to press his siege of Rouen, which was finally starved into submission in January 1419.

By the spring of that year, with all Normandy conquered, Henry was in clear control, and his diplomatic posture hardened. In desperation, Isabel and Burgundy attempted a personal reconciliation with the dauphin. Two months later, when the dauphin met Burgundy for a conference on the castle bridge at Montereau, the Armagnacs knocked the duke's brains out with an axe. Never did a treacherous plot so fail in its ultimate object. The murder of John the Fearless threw the Burgundians, led by John's heir Philip the Good, definitively into the arms of the English. The dauphin's hopes for supremacy in France were swamped in moral revulsion and demands for revenge.

The subsequent diplomacy was exceedingly complicated, but its result was almost inevitable. The treaty of Troyes, signed by Philip the Good, Charles VI, and Henry in May 1420, gave Henry everything he wanted. Charles was to retain the French throne for the rest of his life, but Henry was to be regent for that period and Charles's successor afterward. The dauphin was disinherited. (Isabel herself declared him a bastard, borne by her to an unnamed lover.) The two crowns were to be united in one, namely Henry's, although the two kingdoms were to retain their separate organization. Henry's existing sovereignty over Normandy was recognized. All parties undertook to secure the allegiance of that part of France still under Armagnac-dauphinist control. Twelve days later, Henry married Charles's daughter Catherine. (Although Shakespeare, for obvious dramatic reasons, combines the first encounter of Henry and Catherine with the signing of the treaty, they had actually met at a parley a year earlier.)

The only flaw in this triumph was Henry's incomplete mastery over his new kingdom. French factionalism had greatly assisted him, but it also meant that he could conclude settlements with only one of the factions. Much of France south of the Loire, and a few places in the north and east, were still loyal to the dauphin. They had to be reduced fairly swiftly. In the spring of 1421, when Henry was back in England raising loans, the defeat and death of his brother Clarence in a rather foolish raid at Baugé in Maine proved that the English were not entirely invincible. Henry returned for another campaign, but during the long siege of Meaux in the winter of 1421–1422 he contracted the illness—probably dysentery—from which he eventually died. Meaux fell to him in May and he moved to attack the dauphinist strongholds on the Loire. But he had become too weak to ride a horse. Clearheaded to the last, he dictated plans for the government of his two kingdoms, and then succumbed at Bois de Vincennes outside Paris on 31 August 1422. Since Charles the Mad survived him by two months, Henry was never officially king of France. The double crown descended to his son, who had been born the previous December.

Henry V was unquestionably the most successful of the later

87

Plantagenet kings, and his success is traceable to his own talents and training. He had military genius, diplomatic skill, the magnetic qualities necessary to inspire and to lead others, and the tremendous capacity for hard work that enabled him to keep an expeditionary army in the field for three years while financing and supplying it almost entirely from England. His years as prince of Wales had nurtured these abilities. He was energetic, pious, and personally courageous. Even the French chroniclers praised his devotion to justice. Save that detailed administrative work is no subject for theatrical scenes, Shakespeare's play reflects history fairly accurately in all this. Yet in modern times historians and dramatic critics have sharply disagreed in estimating the value of his success. The goals, motives, and methods of both the historical Henry and Shakespeare's Henry have been vigorously questioned. That, for example, the English eventually lost his French empire (although this occurred thirty years after his death) has been held to show that he should not have sought it in the first place. Much of the criticism visited upon Henry the king and Henry the character reflects the public passions and personal concerns of the critics' own times. In periods when a revulsion against war is strongly felt, or when worldly success is held to be sordid in comparison with refinement of feeling, the career of an exuberant conqueror, one who is dramatically depicted almost exclusively in public oratory rather than private self-exploration, has been treated scornfully or ransacked for undermining ironies. The present book is no place to settle an estimate of Henry V or *Henry V*. It should be noted, however, that, whatever the goals of private persons, a large measure of conspicuous worldly success is demanded of kings. Henry fulfilled that difficult demand. His contemporaries thought that he had ruled spectacularly well, and their admiration lasted as the common English attitude toward him for generations. Over a century after his death, the Tudor historian Edward Hall, in a sonorous passage that was later quoted by Holinshed and must have been pondered by Shakespeare, observed of Henry that "neither fire, rust, nor frettying time shall amongst Englishmen either appall his honor or obliterate his glory, [who] in so few years and brief days achieved so great a conquest."

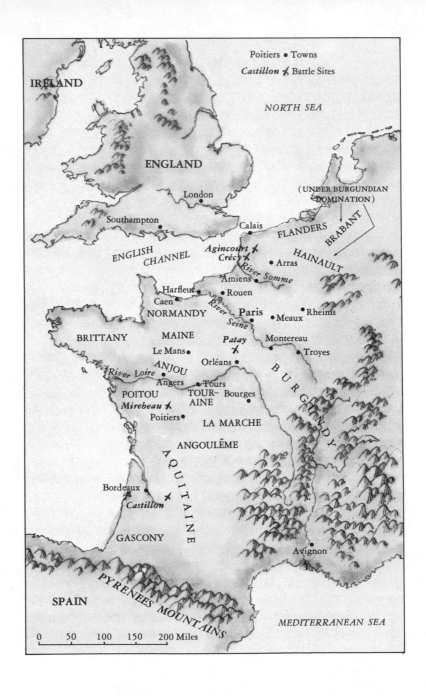

Poitiers • Towns
Castillon ⚔ Battle Sites

IRELAND

NORTH SEA

ENGLAND

London

(UNDER BURGUNDIAN DOMINATION)

Southampton

Calais

FLANDERS

BRABANT

ENGLISH CHANNEL

Agincourt ⚔
Crécy ⚔

River *Somme*

HAINAULT

Arras

Amiens

Harfleur

Rouen

Caen

River *Seine*

NORMANDY

Paris

Meaux

Rheims

BRITTANY

MAINE

Patay ⚔

Montereau

Le Mans

Orléans

Troyes

River *Loire*

ANJOU

BURGUNDY

Angers

Tours

POITOU

TOUR-AINE

Bourges

Mirebeau ⚔

Poitiers

LA MARCHE

ANGOULÊME

A
Q
U
I
T
A
I
N
E

Bordeaux

Castillon ⚔

GASCONY

Avignon

SPAIN

PYRENEES MOUNTAINS

MEDITERRANEAN SEA

0   50   100   150   200 Miles

ɬ V ɬ

ɬeɳɾɣ VI
the loss of empire

Sad tidings bring I to you out of France,
Of loss, of slaughter, and discomfiture.

1. INTRODUCTION TO THE HENRY VI PLAYS

Of Henry VI it has been wittily pointed out that he is the only
king of England to have been twice crowned, twice deposed, and
twice buried. He also reigned over England nearly twice as long
as any of the other later Plantagenets. Born in 1421 to Henry V
and the French princess Catherine, he succeeded to his father's
throne in August 1422, at the age of nine months. He was formally crowned king of England at Westminster in 1429 and king
of France at Paris in 1431. France he lost in 1453 to the successful generals of his maternal uncle Charles VII. England he lost in
1461 to his Plantagenet cousin Edward of York, who deposed
him and assumed the crown as Edward IV. The supporters of the
Lancastrian line, however, rose against Edward nine years later.
In 1470 they forced him to flee abroad and restored Henry to the
throne. But Henry's "re-adeption," as it was called, lasted only
six months. In April 1471 Edward returned in force, destroyed
the Lancastrian cause in two decisive battles, and redeposed

Henry, who perished, presumably by Edward's orders, in the Tower. His body was hastily interred at Chertsey and later moved to Windsor.

The dates of Henry's reign thus enclose an intricate series of events. The loss of the English territory in France was not a swift reversal. The fortunes of battle wavered back and forth: it took the French thirty years to regain what Henry V had conquered in five. In England sundry feuds broke out among the magnates who ruled during the king's minority; these were made more complex when Henry, grown up, attempted to rule, and further embroiled when he married. They climaxed in the wars between Lancaster and York and the eventual establishment of the Yorkist dynasty.

The length and eventfulness of the reign led Shakespeare to devote three plays to it. Although these plays are (rather dully and forbiddingly) entitled *Henry VI Parts 1, 2, and 3*, the king dominates the action in none of them. Henry's inability to dominate anything, indeed, formed a large part of the problem he posed to the country he nominally ruled. *Part 1*, whose action runs from 1422 to 1444, focuses upon the loss of France. Its chief antagonists are the English hero Lord Talbot and the French heroine Joan of Arc. *Part 2*, going from 1445 to 1455, deals with the English quarrels leading to the Wars of the Roses and ends with the first open battle of those wars, the Yorkist victory at St. Albans. Its chief antagonists are Henry's queen, Margaret of Anjou, and Richard duke of York. *Part 3* leads us through the wars, the death of Duke Richard, and Henry's double deposition. It ends with the banishment of Margaret, the re-establishment of Duke Richard's eldest son Edward IV, and the ominous rise to prominence of Edward's brother Richard duke of Gloucester.

The sheer quantity of matter to be contained, then, makes this reign recalcitrant to summary. Two additional circumstances make a brief account of the period and Shakespeare's handling of it difficult. Faced with a tale of frequent reversals of fortune on both sides of the Channel, a tale into which a great many persons enter, Shakespeare performed some acts of radical simplification upon the narrative he found in the Tudor chroniclers Hall and Holinshed. Separate battles are condensed into single engagements; disparate events are linked in unhistorical causal chains; successive holders of the same title (e.g., the dukes of Somerset) are condensed into single dramatic figures; chronology is often telescoped, inverted, or ignored. Further, this stretch of the fifteenth century has so far received relatively little attention from modern historians. The kind of detailed research and re-evaluation that has lately been bestowed on much of the rest of the century is only beginning with Henry VI. Indeed, aside from Edward V (who did not live to grow up), Henry VI is the only king dealt with in this book who has not yet received a detailed modern biography.

The history of these years nonetheless forms an exciting and colorful narrative. It is not astonishing that the youthful Shakespeare, seeking material for his initial ventures in the composition of history plays, turned to England's long recoil from the victories of Henry V and her subsequent civil conflicts. The resulting plays, although they lack the remarkable poetic variety and psychological richness of the mature Shakespeare, are vigorous works that can still hold the stage. Indeed, Shakespeare's drastic manipulation of his material in *Part 1*, probably his first history play and possibly his first play of any kind, shows him to have been already skillful in dramatic construction.*

---

* Shakespearean scholars have long debated in what order the Henry VI plays were composed and whether they are entirely Shakespeare's work (that is, whether he was adapting pre-existing plays). At present there is a consensus favoring Shakespeare as sole author of the three plays written in the natural chronological order. There is no consensus regarding the precedence of *1 Henry VI* over Shakespeare's first work in other genres, *The Comedy of Errors* and *Titus Andronicus*.

2. THE END OF THE HUNDRED YEARS WAR

The Anglo-French war after the death of Henry V falls into three parts. Between the death of Henry and the siege of Orléans (1422–1428), the English maintained and extended their conquest. From the beginning of that siege to the Congress of Arras (1428–1435), a series of thrusts and counterthrusts wildly swung the balance each way by turns. After 1435, despite sundry truces and reverses, the French steadily pushed the English back until they wholly regained control of their own country in 1453.

Two months after Henry's death in August 1422, Charles VI of France followed him to the grave. According to the treaty of Troyes by which Henry had sealed his conquest of France, the French crown was to be united with the English after the death of Charles, both to be worn by Henry and his heirs. Thus before his first birthday Henry VI of Lancaster was sovereign over two kingdoms that had been yoked by violence together.

Acute problems faced his government. In any monarchy where the king has real power, arrangements for a royal minority are delicate. A single man appointed regent may grow overmighty, inspiring the jealousy and anxiety of other nobles; yet rule by a council of theoretical equals risks inefficiency and poor coordination. For the English in 1422, the dual crown exacerbated the problems. Henry VI, descended from both Lancaster and Valois, supposedly governed both kingdoms by right, and emblems of a divinely blessed double monarchy were dramatized in pageants, written up in poems, and circulated on coins and genealogical posters. But mere inherited right, however supported by treaty and backed by propaganda, could not disguise the fact that France was a conquered country, and an incompletely conquered one at that. Henry V's campaigns and his alliance with Philip the Good duke of Burgundy had given him control of Normandy, Paris and its environs, most of northeastern France, and Gascony in the southwest, but the bulk of France south of the Loire remained loyal to the dauphin Charles, who had supposedly been disinherited by the treaty of Troyes. The English not only had to rule what they had gained but also had to extend their conquest until the dauphin and his supporters yielded.

The infant king's four uncles were necessarily prominent in the arrangements for the minority. Two of these were uncles of the full blood, the surviving younger brothers of Henry V, men in their early thirties: John duke of Bedford and Humphrey duke of Gloucester. The others were great-uncles of the half-blood, the surviving bastard sons of John of Gaunt, legitimated after Gaunt married his mistress Catherine Swynford: Henry Beaufort bishop of Winchester and Thomas Beaufort duke of Exeter, both in their forties. Of these Exeter was the least important. A major military figure during the two previous reigns and an executor of Henry V's will, he was given tutelage of the infant king. He died, however, in 1426. The ablest of the four was Bedford. Early trained in the border warfare with the Scots during his father's reign, he had guarded and governed England while his brother invaded France. He shared Henry V's determination, courage, and capacity for hard work, but lacked his magnetism, his easy command over men's devotion. To him fell the regency of France and with it the task of completing Henry's conquest. His brother Gloucester sought a similar regency in England. This youngest son of Henry IV was as energetic and brainy as his brothers. Unlike them, however, he had not experienced an austere youthful training by helping to hold the outposts of their father's usurped kingdom. He grew up headstrong and unstable, often ignoring the public interest in pursuit of his own ambition. In 1424, for example, after contracting a dubious marriage with Jaqueline of Hainault (her first husband was still alive), he nearly shattered the vital English alliance with the duke of Burgundy by invading the Low Countries in order to seize Jaqueline's lands. At Henry VI's accession in 1422, other magnates sufficiently distrusted Gloucester's abilities as a statesman to deny him the regency of

England. He was to be only protector and defender of the realm, first among equals on a council without whose assent he could not act, and he was to yield even this position to his brother Bedford whenever Bedford was in England. Leading the opposition to Gloucester was the fourth uncle, the bishop of Winchester. Clever, vastly rich, ambitious, and possessed of great political experience, Bishop Beaufort had already been chancellor several times and resumed the post in the new government. Henry V had once found it advisable to curb the bishop's ambitions. In 1417 Pope Martin V had offered Winchester a cardinalate and the post of papal legate in England, probably as a reward for Winchester's astute diplomacy at the Council of Constance, where the Papal Schism was resolved by the election of Martin to the papacy. Henry forbade Winchester to accept. (Martin renewed the offer in 1426: this time Winchester took the red hat.) As a churchman, and as a businessman heavily involved in the export of wool to the Low Countries, Winchester had a much better understanding of international politics than did the insular Gloucester. Gloucester, however, was more popular in England. The personal and political rivalry between these two men marked the reign of Henry VI from its inception until their deaths a quarter-century later.

Under these arrangements, English fortunes prospered until late 1428. In 1425, it is true, Gloucester and Winchester were seriously at odds. The duke accused the bishop of denying him entry to the Tower of London (the royal armory as well as a royal residence) and of plotting to assume exclusive control of the king. Feeling ran high enough to inspire mob violence. Bedford was obliged to return from France in December and spend the next year reconciling them and defining the powers of the conciliar magnates. This episode aside, the council governed the country reasonably well during the 1420s. Moreover, English victories continued in France. Bedford was able to provide good generalship, and two other lords were notably successful in the field. Richard Beauchamp earl of Warwick, a loyal Lancastrian since the coronation of Henry IV, was at various times captain of Rouen and of Calais, and prosecuted a successful campaign in Brittany. Upon Exeter's death in 1426, he was appointed tutor to the young king and thereafter alternated between service in the field and attendance upon Henry VI. Thomas Montague earl of Salisbury, whose career under Henry V had been chiefly administrative and diplomatic, maintained an unbroken string of victories and a reputation for all the knightly virtues. The most striking engagement of this period occurred in August 1424 at Verneuil, on the southern border of Normandy. Here an Anglo-Burgundian army under Bedford and Salisbury destroyed the dauphin's army and their Scottish allies in a victory as devastating and significant as that of Henry V at Agincourt. At Verneuil and in other battles Bedford, Warwick, and Salisbury solidified Henry V's conquest of northern and eastern France and extended it to include Anjou and Maine, the counties immediately to the south of Normandy. The summary of this phase of the war given by Shakespeare's source Holinshed is still in the main historically valid: "Such was then the opinion conceived of the English puissance, so oft tried, proved, and prevailing, that the Frenchmen thought the Englishmen would have all which they wished for or wrought for."

Consolidation and gradual expansion, however, were not enough. It was necessary to wreak for more. During the summer of 1428, the English reinforced themselves for a major effort. Orléans on the Loire was the key to central France, the gateway to the dauphin's capital at Bourges. In October Salisbury settled down to besiege Orléans, which was held for the dauphin by the count of Dunois. (Dunois, also known with engaging medieval frankness as the bastard of Orléans, was the illegitimate brother of the city's duke.) Salisbury himself was soon mortally wounded, shot in the face by a cannon from the city walls. Leadership of the English was assumed by a man of somewhat lesser ability, William de la Pole earl of Suffolk, whose father had died during

Henry V's siege of Harfleur and whose elder brother had been one of the two English nobles to perish at Agincourt. Suffolk's generalship appears to have suffered from an excess of caution, but he was assisted by a man of balancing zeal, John Lord Talbot, one of the most distinguished soldiers of the fifteenth century, veteran of Verneuil and later earl of Shrewsbury. Although the English army was not large enough to surround the well-fortified Orléans completely, the French appeared incapable of breaking the siege. They were even unable to disrupt the English supply lines: in February 1429 a French force attempted to intercept a quantity of Lenten food coming from Paris, but in the "battle of the herrings" the small English convoy, led by Sir John Fastolfe, totally repulsed the French attackers and got the supplies through to Suffolk's army. The discouraged dauphin, in any case indolent and unmilitary by nature, disinherited, many times defeated, and now threatened in the very heart of his kingdom, needed a miracle. At this point, Joan of Arc appeared.

The sixteen-year-old farmer's daughter from Domrémy in the eastern province of Champagne, supremely confident that she had been directed by the voices of saints to save France, managed to convince the dauphin of the genuineness of her mission. After being assured by a council of theologians of her orthodoxy and by a council of matrons of her chastity, Charles sent her, along with his cousin the duke of Alençon, to the relief of Orléans. She entered the city at the end of April. Her effect upon the morale of the French soldiers was enormous. Dunois, Alençon, and others actually led the troops, but Joan fired them with the conviction that success was possible. Within ten days, French sorties from the walls persuaded Suffolk to raise the siege. Worse was to follow for the English. In retiring from Orléans, Suffolk split his army, taking a small force up the Loire to Jargeau. There, on 12 June, Alençon and Joan defeated his troops and captured him. A week later, at Patay, Joan, Alençon, and Dunois caught up with the English mainguard led by Talbot and Fastolfe. The English commanders were taken by surprise and overwhelmed. Talbot was captured and Fastolfe forced to flee with the remnants of the army, abandoning guns and baggage.

Although no English army now stood between the French and Paris, the French did not advance upon the capital. Joan's strategy was subtler and ultimately more effective. She took the dauphin on a wide sweep east and north from Orléans. Towns en route opened their gates to her until she arrived at Rheims, the traditional place for the coronation of French kings. On 18 July 1429, in Rheims cathedral, nearly seven years after the death of his father, Charles VII ceased to be a dispossessed heir and became a king. Insofar as it had bastardized and disinherited Charles, the treaty of Troyes was now a dead letter. France had a crowned and anointed king as a focus for loyalty against the English invader, and Charles's own confidence in his position and rights was greatly strengthened.

For the next six years, until the Congress of Arras in 1435, the English struggled to erase the effects of Joan's work. Parliament voted larger subsidies for the war, which during the 1420s had been financed chiefly through taxes on the conquered French population. A symbolic riposte to the coronation of Charles was also thought necessary. The English council had originally postponed the formal coronation of Henry VI until he came of age, but the events in France propelled them to perform the ceremony at Westminster Abbey in November 1429, when the king was still a month short of his eighth birthday. During the next year, the English benefited from luck and from rivalries among the French: misled by court intrigue, Charles withdrew his support from the woman who had made his coronation possible. Joan was subsequently captured by the Burgundians and sold to the English. Charles made no effort to ransom her. The English in turn handed her over to the Inquisition for trial on charges of witchcraft and heresy. She was burned in May 1431. With the Maid safely out of the way, Henry, who had been brought over to Normandy, could be safely taken to Paris. There, in December, Cardinal Beaufort crowned him king of France.

Sporadic fighting continued, but there was no major engagement. Diplomatic wheels churned, however. By various means the pope moved to bring the adversaries to negotiation, and Charles endeavored to detach the duke of Burgundy from his English alliance. The latter task was no less difficult than the former, for Philip the Good, as readers of the previous chapter will recall, had joined the English when Charles's men had murdered Philip's father in 1419. To consort with Charles, Philip had to abandon solemn oaths of revenge as well as his oath of allegiance to Henry V's heirs in the treaty of Troyes. Both developments came to a head in August–September 1435. The English, the French, and the Burgundians gathered at the Congress of Arras, with a papal legate presiding. As a peace conference, Arras was a failure. When the French refused to allow Henry the title of king of France, the English (who of course would not allow it to Charles) left the table and withdrew to Rouen. There, on 15 September, Bedford died; the English thus lost their best general and most respected leader. Meanwhile, the French and the Burgundians continued to talk at Arras. When, on 21 September, the papal legate absolved Duke Philip of his oaths and reconciled him with Charles, the English lost the ally necessary to their continental ambitions. The effect upon the English of the loss of Bedford and the loss of Burgundy was almost immediate. During the next year, after a rebellion of the citizenry, the bastard Dunois took Paris, which had been in English hands since 1420.

It is clear that after the defection of Burgundy the English lacked the resources to take or hold all of France. Charles VII, after all, had the richer and more populous kingdom. It is not so clear, however, that they were bound to lose all that they had already taken, as indeed they did between 1436 and 1453. Quite apart from their supposed right to the French crown, the English had long special claims to parts of France, to Normandy with its capital at Rouen, to Calais and its environs, and to Gascony with its great wine trade centered on Bordeaux. Their claims were reinforced by their long occupation of these regions: many Englishmen had settled permanently in the conquered areas. It is even less clear how the English formed the policies under which they fought this long defeat. The degree of influence exerted by individual persons around the English throne during these years has been disputed by historians and merits much more investigation. The following account must be taken as a tentative sketch.

In negotiations with the French and apparently in English conciliar discussions, the duke of Gloucester manifested a patriotic determination to retain as much of France as possible. Gloucester was now the only surviving brother of Henry V, heir presumptive to the throne, and popular leader of what may be called the war party. Loosely associated with him was another prominent Plantagenet, Richard duke of York. Descended through his father Richard earl of Cambridge from Edmund the first duke of York (fourth surviving son of Edward III), descended through his mother Anne Mortimer from Lionel the first duke of Clarence (second surviving son of Edward III), and the most powerful subject in the kingdom by virtue of the vast inheritances of both York and the Mortimer earls of March, Duke Richard was, at the time of Arras, twenty-four years old. For the next quarter-century his position in England steadily became more crucial. For much of the decade after Bedford's death he served as the English regent in France, keeping Normandy almost intact from repeated French onslaughts.

More influence on English policies was exerted by Cardinal Beaufort and the earl of Suffolk. (Suffolk had been ransomed during the year following his capture at Jargeau, and had been steward of the royal household since 1433.) They repeatedly sought a compromise that would retain for the English only a portion of France. How much influence on the course of events was exerted by the king himself is uncertain. Henry VI officially came of age in 1437. He has traditionally been depicted as a pious man, uninterested and ineffectual in political affairs. Certainly he lacked his father's gift for hard work. Equally certainly, he occasionally exerted his will, and given the powers of a medieval king, no one on the council could really oppose him if he was sufficiently determined. How often he took a hand we do not know, and thus we do not know who was responsible for the ill-advised English policies of the 1440s.

The progress of the war in Normandy showed the English failure to organize themselves effectively. Although York and Talbot dispersed in 1441 a French siege of Pontoise (halfway between Paris and Rouen), forcing Charles and his army into flight, they lacked the resources to follow up their success. When the English got around to reinforcing York in 1443, they foolishly divided their powers. The reinforcing army was put under the command of the duke of Somerset, whose commission made him independent of York's authority. This duke was John Beaufort, son of the eldest of Gaunt's Beaufort offspring and thus nephew to the cardinal. (He has not hitherto figured in this narrative, as he had languished as a French captive between 1421 and 1438.) His independent appointment may reflect suspicions the cardinal and Suffolk (and possibly Henry VI) held about the Gloucester-York party. Not only did Somerset secure equality with York, he also contrived to direct such money as the council had raised entirely to his own forces. York, who had for some time been bitterly complaining about arrears of pay for his troops, got none of the tax revenues that year. Once he arrived in Normandy, Somerset refused to cooperate with York in the field and frittered his expedition away in apparently pointless maneuvers.

In 1444, Winchester and Suffolk managed to secure a two-year truce with France. Although it was later extended, the truce of Tours was merely a truce, not a peace or a treaty: nothing was settled and each side was to stay where it was for the duration. One result of the discussions, however, was to become crucial for the next three decades of English history. Suffolk negotiated the marriage of Henry VI to a French princess, Margaret of Anjou. This lady, a cousin to King Charles, was the daughter of René duke of Anjou and count of Maine, a mild, poverty-stricken, artistically inclined nobleman who held the title—but only the title—of king of Naples and Sicily. Marriage to this daughter of an impoverished branch of the French royal line brought Henry no dowry, no concessions, nothing but fresh expenses and a strong-willed wife around whom contention was to swirl until 1475. Indeed the marriage entailed practical losses for Henry: not only did he forego the opportunity for a more advantageous match, but also he lost a portion of France. In 1445, after Margaret had arrived in England, presumably under her influence and possibly with Suffolk's connivance, Henry upon his own authority ceded René's ancestral counties of Anjou and Maine to his new father-in-law. He thus freely handed back to the French important territories that Bedford and Salisbury had won and the English had kept at the cost of much blood and treasure. If Suffolk was in part responsible for this lavish gesture (there is room for doubt here), he may have been working toward an eventual peace treaty based on realistic compromises, but the loss of Anjou and Maine naturally infuriated many Englishmen.

Suffolk remained at or near the center of power in English politics, especially after the deaths of Gloucester and the cardinal in 1447. York was pushed out of the way by being made lieutenant of Ireland. Command in Normandy was given to Edmund Beaufort, younger brother of the duke of Somerset. (Somerset had died in 1444—supposedly of chagrin at the failure of his military expedition—whereupon Edmund inherited his title.) Thus Edmund had the wretched distinction of being the last English commander in Normandy. King Charles invaded the province in 1449, and by August of the next year, all of northern France except Calais had been recovered for the French crown.

In the next year, 1451, the French took Gascony as well. In

1452 Talbot, now a veteran of nearly seventy, retook Bordeaux and surrounding Gascon towns, but in 1453 his army was wiped out near Castillon, Talbot and his son perishing in the field. Except for Calais, which remained an English town for another century, the English were entirely expelled from the continent. One hundred sixteen years of fighting to enforce the Plantagenet claims to France had ended with Charles of Valois the undisputed ruler of his own kingdom.

3. *HISTORY AND* 1 HENRY VI

Since Shakespeare is creating stage plays out of the long, annalistic, and often digressive chronicles of Hall and Holinshed, he must proceed selectively. He devises dramatic forms by emphasizing some incidents, suppressing others, and importing new episodes from other sources or inventing them outright. Hitherto in this book I have been able to mention Shakespeare's alterations while recounting the history itself. It would have been impractical to mention Shakespeare in the previous section, however, because his procedure in transforming the chroniclers' accounts of the loss of France into *1 Henry VI* is far more radical than the process of selection and shaping used in, say, *Richard II*.

The mere time span of *1 Henry VI* calls for a more ruthless handling of sources. Since the loss of France took thirty years, Shakespeare must select much more radically among persons, events, and details than he does with the two-year story of Richard II's fall. Thus, in order to achieve focus, he concentrates such heroism as the English displayed during these decades into the figure of Lord Talbot, giving him the largest role in the play and bringing him into scenes in which historically he took no part. Thus he also collapses lesser figures: the brothers John and Edmund Beaufort, successively dukes of Somerset, appear as one man. Smaller but still bothersome technical problems call for high-handed alterations of history. If, as it does, the play is to begin with the funeral of Henry V, the title character must be an infant at the opening. Radical changes in the story and a deliberate vagueness about the amount of passing time are needed if Henry VI is to appear as an adult before the play is over. The very character of Shakespeare's sources forced him into his more radical strategy. At their best the Tudor chronicles are loose and baggy, but given thirty years of warfare and a commitment to year-by-year narration, Holinshed can barely start to shape his account of the loss of France. He finds so many decisive turning points (the fortunes of the English "began" to decline when Salisbury died at Orléans in 1428; they also "began" to decline when Bedford died after Arras in 1435) that the notion of a turning point begins to seem meaningless.

Instead of merely selecting and shaping, then, Shakespeare chops the whole story into little pieces, eliminates a large number of them, and rebuilds the remainder into a structure bearing very little resemblance to the original historical sequence. To change the metaphor, he works like a weaver using an old tapestry as material with which to make a new one: he unravels all the threads, discards many, and uses the rest to weave a different portrait of the same subject. The design is new, the colors are remassed, and threads remote from each other in the original end up side by side. *1 Henry VI,* like the chronicles, does of course tell the story of the English loss of France, but the dramatic narrative is analytic rather than historical. Episodes, personalities and chronology have been imperiously rearranged to show *how* France was lost. As a brief review of the play will show, Shakespeare's rearrangement of the episodes points chiefly to English internal divisiveness and the extraordinary influence of scheming Frenchwomen as the chief causes of the English defeat.

In the opening scene, the funeral of Henry V (historically 1422) is interrupted by messengers bringing disastrous news from France. They report the loss of various cities and counties that in fact either never were in English hands or were lost at different times between 1429 and 1451, some of the latter being necessarily treated in subsequent scenes as not yet lost. Paris, for example, is on the list, yet Henry VI is crowned there in Act IV. They also report the coronation of Charles VII at Rheims (1429: here Shakespeare is inconsistent insofar as he makes all his characters, French as well as English, refer to Charles for the rest of the play as dauphin, not as king). They finally report the capture of Talbot and the flight of Fastolfe (also 1429, at the battle of Patay after the English retreat from the siege of Orléans). That the death of Henry V led to general calamity is the effect created, and to create that effect Shakespeare almost randomly picks events scattered over many pages of the chronicles.

Of the following seven scenes (I.ii through II.ii), all but one is devoted to the siege of Orléans in 1428–1429. (The exception, I.iii, deals with the quarrel between Winchester and Goucester at the Tower, an event of 1425.) Joan, presented as a heroic virgin but with an ironic undertone suggesting her sexual attractiveness, is brought to Charles, who falls under her spell. Salisbury, in the presence of the minor historical persons Gargrave and Glansdale who were indeed at Orléans, is shot by cannon. He dies in Talbot's arms, although in fact Salisbury lingered a week before dying and Talbot was not yet present at the siege. Talbot must naturally explain his release from captivity. Since, of course, he was not captured until after the final repulse of the siege, the explanation involves the transposition of later events. Joan's relief of Orléans ensues, although Charles and René of Anjou unhistorically join Joan, Alençon, and the bastard Dunois in leading the French. Then, with a complete disregard of history, Talbot captures Orléans in a night attack that takes the sleeping French by surprise, and vows to bury Salisbury nobly in the chief church. (The night attack is based upon Talbot's capture of Le Mans in Maine the year before; Salisbury's body was actually returned to England for burial; and at no point did the English ever take

Orléans.) This segment of the play, most of it devoted to exalting the heroism of Talbot, ends with a fictional and highly romantic episode (II.iii) in which Talbot evades the wiles of a deceitful French countess.

For three scenes Shakespeare now returns to England to develop the theme of English dissension (II.iv through III.i). Only the third of these is historical, a dispute in parliament between Gloucester and Winchester physically dramatized by a brawl between their servants. This is in fact the quarrel that Bedford settled in 1426, but Shakespeare, eager to introduce his title character, omits Bedford and has the young king play peacemaker. The two preceding scenes, which initiate the enmity between York and Lancaster, are entirely fictional. Somerset, who as a Beaufort represents the Lancastrian side of the royal family, quarrels with Richard of York in the Temple Garden, each plucking a rose to symbolize his faction. Suffolk joins Somerset in choosing a red rose; Warwick joins York in choosing a white. (At this point, Shakespeare is clearly not thinking of Richard Beauchamp, earl of Warwick until 1439 and tutor to the young king, but of his son-in-law Richard Neville, who held the earldom after 1449, became Richard of York's most important ally in the Wars of the Roses, and earned the popular nickname of kingmaker.) In the next scene, the aged Edmund Mortimer, long a prisoner in the Tower, dies after bequeathing to York his claim to the crown and explaining, with some slight inaccuracy, the lineage and history behind that claim. Since he is York's uncle, this Mortimer is presumably the fifth earl of March (the title is not mentioned in the scene), on whose behalf plots had been laid during the reigns of Henry IV and Henry V. (See Chapters III and IV.) March did in fact die in 1425, but he died of plague, at the mere age of thirty-three, while on duty as lieutenant of Ireland. Far from having suffered "loathesome sequestration" in the Tower "since Henry Monmouth [i.e., Henry V] first began to reign," he had been released by Henry V from the house-arrest under which

Henry IV had kept him. Shakespeare here follows the errors of Hall and Holinshed concerning the age and imprisonment of Mortimer. His introduction of this venerable victim of persecution, immediately after the rose-plucking scene, develops the dynastic heritage that makes York a threat to Henry VI and gives importance to the York-Somerset quarrel, not only for this play but for the two plays to follow. In the subsequent parliament scene York's position is further established. After patching up the dispute between Gloucester and Winchester, the king formally restores Richard "to his blood" and grants him the inheritance of York. (Prior to this point in the play, York has lacked a noble title, being called merely Richard Plantagenet. Shakespeare is here following the chronicles in regarding Richard's position as hitherto questionable because his father Richard earl of Cambridge had been attainted for treason against Henry V. Historically, no one seems to have officially regarded York's position as dubious; his lands were indeed held for a time by the crown, but only because York was a minor.) The scene ends with the first of several soliloquies by the king's great-uncle and tutor, Exeter, who reflects upon the "envious discord" growing at the court. Shakespeare ignores Exeter's death in 1426, using him throughout the play as a choral commentator foreseeing English doom.

Act III, scene ii returns to the battlefield for a scene in which Shakespeare has massed together a number of disparate incidents to create a fictional episode stressing the wiliness of Joan and the valor of Talbot. The French win Rouen by stratagem, the English retake the city by storm on the same day, and the aged Bedford dies while watching the English triumph. Rouen in fact remained in English hands from Henry V's conquest in 1419 until the final expulsion of the English in 1449–1450. The devices used by the French (Joan and four soldiers slip into the town disguised as peasants going to market, and Joan signals the waiting French army with a torch) are borrowed from sieges at Cornill (1441) and Le Mans (1428). Bedford indeed died and was buried at Rouen;

he did so, however, at the age of forty-six after the abortive Congress of Arras (1435). The theme of French guile continues in the next scene: by the force and subtlety of her rhetoric Joan persuades the duke of Burgundy to abandon his alliance with England. Joan's two speeches capsulize a whole decade of negotiations by which Charles VII tried to regain Burgundy's allegiance, an effort successful only at Arras, when Joan was four years dead.

The subsequent scenes (III.iv, IV.i) present political wranglings around Henry VI, who has been brought over to France. Henry creates Talbot earl of Shrewsbury (1442) and is himself crowned king of France (1431). York is made regent of France, dual military command being given to him and Somerset (early 1440s). In both scenes two minor persons, Vernon and Basset, both historical and both mentioned in the chronicles but neither in connection with these matters, continue the quarrel between the red and the white roses, drawing their principals, York and Somerset, into the dispute and eliciting from the king a vain effort to quash their enmity.

The remainder of Act IV displays the glorious defeat and death of Talbot and his son near Bordeaux (1453). In a brilliant variation upon history, Shakespeare arranges for this defeat to result from the domestic antagonisms of the English. He takes the noncooperation of the dukes of York and Somerset in the Norman campaign of 1443 and makes it directly responsible for an invented failure to reinforce Talbot at the crucial battle ten years later. For the sake of increased poignancy, young Talbot is unhistorically made the old hero's only son, and his age is reduced. (He was actually in his late twenties, with children of his own.) Thus the contentiousness of the English lords causes the extinction of the noble line of the greatest of England's soldiers.

English heroism thus extinguished, Act V presents the movement toward an ignoble treaty. Much of the act is drawn from the events of 1442–1444: marriage is suggested between Henry VI and the count of Armagnac's daughter, but this plan is abandoned in favor of the betrothal of Henry to Margaret of Anjou as arranged by Suffolk while negotiating a settlement with the French. The emergence of Suffolk as a major character at this point (he closes the play with a soliloquy sketching his dreams of domination) is accurate enough, but the truce of Tours is elevated into more significance as a pause in the war than it actually had. More importantly, Suffolk's motivation for arranging the betrothal is a full-blown Shakespearean elaboration of a mere hint in Hall: Shakespeare has Suffolk himself infatuated with Margaret. Intermingled with these events is the capture and execution of Joan (1430–1431). Throughout the play Joan has been called a witch by the English and a saint by the French. Here the ambiguities fall away: she is revealed as a sorceress, a whore, and a vixen of monstrous pretensions and ingratitude. The real Joan of Arc was of course none of these things, but Shakespeare is dramatizing a common English view of her. He is also arranging a crucial development for the whole sequence of Henry VI plays. Joan is captured just before Margaret enchants Suffolk. Joan's capacity to damage the English is ended; Margaret will go on to sow discord among them for the next two plays. Margaret in effect takes over from Joan the role of the foreign sorceress who scourges England.

The historical material behind *1 Henry VI* has thus been thoroughly recast. Only loosely can one say that the play depicts the loss of Henry V's French empire. France, in fact, is not altogether lost at the end of the play. The last battle of the Hundred Years War is dramatized (Talbot's defeat at Bordeaux), but it is not presented as the last. Shakespeare ends with a peace treaty that he has invented out of the truce of 1444, and the final expulsion of the English from France is not announced until Act III of *2 Henry VI*, a play whose exclusive concentration on domestic politics makes the foreign news appear relatively insignificant. *1 Henry VI* is not a complete narrative but a dramatized demonstration of the forces at work in the years concerned. The Lancastrian empire in France, although temporarily sustained by the heroism of Talbot, cracks under two pressures, the external devices of the French and the internal quarrels of the English.

As a reading of history, Shakespeare's dramatized interpretation may merit severe criticism. The French are of course treated chauvinistically. They are seldom allowed any heroism. They regularly engage in dishonorable stratagems and unchivalric mockery of their enemies. Even in the field, they often rely on gunpowder whereas English exploits are achieved solely by personal combat with traditional weapons. In truth, Dunois probably did more for the French than Talbot did for the English, and Charles had other skillful and successful generals who do not appear in the play. Joan of Arc was of course no witch, and her remarkable achievements in restoring French morale and crowning her king have been thoroughly recognized by subsequent generations.

The presentation of the English quarrels is also problematic. Between Winchester and Gloucester exists the simple contrast of a shrewd ecclesiastical Machiavel, scheming for his own advancement, opposed by "good duke Humphrey," testy but fundamentally anxious for the welfare of the kingdom. This contrast Shakespeare inherited from his sources. Modern historians have found no reason to regard the cardinal as particularly evil. His great wealth was frequently lent to the crown for military expenditure, and although he took shrewd steps to insure himself against loss on these loans and sometimes derived political advantage from them, he was not usurious, and elements of patriotism can be discerned in his behavior. Gloucester certainly equalled him in ambition and far surpassed him in self-centered impetuosity. Shakespeare must omit the episode of his marriage to Jaqueline of Hainault in order to sustain a favorable characterization of him. With York and Somerset, Shakespeare has a more nearly even hand, only slightly tilted in favor of York. Here modern historians have little to say, as nearly all of the antagonism is fictional.

The real York-Somerset quarrel developed in the years covered by
2 *Henry VI;* the Somerset of *1 Henry VI,* as I have mentioned, is
historically two separate persons; and no evidence suggests that
Richard of York seriously contemplated a claim to the crown
before the late 1450s. The modern reader of Shakespeare, as opposed to the modern historian, is more apt to be bothered by the
apparent lack of motivation for their strife. Shakespeare does not
bother to explain why York and Somerset start quarrelling. In the
rose-plucking scene they *enter* in dispute upon a matter that is
never explained, and the subsequent mention of York's dynastic
pretensions merely adds fuel to a fire already raging. A more obvious temperamental incompatibility appears between Gloucester
and Winchester, but their clashes too are so sudden as to look un-
dermotivated, and their charges against each other are seldom
substantiated. With all four of these contenders, Shakespeare does
not much care about the precise genesis of quarrels. That they are
all high-spirited noblemen, more prone to self-assertive passion
than to reasonable self-command, is enough. Far more important
are the results of domestic faction: it weakens a kingdom whose
nominal ruler cannot control his lords.

Even the depiction of Talbot may be historically misleading.
Not that Talbot was really unheroic: far from it. But the concentration of English heroism in Talbot slights the achievements of
others, notably Salisbury (who appears in the play only to die)
and Bedford (who is allowed to do little more). It also slights a
lesser historical personage, Sir John Fastolfe. Fastolfe was a notable veteran, at various times governor or captain of conquered
French cities, whose deeds are approvingly mentioned in the
chronicles. One episode marred his career: his retreat from Patay
after the capture of Talbot could be interpreted as cowardice.
Bedford (not Talbot, as in the play) temporarily stripped him of
his Garter while the matter was investigated. He was exonerated
of cowardice and the Garter was restored, but the one incident,
exaggerated in the chronicles, caught Shakespeare's attention and

led him to depict Fastolfe, for the sake of contrast with Talbot, as a craven consistently fleeing engagements. On a larger scale, the focusing of military glory in Talbot leaves little else for the other English lords to do but quarrel. People so frequently and so vigorously at odds in their counsels as Shakespeare depicts the English to be could hardly have kept France for as long as they did, even though one recognizes (as Shakespeare does not) that rivalries also existed among the French. Indeed, it has been recently argued that, despite a certain amount of personal strife, the English lords managed to cooperate reasonably enough, and that Henry VI himself was responsible for the inept policies that finally lost the war. Certainly it is true that, despite Joan's victories, the war went much better for the English before 1437, the year in which Henry's minority ended, than afterwards, when he occasionally exerted the powers of a medieval king.

On the other hand, however we distribute responsibility among these persons, many modern historians will agree with a point central to Shakespeare's interpretation of history and thus to his play. Henry V, strong-willed, immensely experienced, firmly governing a united country, a skillful diplomat and a shrewd tactician in the field, had in the conquest of France undertaken a task that, if possible at all, only he or someone like him could carry out. To varying degrees Bedford and Salisbury were like him, and they enjoyed considerable success in carrying on his ambition. (Talbot, although fearsome in the field, had few of Henry's other talents.) But the problems of maintaining Henry's kind of authority and directed effort occasionally surfaced in the 1420s, worsened in the 1430s after the successes of Joan, and swamped the English in the 1440s. Although a historian naturally objects to the sweeping generalization, to the telescoping of events and forces implied, Shakespeare has a truth when he punctuates the funeral of Henry V with tidings "of loss, of slaughter, and discomfiture."

Artist Unknown: *Henry VI* (National Portrait Gallery).

❦ VI ❧

⊕ ✠ ḢEṄRY VI ✠ EDWARD IV
the RIVAL kINGS

Hath not thy rose a thorn, Plantagenet?

1. THE DISORDERS OF THE *1440s*

Henry VI Part 2 opens in 1445 with the arrival in England of
Henry's queen, Margaret of Anjou. *Henry VI Part 3* closes in
1471 with the murder of Henry and the permanent establishment
of his cousin Edward IV on the throne. The ten acts of these two
plays thus dramatize twenty-six years of turmoil within the English aristocracy. Although Shakespeare works selectively from
the material offered him by the Tudor chroniclers Hall and Holinshed, compressing events into rapid sequence, the two plays
employ little of the radical rearrangement of chronology practiced
in *1 Henry VI* and discussed in the previous chapter. The chief
difference between what is currently understood to be the history
of these years and the action of *2 and 3 Henry VI* is not a Shakespearean rearrangement but a derivation from the chroniclers.
The Tudor writers clamped a teleological interpretation upon
their material. Because Henry's reign ended in civil war between
the houses of Lancaster and York, with the crown itself changing

hands in 1461, 1470, and 1471, Shakespeare and his historians supposed that dynastic ambition animated events years before the combatants took the field. Ambition for the crown is made primary. Shakespeare has the duke of York soliloquize bitterly upon his exclusion from a crown he considers rightfully his as early as 1445. The earls of Salisbury and Warwick agree to support his pretensions very shortly afterward. In fact, although York attempted to establish a position as heir presumptive to the childless King Henry in the early 1450s, he made no attempt to displace Henry until 1460, and when he tried to do so his claim was rejected by the two earls and his other allies. Most of the chief persons in these events were undoubtedly as truculent and quarrelsome as ever a military aristocracy has been, but outright civil war was a step they took reluctantly, and direct challenge of the anointed king more reluctantly still. They were not initially quarrelling over who should wear the crown, and the allegiance of most individual lords outside the royal family was not consistently "Yorkist" or "Lancastrian." A dynastic interpretation was convenient to the Tudor chroniclers for political reasons, and very convenient to Shakespeare for artistic reasons, but it commands no respect among modern historians.

The main problem afflicting England in the 1440s was the incompetence of the king. In medieval England, the maintenance of general stability, the checking of disputes among magnates, the impartial operation of justice in the courts, the preservation of order among the commons, and a reasonable distribution of the prizes and rewards within the crown's prerogative all required an active, fairly intelligent, respect-worthy monarch. Unfortunately, the accidents of birth to which a hereditary monarchy is subject had produced in Henry VI a king of considerable piety, questionable intelligence, little industry in worldly matters, and no political talent. His incompetence permitted, indeed encouraged, the growth of faction. Without a reliable guardian of national stability, men had to establish and protect their interests by their own efforts. Lesser men did this by seeking the protection of greater, thereby generating armed private retinues that promptly extended any dispute entered into by either the retainer or the lord. Greater men sought to dominate the king, thus bending to their own use the administrative machinery of government and the dispensation of the crown's favors. There ensued a breakdown of order, bitter efforts to dislodge whatever faction currently had the king's ear, a series of shifting alliances as men sought greater leverage for themselves, and private wars between factions. Civil war was the penultimate step. When even that did not avail, the Yorkists broke the impasse by proclaiming their own king. Only then was his supposedly superior right to the crown invoked.

Disorders across the kingdom made plain the lack of effective central government. In Herefordshire, bandits came openly into market towns. The citizens of counties on the Channel complained of riots and murders. Such offenses have occurred in all ages, of course; what stands out about the 1440s is the breakdown of the procedures of justice intended to cope with crime and disorder. In the eastern counties of Norfolk and Suffolk, for example, where the king's favorite the duke of Suffolk was a major landowner, the duke's agents roused the bitter hostility of the citizenry. These agents were accused not only of extortion and intimidation, but also of controlling the appointment of sheriffs and the selection of juries so as to oppress others and prevent their own prosecution. In the southwest, the aristocrats themselves stirred up turmoil. A private quarrel of obscure origin between the earl of Devon and a rising man of affairs called Sir William Bonville (later Lord Bonville) was exacerbated by a ludicrous administrative blunder: in 1440 the king gave Devon the stewardship of the duchy of Cornwall, a post already held by Bonville. Devon and Bonville assembled their friends to fight out the issue. The quarrel continued intermittently into the 1450s, when Devon and his sons besieged Bonville in Taunton Castle, sacked several of Bonville's houses, murdered a prominent Devonshire lawyer, and robbed Exeter Cathedral. Most of these outrages in the east and the southwest are known to us because the victims eventually appealed for redress to the central courts. The north was even more lawless, but history knows less of it. Murder, rape, siege, and the destruction of property by armed bands of ruffians in the service of northern lords became so common, and the processes of justice so ineffective, that resort to legal process was not worth the effort.

Within this violent setting the magnates sought to control the king's government. In the early 1440s the long struggle between Henry's two surviving uncles for direction of royal policy drew to an end. As readers of the previous chapter will recall, Humphrey duke of Gloucester, the last surviving brother of Henry V, had sought the regency of England at the infant Henry VI's accession. It was denied him: he was forced to content himself with the title of protector, a post he naturally lost when the king grew up. Shakespeare inherits from his sources a conception of Gloucester as "good duke Humphrey," patriotically concerned for the welfare of the realm. Gloucester was certainly popular in London and thoroughly earned his reputation as a patron of learning and the arts. The books he gave to Oxford form the nucleus of the present university library. He was, however, a hot-headed man, no less self-seeking than his fellow magnates and more pugnacious than most. His constant opponent in domestic politics, the king's great-uncle Henry Cardinal Beaufort, had clearly gained the upper hand on the king's council by the early 1440s. Gloucester advocated a continuing hostile policy with France; the cardinal sought accommodation with the enemy. Two events of 1440–1441 indicate the failure of Gloucester's influence. First, over Gloucester's strong protest, the duke of Orléans, an English captive since the battle of Agincourt, was released in hopes that he might facilitate a settlement of the long war with France. Second, a bill of charges brought by Gloucester against Beaufort was decisively dismissed by the council.

A more personal blow struck Gloucester in 1441 when his wife was convicted of witchcraft. Eleanor Cobham duchess of Gloucester, originally a mere knight's daughter, gloried in her high rank and yearned for higher. Her husband, after all, was heir presumptive to a childless king. She dabbled in witchcraft; almost certainly she attempted to use it to discover when the king would die, an activity that could be construed as treasonable; she was accused of employing it to encompass Henry's death, a procedure certainly treasonable. She was arrested along with three priests in the Gloucester household, Roger Bolingbroke, Thomas Southwell, and John Hume (or Home), and a woman long held to be a sorceress, Margery Jourdain. All were convicted, Eleanor by both ecclesiastical and secular tribunals that included her husband's opponents on the council. Hume was pardoned. Margery Jourdain was burnt. Southwell died in the Tower the night before he was to be executed. Bolingbroke was hanged, disembowelled, and quartered. Eleanor was obliged to do public penance by walking through the streets of London, and was confined for the rest of her life, first in various English castles and finally on the Isle of Man.

The Tudor chroniclers suggest that the fall of the duchess was entirely contrived by the duke's enemies in order to discredit him. Shakespeare, developing this notion, makes Hume an agent of the cardinal and the duke of Suffolk from the very start of his relationship with Eleanor. Shakespeare further arranges for the dukes of Buckingham and York to eavesdrop on the conjuration in order to arrest Eleanor and her necromancers *in flagrante*. He also establishes a personal jealousy between Queen Margaret and the ambitious duchess. The rivalry of the ladies is pure fiction: Eleanor's downfall occurred four years before Margaret came to England. The plots of the lords are exaggerated. Witchcraft was a serious business in the Middle Ages, and Eleanor was certainly guilty of some of the charges brought against her. Gloucester's opponents did not contrive the whole affair. More modestly, they took advantage of his wife's indiscretions to weaken his political position, exposing her to public trial and imposing upon her the public humiliation of the penitential walks—the sort of punishment usually inflicted upon common prostitutes. The scandal gravely undermined the duke.

The disgrace of the Gloucesters left the cardinal and his party in control. By the early 1440s, however, the cardinal was about seventy. Although in Shakespeare he continues to hatch malign plots, he was in fact gradually retiring from public affairs. The lord who really controlled the government in this decade was William de la Pole earl of Suffolk. Despite his claim in Shakespeare to Lancastrian blood, Suffolk was not a Plantagenet but the descendant of a Yorkshire wool merchant. His grandfather Michael had been raised to the peerage by Richard II. He himself inherited the earldom at the age of nineteen, after his father and elder brother perished in Henry V's Agincourt campaign. As readers of Chapter V will recall, Suffolk assumed command of the siege of Orléans after the death of the earl of Salisbury. He became steward of the royal household in 1433. A partisan of the cardinal, he gradually gained ascendancy over the king. His most significant political act occurred in 1444–1445: he arranged the truce of Tours between England and France, an agreement that entailed the betrothal of Henry VI to Margaret of Anjou. He then proxy-married Margaret and brought her back to England for his royal master. For this accomplishment Henry raised him from earl to marquess, with a further promotion to duke in 1448. (Shakespeare accelerates these promotions: Suffolk gains the ducal title upon his presentation of Margaret to Henry.)

J. R. Lander has strikingly described Suffolk as carrying the fifteenth century's "twin characteristics of greed and piety . . . to schizophrenic extremes." He was cultivated; he endowed religious foundations; just before his death he wrote a letter of lofty spiritual advice to his son. He also profited enormously from direct royal grants, perverted the financial and judicial operations of the crown to the benefit of himself and his supporters, robbed fellow landowners of their estates, and allowed his agents and retainers to terrorize the districts of Norfolk and Suffolk. Above all, he gained Margaret's support and controlled Henry. With Gloucester and the cardinal fading out of the picture, Suffolk monopolized power and barred other lords from the king and the kingly influence. Although some aspects of his character are not touched upon in 2 *Henry VI*, and although he was not Margaret's lover (that is a Shakespearean invention based upon a mere hint in the Tudor chronicles), the unattractive portrait given him in the play reflects the very real hatred in which he was held by the end of the 1440s, hatred that he richly deserved.

Three other lords must enter our survey of this decade. Humphrey Stafford duke of Buckingham, grandson of Edward III's youngest surviving son Thomas of Woodstock, was chiefly loyal to the king. For a time, however, he seems to have been Suffolk's political ally. He certainly enjoyed the rewards of the Tours negotiations: he was raised from earl to duke on the same day that Suffolk secured his marquessate. The two other lords were (for the time being) military rather than political figures: Edmund Beaufort duke of Somerset and Richard duke of York. As related in the previous chapter, Somerset's elder brother had been York's fellow commander (and rival) in the fields of France in 1443, and had died the next year. In 1445 York returned from Normandy, bitter about arrears of payment owed him. He wanted nonetheless to continue as the English commander in France. Somerset was appointed instead and thus presided over the final defeat of the English in Normandy in 1449–1450. York was packed off to be lieutenant of Ireland, remote from the center of power. The leverage of these two men lay partly in their descent. Somerset, the grandson of John of Gaunt by Catherine Swynford, was the senior Lancastrian cousin of Henry VI descended wholly through the male line. Richard, as heir to both the York and the Mortimer branches of the royal family, was the leading prince outside the house of Lancaster and the wealthiest subject in the kingdom.

It should not be thought that all these lords struggled with each other continuously. When Suffolk brought the betrothal of Henry and Margaret before the council, Gloucester voiced no protest. (He had no idea at the time that Henry was going to cede some of the English territory in France to Margaret's father.) At one point in the early 1440s, York asked Suffolk to help him find a suitable daughter-in-law among the French princesses. People were not aligned in clearcut parties. Rather they jockeyed for power, striking opportunistic and temporary alliances while the situation gradually deteriorated around them. The king's council as an established governing and advisory body sank into desuetude, while the clique closest to the king ruled the realm.

A general clarification of the rivalries around the throne occurred in 1447. As related in the previous chapter, Henry VI, in a private letter to King Charles VII, undertook to cede Anjou and Maine to his father-in-law René of Anjou. When the news broke, the public fury was great. As the man closest to the king, Suffolk was held responsible for this wanton generosity. He therefore took steps to protect his position. He arranged for the king to declare in council that he bore no guilt in the matter. Suffolk's great fear was that Gloucester might use the public outrage as a wave upon which to ride back to power. He therefore contrived that the parliament of February 1447 should take place at Bury St. Edmunds, in his own home county and far from the Londoners who provided Gloucester's popular support. When Gloucester arrived at Bury, he was promptly arrested for treason by a deputation including Buckingham and Somerset. After several days of confinement Gloucester died, probably of a stroke or a heart attack brought on by the shock of arrest. (There is no good historical reason for supposing that Gloucester was murdered. As Suffolk's unpopularity increased, however, the suggestion was rumored about and came to be accepted as true. The murder formed part of the Tudor myth of "good duke Humphrey." Thus in Shakespeare's play, Suffolk, the cardinal, the queen, and York agree to have him killed.) Several months later the aged cardinal died. (The Tudors were as hostile to the cardinal as they were favorable to Gloucester. Hence Shakespeare has him die in horror, madly confessing his guilt for Humphrey's death.) It was in this same year that Somerset gained the command in France and York was given the lieutenancy of Ireland. Thus the year closed with Suffolk master of the kingdom.

For two years Suffolk enjoyed the heights of power and the rewards it brought him. Then he fell with extraordinary swiftness. The growing complaints of the commons about royal finances and the maladministration of justice became a howl for Suffolk's blood when the French retook Normandy. For thirty years Normandy had been an English province. In a defeated country, the chief minister is an obvious scapegoat. At the parliament of early 1450, the commons brought in two sets of charges against Suffolk. The first bill blamed him for the loss of France and included wild accusations of treasonable dealings with the French. The second dealt with Suffolk's handling of crown patronage and his interference with judicial processes. The latter charges were more justified and probably more important to the commons. Although Suffolk's foreign policy had contributed to the defeat in France, a single man cannot be held responsible for the disastrous end of the Hundred Years War. The commons advanced the first bill, however, because it constituted the most effective way to destroy Suffolk. A charge of treason was the most powerful weapon with which to combat the king's unquestioned right to select his own ministers. Henry nonetheless strove to protect his favorite. He forestalled a trial by banishing Suffolk as of 1 May 1450. Unfortunately for Suffolk, the ship taking him to the Low Countries was intercepted in the Channel by a vessel known as the *Nicholas of the Tower*. The captain and crew of the *Nicholas* (whoever they may have been) had decided to take justice into their own hands. They gave Suffolk twenty-four hours to prepare for eternity. On 2 May, on the gunwale of a small boat, one of the sailors struck off his head with half a dozen strokes of a rusty sword. Head and trunk were thrown on the beach.

The murder of Henry's favorite did not satisfy the commons. One of Suffolk's chief associates, Bishop Moleyns of Chichester, had already been lynched by soldiers in Portsmouth. At the end of May a general rising occurred in Kent, led by one Jack Cade. Who Cade was we do not know: he claimed to be a Mortimer relative of the duke of York. Whoever he was, his following was not what Shakespeare calls a "rabblement." Drawing on the Peasants' Revolt of 1381, Shakespeare depicts Cade and his men as an ignorant mob who yearn to upset the whole of society and particularly to "kill all the lawyers." Cade's men were actually a reasonably well-organized group of artisans and gentry who made the standard requests of most middle- and upper-class medieval rebels. The formal "Complaint of the Commons of Kent" addressed itself to the loss of France, the extravagance of the royal household, excessive taxation, the undue dominance of the evil councillor Suffolk, and the exclusion from power of the natural advisors of the king, namely such lords of the royal blood as York.

The ruling clique bungled in dealing with Cade. An advance party of royal troops, under the brothers Sir Humphrey and Sir William Stafford, was ambushed and slain by the rebels. Lord Say (the treasurer, a former associate of Suffolk, and a widely detested Kentish landowner) was placed in the Tower as a concession to popular feeling. The government then in effect collapsed, the king withdrawing from the capital to Kenilworth. On 4 July, the Londoners admitted the Kentishmen to the city. Lord Say was hauled from the Tower and executed. The weakness of the royal administration encouraged risings elsewhere in the country. In one of these, a third political associate of Suffolk, Bishop Ayscough of

Salisbury, was dragged from a church while saying mass and beaten to death.

Within several days, the citizens of London tired of the rebels. Aided by the governor of the Tower Lord Scales and his garrison, they pushed the Kentishmen back across London Bridge into Southwark. At this point the council came to terms with the rebels, offering them a free pardon if they would disperse. They did so, most going home. Cade himself did not. Alexander Iden, the sheriff of Kent, later wounded him mortally while trying to arrest him. The other risings were broken up by shows of force.

Thus the decade of the forties, in which the king was disadvantageously married, in which the king's uncle and heir presumptive died in circumstances many found suspicious, and in which an empire was lost, ended in an explosion of discontent during which the commons took it upon themselves to kill four ministers of the crown. The record stands, in R. L. Storey's phrase, as the indictment of a regime. Under the feeble hand of Henry VI, England moved toward chaos. In the first four acts of *2 Henry VI* Shakespeare depicts this disintegration with fair historical accuracy. He naturally tightens the chain of events. The disgrace of the duchess Eleanor is moved forward from 1441 so that Margaret can participate in it and so that the first three acts can present a more closely woven sequence of actions driving toward Gloucester's death at Bury. The revolt of the commons and the fate of Suffolk are then made to arise directly out of the events at Bury. But the only major unhistorical element is the role of York. He is made to cooperate in the undoing of the Gloucesters, to secure the backing of the earls of Salisbury and Warwick for his royal ambitions, and to sponsor Cade's rising. He did not do these things, and the sort of political involvement that they represent is in fact an overhasty anticipation of his career in the next decade. The disorders of the 1440s, however, did provide the circumstances for York's rise in the 1450s. After Cade's rebellion, he ceased to be a commander abroad. He returned from Ireland to become the most potent figure opposing the inept regime of Henry VI.

2. THE FORTUNES OF RICHARD DUKE OF YORK

The death of Suffolk and his three colleagues in 1450 did not destroy the court party that had dominated the king. A new chief minister immediately appeared: the forty-four-year-old Edmund Beaufort, second duke of Somerset. Somerset was a courtier rather than a great landowner like York. He was nonetheless wealthy. At the lavish hand of Henry VI, he had risen, like Suffolk, through the ranks of the peerage and done very well for himself in the way of offices and crown pensions. Even his defeat in France did not disgrace him in his king's eyes. After abandoning Normandy to the French in June 1450, he returned to England to take a seat on the king's council. The surviving adherents of Suffolk grouped around him.

Somerset's ascendancy spurred York into action in 1450. Here was another courtier lord monopolizing the king's ear and directing the king's policies, keeping York in Ireland and failing to pay him the large sums he was owed for his military services. Indeed, to York Somerset was more loathesome than Suffolk had been; the rivalry was more direct. Somerset had completed the English disgrace in France, whereas York felt that, had he been given the command there, he could have held the French back. Furthermore, a tricky dynastic matter set them at odds. After the death of Gloucester in 1447, Henry VI himself was the only living descendant of the first Lancastrian king, Henry IV. York, as the senior Plantagenet prince outside the Lancastrian line, regarded himself as heir presumptive to the crown. But Somerset was a Beaufort, the senior male of the family descended from John of Gaunt (Henry IV's father) and his third wife Catherine Swynford. The status of these Beauforts within the royal line was curious.

The children of Gaunt and Catherine had been born bastards, the fruit of double adultery. When their respective spouses had died, Gaunt and Catherine had married, and Richard II had kindly legitimated their offspring by act of parliament. The next king, however, Henry IV himself, amended the act by inserting a phrase excluding the Beauforts from royal inheritance. Only this phrase, and whatever royal or constitutional authority it might be construed to possess, stood between Somerset and potential recognition as the nearest male heir to the childless Henry VI. Although the matter is murky, it was certainly conceivable that Henry VI might try to reverse the action of Henry IV. York probably feared that Somerset's influence over the king would result in diversion of the crown to his enemy.

It is difficult now to discern the real character of Richard duke of York. He appears to have been steadfast and persistent rather than clever; occasionally rather arrogant; sometimes politically inept and often tricked by his opponents. He was also widely popular among the commons. As a royal duke and a great landowner, he was (according to contemporary political thought) a proper advisor to the king. His military reputation, unlike Somerset's, was untarnished. His brief rule in Ireland was reasonably moderate and just, making Dublin a bastion for the house of York in later years.

Repeatedly York endeavored to stir up popular feeling against the court party and to assume Somerset's place next to the king. It was probably Somerset's return from France to power and influence in England (rather than Cade's rising, as Shakespeare has it) that brought York from Ireland in September 1450. The court showed their hostility to him by attempting to waylay him on the road to London. Reaching the capital safely, however, he pushed his way into the king's presence and demanded a high place at court for himself and the trial of Somerset for treason in France. The king promised a major council to resolve such matters, but failed to act on the promise. Espousing the complaints of commons, York then attempted to work through parliament, which was in session from November 1450 to May 1451. This parliament attempted to control Henry's generosity with royal lands and pensions, and complained about the maladministration of justice. Nothing was done about Somerset, however. Indeed, he was given the captaincy of Calais, the largest English military garrison. A member of commons who proposed the recognition of York as heir presumptive was clapped into the Tower. York had gotten nowhere.

In 1452 he tried again to dislodge Somerset and reform the government, this time by threat of force. Perhaps taking a hint from the temporary collapse of Henry's administration during Cade's rebellion, he worked to inspire widespread civil uprisings timed to coincide with a military march on the capital. His army eventually confronted the royal forces at Dartford, southeast of London. Probably no one at Dartford really wanted an armed conflict. In negotiation with the king's representatives, York agreed to dismiss his army if Somerset were arrested and held for trial on charges arising from his conduct in Normandy. After this bargain was struck, York, who was an honorable man, sent his troops home. He then entered the king's tent, only to discover Somerset still in attendance upon Henry. York himself was arrested and paraded through London as a prisoner. Although Somerset probably wanted to try him for treason, the council eventually released him upon oath never again to raise forces against the king. York was disgraced and politically isolated.

Among York's weaknesses in these two efforts was a lack of support from other lords. Popularity among the commons was all very well, but real power lay with the greater nobles. His only significant allies in 1450 had been the duke of Norfolk (grandson of Richard II's Mowbray) and the ruffian earl of Devon. By 1452 Norfolk's support had waned. In 1453, however, a genuine Yorkist party began to form. York achieved an alliance with the house of Neville.

The Nevilles were the descendants of Ralph Neville, Henry IV's earl of Westmorland. As readers of Chapter III will recall, Westmorland begot sixteen surviving children by two wives. The progeny of his first marriage proved to be of comparatively little significance. Since Westmorland rather illegally arranged for his second brood to receive larger inheritances, the first lot were in fact less powerful. Westmorland's grandson by his first marriage, Ralph the second earl, was perhaps an invalid—at any rate, he played no part in the Wars of the Roses. (Hall and Holinshed err by including him in the conflict, and thus Shakespeare has him appear briefly in *3 Henry VI.*) The second family was of great importance. Its senior member, Richard Neville, married the heiress of the earl of Salisbury and thus became earl in his wife's right. His eldest son, another Richard, in turn scooped up an even greater heiress: by marrying the daughter of the distinguished general Richard Beauchamp earl of Warwick, he became earl of Warwick. The holder of this title was traditionally considered the premier earl of the realm.

Some historians have supposed that the alliance between York and the Neville earls of Salisbury and Warwick was made inevitable by ties of acquaintance and marriage. A three-year-old orphan after his father's execution in 1415, the duke of York had been reared by the first earl of Westmorland and had married Salisbury's youngest sister, Cecily. But the Neville earls did not support York in 1450; they had indeed represented the king in the Dartford negotiations in 1452. By 1453, however, they had their own reasons for joining the duke who opposed Somerset's rule. The Nevilles' chief power lay in the north. Salisbury was one of the wardens of the marches, the border area between England and Scotland. His major rival in that region was Henry Percy, second earl of Northumberland. (This was Hotspur's son, the child who had been left in Scotland when the Percy revolts against Henry IV collapsed.) Throughout the reign of Henry VI, Neville influence in the north had gradually increased at the expense of the

Percies and their relatives, the Cliffords. (Thomas Lord Clifford, who appears in 2 *Henry VI,* was the son of Hotspur's daughter Elizabeth.) By the early 1450s, Salisbury's younger sons were feuding with Northumberland's younger sons. Allied with the latter were the Cliffords and the obstreperous young Henry Holland duke of Exeter. (Exter was a descendant of a sister of Henry IV. He appears as a minor character on the Lancastrian side in *3 Henry VI.*) In the feud, the Percy side manifested a degree of hooliganism unusual even for the fifteenth century. They pushed their maraudings to the point of private war with the Nevilles. In the summer of 1453, both sides were calling out large retinues, and the Percies turned a Neville wedding celebration into a bloody clash. In the view of one modern historian, R. L. Storey, the Wars of the Roses were simply the outgrowth of the northern war between Percy and Neville. That is probably an over-statement, but certainly the Percy-Neville hostility drove the participants to seek allies. The only question to be raised was which side should ally itself with York and which with Somerset. That Salisbury was York's brother-in-law counted for little. Oddly enough, he was also Northumberland's brother-in-law. When Somerset started a quarrel with Warwick by trying to seize lands that formed part of the countess of Warwick's inheritance, the question was settled. The Nevilles joined the government's chief critic, whereupon the Percies, the Cliffords, and Exeter joined the government's chief minister.

While the alliance between York and the Nevilles was being formed, a startling event revised the political map of England much more thoroughly. In August 1453, Henry VI went mad. He had apparently inherited the debility of his French grandfather, Charles VI, but Charles's first fit was violent and noisy. Henry, by contrast, fell into a speechless and motionless stupor, unable to recognize or respond to anything. The lords closest to him could not long disguise his incapacity. Although it is not certain how much ruling Henry ever did, it was necessary at least that he appear to rule. Two months later Queen Margaret bore him a son. The madness of Henry and the birth of Prince Edward released Margaret as a potent political force.

Shakespeare is unhistorical in assigning Margaret a major part in events from almost the moment of her arrival in England in 1445. At that time she was fifteen, inexperienced, and ignorant of the country to which she had come. (She never did become very knowledgeable.) She naturally associated herself with Suffolk, who had arranged her marriage, and with Somerset, who succeeded him, but it is hard to trace any effect on affairs prior to 1453 that can be definitely attributed to her. Assertive females had been common in her family, however, and when her personal interests were threatened she became the fiercely energetic queen that Shakespeare depicts. A fifteenth-century letter describes her as "a great and strong-labored woman, for she spareth no pain to sue her things to an intent and conclusion to her power." Fired by the desperate situation of the house of Lancaster incapable king, infant prince she attempted to claim the regency with full powers of government and patronage.

Rule by a Frenchwoman was an arrangement that only the most ardent members of the court party could accept. In late 1453, a great council was called—that is, a meeting of the upper house of parliament, the temporal and spiritual lords. To this meeting York had to be invited; although no one could consider him heir presumptive any longer, he was still the greatest of the peers in blood and wealth. It was probably at this council that the Nevilles settled their alliance with York. The duke of Norfolk once again inclined to York's side. York was thus strong enough to act against Somerset, reviving the charges of treason against him and confining him to the Tower. But debate on the means of government during the king's insanity dragged on until March of the next year, when the death of the chancellor (who also happened to be the archbishop of Canterbury) made it obligatory that someone have power to appoint a successor. York was then made protector and head of the council.

York's protectorate showed him capable of reasonable government. He took to himself the captaincy of Calais, and made Salisbury chancellor, but his administration was not nakedly partisan. Somerset, although imprisoned, was not further harassed. York even managed to calm some of the northern feuds, imprisoning the hooligan duke of Exeter. Unfortunately for him and the country, King Henry recovered his wits (such as they were) around Christmas. The protectorate lapsed. Somerset was released, restored to favor, and regranted the captaincy of Calais. By early 1455, York's allies were relieved of their offices, and York himself was once again out in the cold.

York and the Nevilles left London in the late winter of 1455, fearing that Somerset would move against them. Their fear was justified. Somerset called another great council, this one to meet at Leicester in May, announcing that his purpose was to provide for the safety of the king. That was indeed ominous to the Yorkists, so they arranged that the court never got to Leicester. York and the Nevilles, with an army, met the royal party at St. Albans, some twenty miles north of London. (York had secured a papal dispensation from his vow not to raise troops against Henry.) Somerset, not expecting such swift action, was off guard and outnumbered. Henry attempted to negotiate with York, employing the relatively moderate duke of Buckingham as spokesman. York was not so easily taken in this time as he had been at Dartford. Again the crucial issue was the fate of Somerset: York demanded his trial and Henry would not give him up. Negotiations collapsed and, probably at the instigation of Warwick, fighting broke out.

The first battle of St. Albans (another took place there six years later) is conventionally said to have begun the Wars of the Roses. It was little more than an armed clash. The armies were small.

The dead numbered no more than sixty. The chief persons on the Yorkist side were the two Neville earls, York himself, and possibly his thirteen-year-old son, the earl of March. (In the fifteenth century men took up arms at an early age. But not ridiculously early. Shakespeare also brings into the battle York's youngest son, the future Richard III, already displaying a wonderfully sardonic bloodthirstiness. This is sheer invention: Shakespeare knew that in 1455 Richard was only two.) On the court side were Henry (who did no fighting), Somerset, Buckingham, Northumberland, Thomas Lord Clifford, and, rather oddly, Salisbury's brother Lord Fauconberg. (Shakespeare omits Fauconberg—or Falconbridge—from this episode, bringing him in on the Yorkist side in later battles. He includes the queen, who was not present at St. Albans and whose role in these events is not known.) The ill-prepared Lancastrians were overwhelmed. York captured the king. Somerset, Northumberland, and Clifford all died. That casualty list demonstrates the extent to which the battle was the outcome of the two superimposed feuds, York vs. Somerset, Nevilles vs. Percies and Cliffords. Once the principal personal enemies of York and the Nevilles were dead, the battle was over.

The first battle of St. Albans returned the Yorkists to power. Under pressure from the commons, who were anxious about a fresh outbreak of private war in Devon, York was reestablished as protector. Among the offices gained by his colleagues, the most important was the captaincy of Calais, which went to Warwick. But the long-run effect of the Yorkist victory was not to settle matters but to embroil them further. York's brief protectorate (November 1455 to February 1456) ended when the king again appeared in parliament. Henry himself was willing to retain York as his chief councillor, but Margaret would not hear of it. Fearing that York's ascendancy would destroy her power, her husband's, and eventually her son's, she contrived to gain control of the administration by securing the privy seal, under which government warrants were issued, for the chancellor of her own household.

Further, she welded together a party fanatically hostile to the Yorkists, a party that included the sons of those lords who had fallen at St. Albans: Henry Beaufort third duke of Somerset, Henry Percy third earl of Northumberland, and John Lord Clifford. (The last is Shakespeare's Young Clifford, known for his later slaughters as "the butcher" and "bloody Clifford.") A passion for revenge without quarter had entered English politics.

For the next two years, matters further deteriorated. Henry touchingly tried to reconcile his bickering peerage. Margaret encouraged further bitterness. Significantly, she moved the court out of London, always Yorkist in sentiment, to the Lancastrian estates in the midlands. Eventually, at a great council held at Coventry in 1459, the court party apparently decided to crush its enemies by force. Alarmed, the Yorkists rallied at Ludlow, York's castle in the Welsh marches. The two armies met at Ludford Bridge near Ludlow on 12 October 1459, the Yorkist lords confronting Margaret, her captains, and the king himself. Ludford was a complete rout for the Yorkists. Their army was smaller, and the presence of the king (not a combatant but still a sacred personage) caused some of Warwick's troops to change sides. The Yorkist lords were forced to flee. The two Nevilles and the earl of March (now seventeen) scampered to the Devon coast and sailed off to Warwick's stronghold at Calais. York and his second son, the earl of Rutland (aged sixteen), crossed to Dublin. The duchess of York and her two younger sons, George and Richard, were taken by the royalists.

Margaret swiftly capitalized upon her victory. The parliament that met at Coventry the next month, later dubbed the Parliament of Devils, passed an act of attainder against York, his sons, and the Neville earls, making them legally guilty of treason and declaring their lands forfeit. But this move was bound to provoke an extreme response. Faced with a sentence to death and complete dispossession, the Yorkist lords had to retaliate simply to survive. In the summer of 1460 they did.

It is not altogether clear why the party of York went from the bottom to the top of the wheel of fortune in the nine months between the rout of Ludford in October 1459 and the battle of Northampton in July 1460. They had the advantage of retaining Dublin and Calais, of course, potent bases from which to strike. They enjoyed popular acclaim, fueled chiefly by generally disgust with the Lancastrian government and supported by their own diligent propaganda. Except during the two periods when York was protector, nothing had been done to cure the abuses of administration that had moved the commons to topple Suffolk a decade earlier. Perhaps most significantly, a greater number of lords joined the Yorkist cause in these nine months. The York-Neville alliance had never previously amounted to more than a narrow faction within the peerage, but the wholesale condemnation of the Yorkists at the Parliament of Devils excited one of the strongest sentiments of the age: the nobleman's feeling of the sanctity of property and inheritance.

The success of the Yorkists in 1460 still remains a remarkable turn of events. The Neville earls, March, and Salisbury's brother Fauconberg landed on the Kentish coast in June. Canterbury welcomed them on 26 June, London on 2 July. On 4 July, they marched north to confront the king at Northampton. They asked for the usual parley, but this time no negotiations preceded the battle. The duke of Buckingham, who had always been a moderate political figure—loyal principally to the king, uninfluenced by Margaret, and not particularly hostile to York—now argued against talking with the invaders. In a battle lasting only half an hour, the Yorkists triumphed, Buckingham perished, and the king was once again captured. Margaret fled northwards.

The state of affairs after the battle of Northampton closely resembled that after St. Albans. The king was escorted back to London, and a parliament was summoned in order to reverse the attainders of the previous year. Important posts were distributed among the Yorkists. The king was not mistreated. There was no thought of deposing him: the earls planned to rule in his name as their opponents had done. The one major difference was the absence of York himself. He had lingered in Ireland, allowing March and the Nevilles to do all the work, hatching plans of his own. He finally crossed the Irish Sea in September, advanced to London with all the accoutrements of a royal progress, and timed his arrival to coincide with the opening of parliament. He strode into Westminster Hall, passed the assembled lords, and laid his hand on the empty throne to claim it. The response was a stunned silence. York had miscalculated by turning a struggle for power under the king into an effort to replace the king.

In the next few days he formally asserted his claim to the crown, for the first time publicly stating his rights as the heir to Edward III through Lionel of Clarence and the Mortimer line. All the acts of parliament since 1399 that confirmed Lancastrian possession of the throne he condemned as void. The assemblies that had enacted them were not true parliaments, he said, because the Lancastrian kings who summoned them were usurpers. He admitted that he had long refrained from pressing his claim; nonetheless, he argued, "Though right rest for a time and be put to silence, yet it rotteth not nor shall it perish." The lords were appalled. They had no wish to open the matter of the royal title, despite the fact that many were York's supporters and the most ardent partisans of Lancaster were not present. Divinity still hedged the anointed king. They passed York's claim to the judges, who promptly passed it back as beyond their learning: it should be settled by the lords of the blood royal and the peerage. Finally the latter stuck on one point: they had all sworn allegiance to Henry VI. They consequently arrived at an act of accord. Henry was to reign for his lifetime, or until he should decide to abdicate. The crown would then pass to York and his heirs. The solution strongly resembled the arrangements made in 1420 about the French crown in the treaty of Troyes.

Margaret naturally found little occasion for joy in the Yorkist victory, and none whatever in the act of accord that disinherited her son Prince Edward. She and the ardent Lancastrians—Somerset, Exeter, Northumberland, Young Clifford—raised a large host in the north. In December, York, Salisbury, and Rutland marched to York's castle near Wakefield to oppose them. On 30 December, with a small force, they left the castle to meet the Lancastrians, too rash to await the return of troops that York had sent foraging. Wakefield was a disaster for the Yorkists. The duke and his son were killed in combat. (Tradition has it that Young Clifford killed Rutland, crying out, "Thy father slew mine, and so will I do thee and all thy kin!") Salisbury was captured and executed after the battle, possibly as a private act of vengeance by Northumberland. The severed heads of York and Salisbury were placed on the walls of York city, York's being derisively decked with a paper crown.

Few men in English history have experienced so many reversals of fortune so swiftly as Richard duke of York. In a single decade he bid for power—power either under the nominal lordship of King Henry or above it—six times. Thrice he was successful—during Henry's madness, at St. Albans, and after Northampton—but never for long. With elegant economy, Shakespeare manages to compress a remarkable amount of this whirling career into seven scenes. The first three constitute the last act of *2 Henry VI*. After the death of Suffolk and the rebellion of Cade, York returns from Ireland (1450). His negotiations with Buckingham and the king, however, are drawn from the confrontation at Dartford (1452). Breaking the bargain arrived at, Somerset appears in attendance on the king. This episode leads directly to the battle of St. Albans (1455). Thus several reversals, York's first protectorate, and the king's insanity are omitted. With the Yorkist victory at St. Albans the play ends.

The rest of York's career occupies the first act of *3 Henry VI*. The play opens with a parliamentary scene in London after the victory at St. Albans, but the events are actually those of 1460.

The aftermath of St. Albans has been telescoped with the similar aftermath of Northampton. York claims the crown. Since in Shakespeare his royal ambition has long had the backing of the Nevilles, the opposition comes, not from Yorkist and neutral lords, but from the committed Lancastrians, Young Clifford, Northumberland, and Exeter, who historically were not present at this parliament. (Neither, of course, was the future Richard III, who in Shakespeare vigorously urges his father on.) The assembly then arrives at the act of accord, which is immediately denounced by Margaret on her son's behalf. After York's sons unhistorically persuade York to ignore the act, Shakespeare proceeds directly to Wakefield. Two Mortimer uncles of York, persons of dubious historicity, appear in the battle. The killing of Rutland by Young Clifford becomes a scene of great pathos, since Shakespeare unhistorically makes Rutland a child instead of a seventeen-year-old soldier. The death of York himself receives the major emphasis. He dies, not in battle, but afterwards, captured by Young Clifford, paper-crowned and taunted at length by Margaret, and finally stabbed by both. Throughout the whole portrayal, York appears as an unsympathetic figure, fierce, blustering, and duplicitous. Only in his death scene, when he is helpless before the equal ferocity and greater cruelty of Margaret, does he gain a measure of tragic dignity. It is a harsh portrait of a man who was essentially upright, whose firmness and moderation might have made him a good king, and who was undone by the intractability of his circumstances and his own occasional rashness.

3. EDWARD IV, 1461–1471

Within three months of the duke of York's death in December 1460, his eighteen-year-old son, Edward earl of March, became king of England. Once again the house of York made a remarkable recovery from disaster. Edward had not been at Wakefield. Early in December he had gone to collect Yorkist forces in the Welsh marches. There he encountered a Lancastrian army under the leadership of the Welshman Owen Tudor, second husband to Henry V's widow Catherine, and Owen's son Jasper, half-brother to Henry VI. On this, his first independent command, Edward proved himself an aggressive general. By the energy of his attack, he triumphed over the Lancastrians at Mortimer's Cross, driving Jasper Tudor into flight and executing Owen Tudor after the battle. At Mortimer's Cross, a peculiar meteorological phenomenon occurred: three distinct suns were seen shining in the heavens before the battle. According to a fifteenth-century chronicle, Edward opportunistically interpreted the triple sun as a token affirming that the Trinity was on his side. This marvel is the only incident Shakespeare uses from the battle of Mortimer's Cross. In the play, Edward and his brother Richard (whose presence is again unhistorical) take the suns to symbolize eventual triumph for the three sons of York. After this incident, according to both Shakespeare and his source Hall, Edward used the "sun in splendor" as a personal badge.

Although Mortimer's Cross showed Edward to be a capable soldier in his own right, the house of York required more than a Welsh victory and an odd atmospheric effect. Margaret and her forces, flush from their triumph at Wakefield, were at large in the north. Securing aid from the Scots, Margaret marched her army south to rescue her husband from Warwick in London. With her were Somerset, Exeter, Young Clifford, and Northumberland. On 17 February 1461, they encountered Warwick and the king at St. Albans, inflicted upon Warwick a heavy defeat, and took possession of the king. But Warwick himself escaped and Margaret was unable to follow up on her victory. Had she marched straight into London after the second battle of St. Albans, the Yorkist cause would have been in ruins. As it happened, however, the Londoners locked their gates against her. On the march south from Wakefield, she had given her army license to sack as they came, thus allowing the single episode of widespread devastation, slaughter, and looting that took place during the Wars of the Roses. The Londoners dreaded similar treatment from her marauding northerners. Indeed, the duchess of York, in London at the time, swiftly sent her two younger sons, George and Richard, across the sea to refuge in Burgundy. Margaret's own miscalculated tactics had stiffened Yorkist sentiment in the south. While she angrily retired north once again, London welcomed Edward and Warwick.

The second battle of St. Albans, however, created a political crisis. Having lost the person of the king, the Yorkist government, which had held sway since the battle of Northampton the previous July, lost all legitimacy. Aside from Duke Richard's claim to the throne in October, set aside by his own followers, the Wars of the Roses had hitherto been conducted as a struggle to gain control of King Henry and thus of his government. Three times the Yorkists had seized the king, only to lose him again to the determined queen and her party. After second St. Albans, it must have seemed to Edward and Warwick that, as long as the struggle persisted in these terms, it would continue indefinitely, or at least until they themselves fell as York had. They thereupon changed the terms radically. On 1 March, Warwick's brother George Neville, who was bishop of Exeter and had been the chancellor of the Yorkist government, addressed the London populace; on 3 March, a council of lords met; on 4 March, Edward was declared King Edward IV at Westminster. He was proclaimed as the legitimate heir of Edward III through Lionel of Clarence. Henry VI was set aside as a usurper whose reign had brought crime and chaos to England.

Before the month was out, the new king's asserted authority over England became authority in fact. Accompanied by Norfolk,

Warwick, and Warwick's uncle Fauconberg,* Edward marched north to engage the Lancastrians at Towton in Yorkshire. In a preliminary skirmish on Saturday 28 March, the butcher Clifford was killed. On the next day, Palm Sunday, in a blinding snow- storm, the largest, longest, and bloodiest of the battles of the roses was fought. As many as 50,000 men are said to have partic- ipated, including three-quarters of the surviving adult peerage. The slaughter was very great. For centuries after, it was believed that Towton exemplified the most horrible results of internecine warfare: men were thought to have slain unknowingly their own fathers or sons. Accordingly, Shakespeare, in his depiction of the battle, interrupts his scenes of combat to present the lamentations of "a son that hath killed his father" and "a father that hath killed his son." Among those slain or executed afterward were Northumberland and Devon. Finally the Lancastrians fled. Margaret, Henry, and their son escaped to Scotland, where they were later joined by Exeter and Somerset. Edward IV was king of England in deed, and the power of the northern houses opposing the Nevilles—Percy, Clifford—was decisively broken.

Edward IV was formally crowned in June 1461, and his title was confirmed by parliament in November. No formal deposition of Henry VI was thought necessary, he and all his line being deemed usurpers. (Henry himself was captured four years later, wandering in Lancashire, and thereafter dwelt a prisoner in the Tower.) The new reign was inaugurated by the usual bestowal of honors upon the new king's supporters. Edward's surviving brothers, George (aged eleven in 1461) and Richard (aged eight), returned from Burgundy to be created dukes of Clarence and Gloucester respectively. Edward's faithful retainer, William Hast- ings, became Lord Hastings. William Herbert of Raglan became

---

* Shakespeare is confused about Warwick's relatives. In the battle of Towton as depicted in *3 Henry VI*, it is Warwick's brother John Lord Montague rather than his uncle William Lord Fauconberg who takes part. Historically, Montague was Margaret's prisoner at the time.

Lord Herbert and later earl of Pembroke (Shakespeare uses only the latter title). The Nevilles were variously rewarded. Warwick's brother the bishop of Exeter and chancellor became archbishop of York. His other brother John became Lord Montague and then (displacing the Percy heir) earl of Northumberland. Warwick himself received no new title, but he garnered a slew of profitable offices: great chamberlain of England, warden of the Cinque Ports, constable of Dover.

Edward ruled England for twenty-two years, but his reign was split almost in half by a Lancastrian restoration in 1470–1471. Since *3 Henry VI* ends in 1471, and since Edward was more successful in the dozen years after that date, we will postpone consideration of his qualities as a king to the next chapter. The decade before that restoration is marked in Shakespeare, and to a large extent in history as we currently understand it, by a growing division between the king and his chief supporter, Warwick. Warwick was unquestionably the greatest of Edward's subjects, not only because of his services in making Edward king, but also by reason of his territorial power. He enjoyed the offices abovementioned; he was still captain of Calais; and he held his wife's earldom of Warwick, his mother's earldom of Salisbury, and numerous other estates brought to him by the successes of the Neville family. He was a popular and glamorous figure, but also a difficult man, an ambitious adventurer capable of sullen resentment. For a time Edward and Warwick were close: until Somerset was executed after the minor battle of Hexham in 1464, they had to cooperate in order to wipe out remaining pockets of Lancastrian resistance. Once that was done, the relationship between king and kingmaker became increasingly strained. Edward was his own man, not a mere protégé of his older cousin. As had been the case at the beginning of the century with Henry IV and the first earl of Northumberland, the new king's indebtedness to his loyal earl became a source of rancor as soon as the king decided not to follow the earl's advice about governing the realm.

The first fissure opened over Edward's marriage. (Although some modern historians have doubted this traditional view, there is a good deal to be said for it.) Warwick sought to arrange an alliance between England and France, and to cement it by wedding Edward to Bona of Savoy, the sister-in-law of the new French king, Louis XI. Negotiations to this effect had been scheduled for October 1464. A month before Warwick set out for Paris, however, Edward announced to his council that he already had a wife. The previous May he had secretly wed an English widow, Elizabeth Woodville. Warwick was astonished and chagrined.

The marriage, indeed, caused general astonishment. Edward had consulted no one about it. He was, moreover, the first English king since the Norman Conquest to marry a subject, let alone the widow of a commoner. (Henry IV had married the earl of Hereford's daughter, but this took place long before there was any prospect of his becoming king. All the other Norman and Plantagenet kings had married foreign princesses.) The Tudor chroniclers, followed by Shakespeare, made much of Queen Elizabeth Woodville's lowly origins. Romantic stories soon appeared that Edward, who was a considerable ladies' man, married her only because she stoutly refused to become his concubine. In fact, the Woodvilles had some claim to noble connections. But certainly the marriage constituted a slap in the face of Warwick's diplomatic efforts. It also came to inconvenience Warwick in a more personal way. Elizabeth had two sons by her first marriage, as well as five brothers and seven sisters. Thanks to her elevation, her relatives were able to sweep the aristocratic marriage market, snagging the holders or the heirs of the earldoms of Essex, Arundel, Pembroke, and Kent, and the duchies of Exeter and Buckingham. Their marital greed went to an extreme when Elizabeth's twenty-year-old brother, John, became the fourth husband of the wealthy dowager duchess of Norfolk, a lady well into her sixties. Aside from this last union—described in its own time as a diabolical marriage—there was nothing particularly extraordinary about this behavior. The prolific Nevilles, including Warwick himself, had been marrying to equal or greater advantage for the last sixty years. The Woodvilles' success, however, posed Warwick a problem: they had left no one eligible to marry his own daughters, Isabel and Anne, unless the girls married the younger brothers of the king himself, an arrangement Edward would not permit.

The conduct of foreign policy apart from marriage negotiations further estranged Edward and Warwick. In the 1460s, France and Burgundy became increasingly hostile to each other. The vigorous and wily Louis XI resented the near-independence his supposed vassal, the duke of Burgundy, had gained during the latter decades of the Hundred Years War. In this potential conflict, Warwick inclined toward France. Having been acquainted with Louis before the latter became king, Warwick fancied that a special relationship existed between them. Louis, however, was by far the craftier diplomat. Anxious to secure English help, he strung Warwick along by allowing him to dream of dominion over portions of a dismembered Burgundy. Warwick was to expand his captaincy of Calais into a great continental lordship with an appropriately exalted title. Edward, on the other hand, sought alliance with Burgundy. England's most important commercial ties lay with the Low Countries ruled by Burgundy, and Burgundy was the traditional ally with whose aid England might once again conquer northern France. Therefore, defying Warwick's counsel, Edward married his sister Margaret to Charles the Rash, the heir (and after 1467 the duke) of Burgundy. He also attempted to marry his brother George of Clarence to Charles's daughter. Here he met an obstacle. Clarence had fallen under Warwick's sway, and Warwick's brother the archbishop had undertaken to secure papal dispensation for a marriage between Clarence and Warwick's daughter Isabel. (They were first cousins.) Edward angrily forbade the marriage and dismissed the archbishop from the chancellorship.

Thwarted on the marriage market, ignored in matters of foreign policy, Warwick grew increasingly hostile to the king. The man who had been so necessary to the ambitions of the house of York seemed no longer necessary, or even important, once those ambitions had been realized. In 1469 Warwick resorted to conspiracy and rebellion to regain his power. In this he was assisted by Clarence, now nineteen and possibly the shallowest of the later Plantagenet princes. Clarence was good-looking, eloquent, greedy, skittish, perpetually discontented, perpetually engaged in foolish schemes—in Shakespeare's phrase, "false, fleeting, perjured Clarence." Possibly inspired by dislike of the Woodvilles, he ran off with Warwick to Calais and there married Isabel in July 1469. Next, they recrossed the Channel, entered London, and marched north. Edward, distracted by a northern rising inspired by Warwick, was caught off guard. The rebels won a short skirmish at Edgecote against Edward's supporter Pembroke. Warwick then captured the king himself, his brother Richard of Gloucester, and his close friend Lord Hastings. The queen's father and her brother John (he who had married the elderly duchess) were not only captured but executed as well.

Warwick then attempted to rule England under Edward's nominal authority in the same way that the duke of York had attempted to rule in Henry VI's name. His official complaint against Edward was the same that had been raised against Henry's regime, namely that the king was dominated by a clique of evil counsellors (i.e., the Woodvilles) to the exclusion of his proper advisors, the great lords of the realm (i.e., Warwick himself). But Edward was very different from Henry, and Warwick's faction was even narrower than the old duke of York's had been. Under Warwick's restraint, Edward smiled blandly, signed whatever was put before him, and bided his time. Warwick attempted to call a parliament, possibly for the purpose of deposing Edward in favor of Clarence. (He had it rumored about that Edward was illegitimate and that therefore Clarence was the rightful Yorkist heir.) But he discovered that he could not rule the kingdom without the king. Only Edward's personal authority would be recognized. After insurrections broke out, Warwick was obliged to release Edward. Edward continued to smile blandly, promising the reconciliation of all difficulties. He also quietly ensured himself of the support of loyalists, among whom the most important were Hastings and Richard. By April 1470, after the revelation of Warwick's complicity in another rising, Edward was strong enough to act. He declared Warwick and Clarence "great rebels" and chased them out of the kingdom. Upon his orders, refuge was refused them at Calais.

Warwick was now a ruined man, and in desperation adopted an astonishing expedient to restore himself. The fertile, cunning brain of Louis XI had hit upon the notion of reconciling Warwick with Queen Margaret, who had been begging her French relatives to help her back to the English throne. Warwick was to reestablish the house of Lancaster. Louis's purpose was, of course, to pull England out of the Burgundian alliance and into the French orbit. Margaret naturally wanted to regain her son's inheritance. Warwick, although he must have realized that it would be as difficult to dominate England under Margaret as it had been under Edward, fell in with the scheme as the only way to regain anything at all. Although it took much diplomacy, Louis brought Margaret and Warwick together. Each had freely slaughtered the other's relatives and adherents a decade before, but Louis induced Warwick to beg Margaret's pardon and induced Margaret to forgive Warwick. To seal this strange new alliance, Margaret's son Prince Edward was married (or at least betrothed: see note on page 166) to Warwick's younger daughter Anne. With Louis's backing, an invasion was launched. In September 1470, Warwick, Clarence, and the Welshman Jasper Tudor landed on the south coast of England. With them also was Warwick's brother-in-law, John de Vere earl of Oxford. An ardent Lancastrian whose father and brother had been executed by Edward IV, Oxford had joined Margaret in France the previous year. Margaret herself, her son Edward, and his bride Anne remained in France to await the issue.

Although Edward IV had easily driven Warwick out of the country, England had remained restive during the interlude before the new invasion. While trying to secure his position, Edward made a bad blunder. Having been betrayed by the house of Neville, he decided to restore the house of Percy as a bulwark in the north. He returned the earldom of Northumberland to the Percy heir, who had been dispossessed since the death of his father at Towton nine years before. Unfortunately, he had already given the earldom to Warwick's brother John, formerly Lord Montague, the one Neville still loyal to him. Edward tried to compensate John for the loss of Northumberland by inventing another title for him, marquess of Montague, but John of course lost the Percy lands and the income that went with them. His new title, although loftier in the peerage, carried no great estates with it. Edward thereby alienated Montague, and the effect was to be crucial. When Warwick landed in the south, Edward was in Yorkshire. Montague, who was nearby with forces larger than Edward's, promptly declared for Warwick. Edward fled. He and a few followers, notably Hastings and Richard, hastily sailed to the Low Countries and took refuge with Charles the Rash. Warwick entered London, plucked poor old Henry VI from the Tower, and put him back on the throne.

The so-called re-adeption of Henry VI lasted only six months. The new government was shaky, founded upon alliances impossible to maintain for any length of time. Archbishop Neville opened parliament with a sermon on the text, "Return, O backsliding children," but the past to which these particular children were thus invited to return was criss-crossed with their own hatreds. Clarence's allegiance was uncertain: he yearned for a throne, but with Lancaster restored, the best that could be offered him was a promise that he should inherit if Henry and his son died without issue. Edmund Beaufort, fourth duke of Somerset since the execution of his brother in 1464, was no friend of Warwick's: too many of his relatives had fallen while fighting Warwick. Exeter, Jasper Tudor, and other fairly consistent Lancastrians resented the new triumph of their old enemy. The Tudors had a particular cause for irritation. Jasper's thirteen-year-old nephew, Henry Tudor, was heir to the earldom of Richmond, but this earldom had been given by Edward IV to Clarence, who naturally hung on to it now that he was a powerful Lancastrian. (Shakespeare uses Henry of Richmond's appearance in London during the re-adeption as an occasion for Henry VI to prophesy the eventual elevation of the Tudor to the throne.) Finally, Margaret was so distrustful of what might occur in England that she and her son stayed in France.

This jerry-built regime soon collapsed before the energy and good luck of Edward IV. In March 1471, Edward, Richard, and Hastings landed at Ravenspur on the Yorkshire coast with a small force given them by Charles the Rash. (Charles's motives duplicated Louis XI's: he too wanted the English alliance.) The Percies, although not assisting Edward, made no move against him. To that extent, Edward's regrant of the earldom of Northumberland worked to his benefit. Borrowing from the actions of Henry of Bolingbroke, who had landed at the same place in 1399, Edward claimed that he sought only his duchy, not the crown. On this pretext, he gained entry into the city of York. He then dropped the pretense and marched south with a swelling army. Warwick had difficulty mobilizing: several of his supposed allies preferred to await Margaret's arrival. At this point, Clarence was persuaded by Yorkist emissaries to turn his coat once more and rejoin his brothers. Finally, Somerset, Oxford,

Exeter, and Montague massed their troops with Warwick's at Coventry. They declined Edward's invitation to battle there, whereupon Edward dashed for London and took possession of the hapless Henry VI.

On Easter Sunday, 14 April, the two armies at last confronted each other at Barnet, ten miles north of London. Early morning fog, a difficult terrain, and a wildly shifting battle line made Barnet a very confused fight. The end came when Oxford's forces, after straying for a time in the mist, returned to battle only to fall mistakenly upon their own allies. The Neville-Lancastrian army then broke up in complete rout. Exeter, severely wounded, was taken by the Yorkists. Oxford and Somerset fled, the former escaping to Scotland. Warwick and Montague both died in the field. Edward arranged for their bodies to be exhibited at St. Paul's Cathedral, so that no doubt might linger as to the fall of the Nevilles.

On the same day, far too late, Margaret, Prince Edward, and Anne arrived on the Dorsetshire coast. Linking up with Somerset, they hastened north, hoping to get into Wales where Jasper Tudor could reinforce them. Edward IV was too swift for them. Proceeding across England by forced marches, he brought Margaret's troops to bay at Tewkesbury, near Gloucester, on 4 May. There he inflicted upon the Lancastrians a final defeat. Prince Edward was killed in the battle, along with Somerset's younger brother John Beaufort. Somerset himself was taken prisoner and executed. Margaret was brought a captive back to London. Four years later, Edward permitted Louis XI to ransom the ruined queen. She died in France in 1482.

With the deaths of Prince Edward of Lancaster, the duke of Somerset, and John Beaufort, only one man remained alive who was descended from old John of Gaunt entirely in the male line: Henry VI himself. On the night of King Edward's return to London, 21 May 1471, the roll of Lancastrian deaths was completed.

The official account of the restored Yorkist government later announced that Henry had received the news of Tewkesbury "with such hatred, anger, and indignation, that of pure displeasure and melancholy he died." It is difficult to imagine anyone believing this disingenuous tale. Modern examination of Henry's remains has suggested that he died of a fractured skull. The Tudors, including Shakespeare, held that Richard of Gloucester personally despatched Henry on his own initiative, but this is quite unlikely. The death of the last Lancastrian king must have been ordered by Edward IV, possibly with the advice of his council. Richard, as constable of England, would probably have been charged with seeing that the decision was carried out.

The events between the duke of York's death at Wakefield in December 1460 and Henry VI's death after Tewkesbury in May 1471 provide the material for the last four acts of *3 Henry VI*. Although they are condensed in Shakespeare's usual way, so that the pace of the play is extraordinarily vigorous, Shakespeare manages to preserve a large amount of detail. In these four acts the playwright elides and omits less historical fact than he does elsewhere in the trilogy on Henry VI. Of course, certain episodes are subordinated for the sake of dramatic focus. In Act II, which presents Edward IV's rise to power after his father's death, the battle of Mortimer's Cross is omitted save for the three suns, and the second battle of St. Albans is reduced to a report of offstage events. Thus full emphasis can fall upon the decisive battle of Towton, which receives elaborate treatment. In Act III, the gradual estrangement between Warwick and Edward is simplified by the omission of much international diplomacy. Edward's surprising marriage to Elizabeth Woodville becomes the single cause of Warwick's alienation and his subsequent alliance with Margaret and Louis XI. Here the events of 1464 (the marriage, the consequent collapse of negotiations for the hand of Bona of Savoy) are telescoped with the events of 1470 (Louis's reconciliation of

Margaret with Warwick, their plan to restore Lancaster in England) to form a single scene in which Bona, Margaret, Prince Edward, Oxford, and Warwick all appear at the court of King Louis. Acts IV and V dramatize the many reversals of fortune between 1469 (Clarence's desertion, Warwick's brief capture of Edward) and 1471 (the return of Edward, the confrontation at Coventry, the battles of Barnet and Tewkesbury, and the death of Henry) with remarkable comprehensiveness and very few changes. Some minor alterations keep the lesser characters in tidier order: Oxford, for example, is present at both Barnet and Tewdesbury instead of fleeing the kingdom after Barnet, and the third and fourth dukes of Somerset become a single person.

Shakespeare's version of the 1460s is also true to a large-scale element of the struggle between the houses of Lancaster and York. As was noted at the beginning of this chapter, Shakespeare focuses throughout the Henry VI trilogy upon the personal ambitions of individuals. This focus drew him into what is now perceived as historical falsehood in the earlier scenes of the trilogy. The duke of York was not pressing for the crown as early as 1450, although Shakespeare represents him as doing so. But by the 1460s, the civil struggle had become much more a matter of naked personal ambition. Warwick's astonishing change of sides in 1469–1470 was provoked by mere disgruntlement with Edward's behavior. Warwick had lost power, and he turned to Lancaster simply as a way to recoup. Although his propaganda condemned Edward's government for the same kind of misrule that the Yorkists had complained of under Henry VI's regime, Edward had in fact exerted himself to strengthen the monarchy and pacify the local feuds that had vexed the 1440s and 1450s. He did not fully succeed in restoring the prestige of the crown and the peace of the kingdom until after Tewkesbury, but he had made a considerable start in the first decade of his reign. Warwick's revolt did not arise from any significant concern for the method of government, the state of the realm, or the constitutional legitimacy of the ruling house. In other words, by 1470 the Wars of the Roses involved no principles concerning the proper nature or use of power. Men fought simply to determine which individuals should wield power. Thus by the middle of *3 Henry VI*, Shakespeare's view of history as governed by the passions and power-lusts of influential persons has coincided with our present understanding of events.

But Shakespeare goes further. He entertains (with perhaps some qualifications) a notion no modern historian would espouse, the notion that the passions of individuals mesh into a large-scale, divinely guided pattern. His Yorkists and Lancastrians are locked in a chain of appropriate disasters: revenge follows murder, punishment follows crime to the entire extermination of the Plantagenets and their noble supporters. Working out of Hall and Holinshed, he unhistorically molds events so that the balancing design of a savage justice emerges. In particular, he elaborates and emphasizes certain characters and episodes to create the appearance of a doomed heritage for the Plantagenets, a well-merited curse upon the royal house that works with a relentlessness suggesting the second law of thermodynamics.

The chief character so developed is Richard of Gloucester. He is made the final and most awful embodiment of Plantagenet savagery, who will eventually usurp the throne after Edward IV's death. Consideration of the character of Richard III must wait until the next chapter, but it must be pointed out here that his role in *3 Henry VI* is almost entirely unhistorical. Following the Tudor conjecture that Richard cherished ambitions for the throne from his earliest days, Shakespeare gives him several brilliant soliloquies expressing his yearning for absolute power and his hatred for all his relatives. He goes beyond the Tudor historians by introducing him as a major figure far before his time. Thus throughout the middle and late scenes of *3 Henry VI*, the ominous figure of the future Richard III looms over hopes for peace and prepares for the final play of the Yorkist tetralogy, the play that bears his own name. In sober fact, Richard was too young to participate in most of the events of *3 Henry VI*. His part in history began in 1469, when, at the age of seventeen, he supported his brother Edward against Warwick. The first battle he fought in was Barnet. Whatever his actions may have been after Edward's death thirteen years later, he displayed unfailing and energetic loyalty to his brother during the latter's lifetime.

The chief episodes that Shakespeare elaborates to suggest a doomed heritage concern the murder of children. In Act I of *3 Henry VI*, York's son Rutland is slaughtered at Wakefield by the butcher Clifford. In Act V, Henry VI's son Prince Edward is even more savagely cut down after the battle of Tewkesbury by the three York brothers, Edward IV, Clarence, and Richard of Gloucester. Again following the Tudor chronicles, Shakespeare makes much of the blood-lust of the killers and the pathos of the slain. In fact, Edward of Lancaster was not wantonly murdered after capture: he was killed (by whom no one knows) in the battle itself. Rutland also died in battle. Both were men in their late teens at the time, adult soldiers by medieval standards. Prince Edward was indeed only a year younger than Richard of Gloucester. But the child-murders given the playwright by his sources were far too good a symbol of the internecine strife of late Plantagenet England for Shakespeare to ignore. The killing of a child, the ultimate act of tyranny in a Christian society that well knew the story of Herod and the Innocents, marks out the appalling savagery of Clifford and Margaret. It then recurs to mark the sons of York as avengers who will sink as low as their enemies.

Finally, one suggestion implicitly made by the whole of *2 and 3 Henry VI* must be countered. It would appear from the plays that between 1445 and 1471 England experienced continuous turbulence on a national scale, that the whole country suffered from unceasing uproar, punctuated by episodes of hideous atrocity, while the nobles sought to control or seize the crown. It is not so. "The lack of politic rule and governance" under Henry VI (the phrase is that of a fifteenth-century judge and political theorist) did allow riot, feud, and extortion to proceed, often unchecked by justice; and the escalation of private quarrels did of course lead to war and changes of dynasty; but Shakespeare's plays greatly exaggerate the turmoil. Risings of the commons were exceptional. Despite the occasional outrages and disorders, peasants mostly tilled their fields and merchants mostly tended to trade. The wars of the lords were confined to a skirmish in 1455 (first St. Albans), six battles in 1459–1461, and three (including the brief clash at Edgecote) in 1469–1471. In other words, very little time was spent in actual campaign. Only at Towton was there a really long casualty list. The marauding march of Margaret's northerners before the second battle of St. Albans provided the only episode of extensive sack. England did not suffer the devastation that had occurred in northern France during the Hundred Years War. During the Wars of the Roses, those who suffered most were the noble combatants themselves and their immediate retainers, a tiny group in comparison to the whole population. Villagers, of course, derive no benefit from having a battle take place in their fields, and the citizens of St. Albans must have been vexed to find themselves twice visited by grandees spoiling for a fight, but their sufferings bear no comparison to the horrors of civil war in more recent centuries. The Tudor vision of catastrophic convulsion in mid-fifteenth-century England was born largely of propaganda. Tudor Englishmen feared a repetition of the dynastic struggle, and the chronicles served as celebrations of the strength of Tudor rule and as warnings to any who might be discontented with the Tudor monarchs. Shakespeare converts that propaganda into eloquence, but no specialist in medieval English history has yet identified "the father that hath killed his son."

Still and all, the eloquence is germane, regardless of Shakespeare's misinformation on the extent of the wars. Whether you are nine or nineteen, whether you have a handful of soldiers beside you or a host, to fight and die is still to fight and die.

RICARDVS · III · ANG · REX ·

Artist Unknown: *Richard III* (National Portrait Gallery).

⚜ VII ⚜

RICHARD III
the last plantagenet

What heir of York is there alive but we?
And who is England's king but great York's heir?

1. EDWARD IV, 1471–1483

The Tudor imagination revelled in Richard III. Archvillain and
devil incarnate, he supposedly started his infamous career by lin-
gering sullenly in the womb for two years, finally coming to term
with teeth and shoulder-length hair. Having thus discommoded
his mother, he murdered his way through the royal house, slaughtering his cousin the last Lancastrian king Henry VI, Henry's
son Prince Edward, his own brother the duke of Clarence,
his nephews the child-king Edward V and Richard duke of
York, and finally his wife Anne. He was the bane of his brother
Edward IV's wife Elizabeth Woodville and of her relatives;
he contrived the judicial murder of Edward's loyal chamberlain
Lord Hastings; and he spun his plots whilst seated in a privy. He
was the final embodiment of the wrath of God visited upon England for the crimes of the Plantagenets since Richard II's deposition in 1399. He was a criminal so appalling that his own death
was not a further crime requiring still more retribution, but a

purgation of all England. After his defeat at Bosworth, the kingdom could rest united and secure under the Tudor dynasty that had conquered him.

This lurid king, hunchbacked, clad in blood-spattered black velvet, forever gnawing his nether lip or grasping for his dagger, has an enduring place in English mythology. He owes something to the facts about the historical Richard III. He owes far more to rumor and to the political bias, credulity, and especially the literary talent of Tudor writers. A Warwickshire antiquary of Henry VII's time started the tale about Richard's prolonged prenatal life. Polydore Vergil, the Italian humanist hired by Henry VII to write the history of England, placed Richard in the framework of God's providential scheme for the fifteenth century. Early in the reign of Henry VIII, St. Thomas More started a history of Richard III, a gem of ironic narration that established the popular image of the king (the crooked shoulders, the withered arm, the gnawed lip) and the popular account of the fate of his nephews. More reported many details as mere rumor, but his readers tended to accept them as fact. The chronicler Edward Hall, completing a corrupt text of More's tale and fitting it within his own elaboration of Polydore's providential scheme, fused the two to form the climax of his *Union of the Two Noble and Illustre Houses of Lancaster and York.* Raphael Holinshed, in his *Chronicles of England,* stole from Hall, and out of them Shakespeare created his *Richard III.* In Shakespeare the providential scheme is articulated by Henry VI's widow Queen Margaret (who was in fact dead at the time of Richard's accession): cursing the Yorkists, she predicts the punishments they will receive for their crimes in destroying the Lancastrians. Richard himself appears as a monster, More's villain endowed with superb dramatic exuberance and a rich vein of sardonic humor:

> March on, join bravely, let us to it pell-mell!
> If not to heaven, then hand in hand to hell!

As myth, the Tudor Richard is indestructible, nor should one try to destroy him. This demonic jester and archetypal wicked uncle is far too satisfying a creation, and the works of More and Shakespeare are far too vigorous, for us to wish them otherwise. As history, however, the Tudor Richard is unacceptable. Some of the legend is incredible, some is known to be false, and much is uncertain or unproved. The physical deformity, for example, is quite unlikely. No contemporary document or portrait attests to it, and the fact that he permitted himself to be stripped to the waist for anointing at his own coronation suggests that his torso could bear public inspection. Concerning Richard's character and career as a whole, much controversy has raged. Richard has had ardent defenders in modern times, some of whom have described a king as virtuous as the Tudor villain is monstrous. This Richard commits no crimes; his claim to the crown is altogether just; he is unwaveringly loyal to his family; and his conqueror Henry VII is the real villain, responsible first for the murder of the princes and then for the murder of Richard's reputation. This chapter cannot change the minds of readers who happen already to be partisans of either Richard the Monster or Richard the Good. It can perhaps set forth briefly what is known of Richard and relate that to Shakespeare's play.

Richard III begins where *3 Henry VI* left off, with the restoration in 1471 of the first Yorkist king, Edward IV. Compressing selected events of a dozen years into half a dozen scenes, it rapidly proceeds to Edward's death in April 1483. It then dramatizes more carefully the three-month interregnum, the nominal reign of the twelve-year-old Edward V that ended with Richard's accession in late June. The last two acts deal with Richard's own reign, cut short in August 1485 by Henry Tudor's victory at Bosworth. Richard, however, dominates the whole play. His brother Edward IV, indeed, appears only in one scene, on his deathbed. The first historical injustice that Shakespeare commits victimizes, not Richard, but Edward IV.

Of all the English kings in Shakespeare's double tetralogy, Edward IV is most neglected by the playwright. Shakespeare's telescoping of time so elides Edward's twenty-two years on the throne that he does not even have a play named after him. Yet the reign was prosperous. Aside from Henry V, he was the most successful of the later Plantagenets.

In justice to Edward then, and by way of supplying background frequently alluded to by the characters of *Richard III,* the history of the house of York prior to Richard's accession must be recounted here. As readers of the previous chapter will recall, throughout the 1450s Richard duke of York repeatedly attempted to gain control over the government of his pious but disastrously incompetent cousin Henry VI. In December 1460, an army gathered by Henry's fierce queen, Margaret of Anjou, defeated and killed Duke Richard at Wakefield. Also perishing in this battle was the second of York's sons by his duchess, Cecily Neville: the seventeen-year-old earl of Rutland. (Following the Tudor historians, Shakespeare made Rutland a child at the time of his death. The cruelty of Rutland's slaughter, compounded when Margaret flourished in York's face a handkerchief dipped in Rutland's blood, is an outrage many times recalled by the Yorkist characters in *Richard III.*) The Yorkist cause then descended to the duke's three surviving sons, Edward, George, and Richard, aged eighteen, eleven, and eight respectively. In March 1461, three months after Wakefield, Edward was proclaimed king by a faction of Yorkist lords, of whom the most powerful was the Duchess Cecily's nephew, Richard Neville earl of Warwick. A few weeks later, Edward and Warwick inflicted a decisive defeat upon the Lancastrians at Towton, driving Henry and Margaret into flight and securing the Yorkist hold on the crown.

Edward then settled down to rule England, and his young brothers George and Richard became dukes of Clarence and Gloucester respectively. He married a beautiful widow, Elizabeth Lady Grey, née Woodville. He also alienated his chief supporter

Warwick. The king's marriage embarrassed Warwick: he had been negotiating a diplomatic betrothal between Edward and the French king's sister-in-law when Edward secretly wed Elizabeth. The results of the marriage also annoyed Warwick: led by the queen, numerous Greys and Woodvilles began to secure influence at Edward's court. Most significantly, Edward ignored Warwick's advice in matters of foreign policy. Finally, in 1469–1470, Warwick the kingmaker revolted against the king he had made. Seducing Clarence to his side and marrying him to his eldest daughter Isabel, Warwick allied himself with Queen Margaret and drove Edward into exile. He then put back on the throne poor Henry VI, who had spent most of the previous decade in the Tower. The so-called re-adeption of Henry VI was, however, a short-lived affair based on a strained alliance. Edward, vigorously supported by his loyal brother Richard of Gloucester and eventually regaining the allegiance of his turncoat brother George of Clarence, returned to England in 1471 and seized the kingdom once again. Warwick was defeated and killed in the battle of Barnet (14 April). Margaret was defeated and captured in the battle of Tewkesbury (4 May). During the latter battle, the only son of Henry and Margaret, Prince Edward of Lancaster, fell. (As with Rutland, the Tudor writers converted this death of a young prince in battle into an atrocity. In *3 Henry VI,* Shakespeare has the three York brothers, Richard in the van, savagely cut young Edward down after he has surrendered. This outrage is also extensively recalled in *Richard III:* old Margaret curses each of the Yorkists for his role in the destruction of her "sweet son.") Some days after Tewkesbury, the final extinction of the house of Lancaster was achieved by the assassination of Henry VI, once again a prisoner in the Tower. Edward, or Edward and his council, presumably ordered the deed. Thomas More, however, reported the dubious tale that Richard of Gloucester personally slew Henry on his own initiative. The Tudor Richard now had two crimes to his credit.

Thus by late May 1471 Edward reigned secure, without a rival dynasty or an overmighty subject to harass him. During the next twelve years he enjoyed himself thoroughly. It may have been a stroke resulting from self-indulgence that killed him at forty. Certainly he grew rather fat from the pleasures of feasting, and he thoroughly earned a reputation for lechery unrivalled by any other English king except Charles II. (His most famous mistress, Jane Shore, is often mentioned in *Richard III*. The wife of a London merchant and supposedly the merriest harlot in the realm, she long outlived her royal lover, surviving well into the next century.) But lust and gluttony did not so preoccupy Edward that he failed to rule well. Despite his pleasures, his chief concern was the business of government. Under his guidance the kingdom prospered. He may have lacked the kind of overmastering will and single-minded devotion by which Henry V bent all his own and his subject's energies to clearly conceived goals: Edward was more pragmatic, less forethoughtful. Yet during his reign England recovered from the Wars of the Roses, and Edward managed to cure some of the disorders that had led to those wars.

He restored to the monarchy the prestige it had lost during Henry VI's long and wretched reign. Unlike the shabby, vacant-faced Henry, he looked like a king. He was over six feet tall, remarkably handsome, and fond of magnificent clothes: his personal appearance fixed in his subjects' minds the power and glory of the crown. Although he had the unattractive habit of handing over to his friends the women whose charms he had wearied of, his rampant sexuality seems to have enhanced rather than detracted from his reputation. Of greater significance was his firm rule. The orders of the king, or the king and his council, were obeyed in a way they never had been under Henry VI. He qualified his firmness with a leniency designed to heal past wounds. By a practice of judicious mercy, he allowed the surviving Lancastrian lords or their heirs to secure reversals of their attainders for treason, and thus to regain their titles and at least some of their lands. His handling of financial matters was particularly notable. He introduced into the administration of the royal estates financial reforms that enabled him to garner the true wealth of the crown. The commons had long complained to Henry VI (and to his two predecessors) that crown income was thriftlessly managed. By reinvigorating the methods of accounting, by replacing some of the cumbersome exchequer machinery with simpler arrangements, by entering into trade on his own behalf, and above all by securing a hefty pension from Louis XI in return for cancelling an invasion of France, Edward contrived to pay off crown debts, achieve solvency, and even to establish a comfortable surplus. Between 1475 and 1482, for the first time in the fifteenth century, the king was able to do what the commons had always begged the king to do: namely, to "live of his own," to pay all the expenses of his household and his government out of the regular crown income without asking parliament for taxes. That he was fighting no war, civil or foreign, naturally assisted him. Here Edward IV may deserve credit even above Henry V. During his reign, partly because of his own good sense and partly because of developments in continental politics, the English set aside the old dream of conquering France and thus saved the price in blood and treasure attached to that dream. Finally, he even managed to make some inroads upon the disorders and feuds that had long prevailed in the remoter parts of the kingdom. Here his achievement was less spectacular than it was in finance. The Welsh and the northerners could not quickly unlearn obstreperousness. But a good start was made. Edward made his brother Richard a kind of viceroy in the north by giving him extensive authority and estates on the Scottish marches and in Yorkshire, Cumberland, and Westmorland. To rule Wales he established a council at Ludlow in the Welsh marches. This body, nominally headed by his eldest son the prince of Wales, was directed by the queen's brother Earl

Rivers. Rivers and Richard exercised their power effectively, suppressing the sort of treason and insurrection that had led to the civil wars.

Had Edward lived until his sons were grown, there would have been little after 1471 to mar his record as a king. Except for his brother Clarence (of whom more later), the great lords were loyal to him, and he was able to cope with the jealousies that sprang up among them. His coping, however, was entirely ad hoc. He made no lasting arrangement to ease or defuse court rivalries and thus to ensure a smooth succession in case he died betimes. These rivalries were the more dangerous because his policies had made Richard, Rivers, and others so powerful. They arose chiefly from Edward's startling and imprudent marriage.

Insofar as the marriage was fruitful, it was a success. Edward's dynasty was apparently secured by the birth of two sons, Edward prince of Wales (b. 1470) and Richard duke of York (b. 1473). Five daughters also survived infancy, of whom the most important was the eldest, Elizabeth (b. 1466). But Queen Elizabeth Woodville also brought to her husband a throng of relatives: a flock of brothers and sisters as well as two sons by her previous marriage. The Woodville clan, deeply responsive to the dictates of self-interest, swiftly capitalized upon their new royal connection by cornering the aristocratic marriage market and securing for themselves various titles and court offices. Now the Woodvilles were not complete upstarts. The queen's father had been made a baron long before she married Edward. Her first husband had had connections among the nobility. Her mother had been Jaquetta of Luxembourg, widow of Henry V's brother the duke of Bedford and daughter to the count of St. Pol, a distinguished European nobleman. Nor was the advantage the Woodvilles took of their new position unprecedented: other families had risen in comparable ways during the previous century. The extraordinary swiftness and success of the Woodvilles' rise, however, together with the irresponsible behavior of some of them and their previous participation on the Lancastrian side of the civil war, caused them to be *regarded* as upstarts by the older nobility and those who had shared the Yorkist struggle for the throne. At the time of Edward's death they were both powerful and unpopular. Aside from the queen herself, four of these Woodvilles crucially enter the story of Richard III. Elizabeth's eldest brother Anthony, who became Earl Rivers in 1469, was governor to the prince of Wales. The most interesting member of the family, he was a polished, educated, pious, rather nonpolitical peer, famous for chivalric jousting. Another brother, Sir Edward Woodville, served as a military commander. The queen's first-marriage sons, Thomas Grey marquess of Dorset and Lord Richard Grey, were playboy courtiers. Their chief occupation seems to have been debauchery, an activity in which they sometimes joined their stepfather.

Four important men were at odds with the Woodvilles. the king's brothers Richard and Clarence, the king's chamberlain Lord Hastings, and the most eminent peer outside the house of York, the duke of Buckingham. In the veins of Henry Stafford duke of Buckingham ran Plantagenet blood: he was great-great-grandson to Thomas of Woodstock. He had succeeded to his duchy at the age of five, after his grandfather's death at the battle of Northampton (1460). A royal ward until 1473, he had been married off to the queen's sister Katharine at about the age of ten. Youthful marriages were common practice among the aristocracy, but Buckingham came to resent being thus saddled with a comparatively humbly born wife. Perhaps because of this, he took very little part in public events during Edward's reign despite his rank and descent. By contrast, William Lord Hastings was at the center of the court. Having shared all Edward's perils since 1460, he was the king's closest friend and most trusted councillor. Rivers resented Hastings for gaining a post both had wanted, the captaincy of Calais. Dorset and Hastings maintained a private quarrel, probably arising from rivalry over mistresses.

The entire Woodville clan was jealous of Hastings's intimacy and influence with the king. In 1482 they contrived to get him into serious, although temporary, trouble with Edward, an incident mentioned several times early in Shakespeare's play.

Richard seldom came to court. For a dozen years he served Edward as his deputy in the north, occasionally travelling to London when the king's business required it. There is no evidence whatever that during this time he was anything but loyal to his brother. The Tudor story of Richard's early schemes for the crown is entirely unfounded. He could not in any case have anticipated that Edward would die at forty, leaving a minority that would afford him the opportunity to seize the throne. In the north he earned a reputation as an able administrator, a successful general in several forays against the Scots, and an upright man. He dwelt chiefly at Middleham in Yorkshire, with his wife Anne Neville. Anne's father Warwick had previously married her, or at least betrothed her, to Prince Edward of Lancaster as the seal on his alliance with Queen Margaret.* She married Richard in 1472, a year after the death of her first husband. In Shakespeare their courtship forms a macabre scene: the murderer of Anne's husband and father-in-law zestfully woos the poor widow over the corpse of the father-in-law. No such melodramatic episode took place. Recent defenders of Richard have claimed that the marriage was a love-match, but there is little more evidence for this rosy view than for Shakespeare's grim one. It is more to the point that Anne and her sister Isabel (Clarence's wife) were the greatest heiresses in the kingdom. Richard, like most lords of his time, presumably wanted to marry well, and Anne may have wanted a husband who could prevent Clarence from swallowing her half of the Warwick estates. Clarence did indeed try to prevent the match: he thrust

---

* There is no actual record of a marriage between Anne and Prince Edward. Unlike a modern enagagement, however, a fifteenth-century betrothal was a binding contract in the eyes of the institution under whose jurisdiction such matters fell, the church.

her, disguised as a kitchen-maid, into a friend's house, whence Richard rescued her; and then he challenged the division of the Warwick properties. Aided by the moderation of Richard's demands, King Edward settled the quarrel over the inheritance after it had gone on for three years. This awkward dispute, however, did not create lasting resentment in Richard. Apparently he tried to prevent Clarence's execution in 1478. Certainly he held the Woodvilles responsible for Clarence's death. His lasting resentment was directed toward them.

Clarence was very unlike Richard. Where Richard was stable, reliable, and faithful to the king, Clarence was an ambitious will-o'-the-wisp. He had already betrayed Edward once by joining Warwick's revolt: he was lucky to be alive, free, and rich after Edward's restoration. Yet this skittish prince continually hatched plans for self-aggrandizement, indulging finally in behavior so foolish that one may doubt his sanity. Clarence was a royal nuisance. In the early 1470s he not only upset the family by quarrelling with Richard, he also seems to have dabbled in trivial Lancastrian plots. In 1477 his activities became a scandal. In that year, after the death of Isabel, he schemed to marry the heiress of the duchy of Burgundy. Edward firmly scotched that plan, which would have dragged the English into a continental war. Next, entirely on his own authority, he tried and executed a servant on the ridiculous charge that the unfortunate woman had poisoned Isabel. (The poison, according to Clarence, was administered two months before Isabel died. No such slow-acting poison was then known.) Clarence thus not only committed a reasonless judicial murder, but took the king's justice into his own hands to do it. The offense to Edward was all the greater since Edward had been trying to reestablish the probity of the law courts after the abuses they had suffered in Henry VI's time. Next Clarence protested Edward's execution of another servant of his, a man convicted of witchcraft: with truly remarkable folly, he chose as his spokesman a friar who had publicly expounded the Lancastrian right to the throne during the re-adeption of Henry VI. Finally, he stirred up a small, ineffective rising in Cambridgeshire. The king's patience broke. Arresting Clarence, he introduced into parliament a bill of attainder of treason against him. Clarence was charged with perverting the king's justice, with trying to alienate the king's subjects, and with spreading rumors that the king was illegitimate. He was also charged with preserving a copy of an act of the re-adeption parliament, an act that declared Clarence himself heir to the crown should Henry VI and his son die without issue. (The last charge is dubious: there is no other evidence that such an act was passed. Clarence may have forged the thing in a wild dream of securing the throne, or Edward may have invented it to seal Clarence's fate.) Clarence had been many times forgiven. Now he was officially found "incorrigible." In February 1478 he was condemned. Ten days later he was privately executed in the Tower. Surprisingly enough, the story (used by Shakespeare) that he was drowned in malmsey may be true.*

The responsibility for Clarence's death has been debated. In Tudor times Richard was blamed. In Shakespeare, Richard contrives both the arrest and the execution in order to remove an obstacle in his path to the throne. This he certainly did not do. Contemporary reports suggest that he was grief-stricken at the whole affair. He held the Woodvilles responsible and thereafter came to court even less frequently than before. The Woodvilles *may* have encouraged the king in the deed. Any threat to the king threatened their power and position. They disliked Clarence anyway because of his participation in the re-adeption, during which several Woodvilles had died. Many did hold them guilty during the next few years. But the chief responsibility for Clarence's death must lie with Edward. He initiated proceedings. He took

---

* On the other hand, Professor Charles Wood informs me that, six years later, Richard III's only parliament passed "An Act for the Contents of a Butt of Malmsey." The statute does not mention royal dukes as a necessary ingredient of the wine.

the very unusual step of acting as Clarence's prosecutor in parliament—normally kings arranged for someone else to do this. It was his power that Clarence's schemes and follies threatened. The death of Clarence demonstrates Edward's authority in England and the length to which he would go to maintain that authority. He would have no subject opposed to him, not even his own brother. His own strength, the legality of the procedure, and Clarence's manifest guilt enabled him to escape the retribution that Richard II had suffered eighty years earlier for taking similar measures against a close royal relative.

2. THE ACCESSION OF RICHARD III

Edward IV died on 9 April 1483. Two days later his eldest son was proclaimed king. On 26 June, however, Richard of Gloucester was proclaimed in his stead, and on 6 July he and his wife were crowned King Richard III and Queen Anne at Westminster Abbey. The intervening three months were busy with plots and counterplots, not all of which can be clearly discerned now.

April saw a struggle for possession of the prince. Edward had made the obvious appointment of Richard as protector during the minority. Richard was, after all, the only surviving adult male in the house of York, a loyal, long-tested prop of the Yorkist throne, and the most powerful man in the realm. Edward had also, however, left the prince himself in the hands of Richard's enemies the Woodvilles. The struggle was the more acute because the persons concerned were geographically scattered. Richard was in the north. Buckingham was on his own estates at Brecon (Brecknock) in southern Wales. The twelve-year-old prince, together with his governor Rivers, was at Ludlow in the Welsh marches. The rest of the Woodvilles, the little duke of York, and Hastings were in London where the king died. (Shakespeare does not adhere to this geographical scattering. For dramatic convenience, all his characters except the prince are in London.) Those in London, moreover, were deeply suspicious of one another. Despite Edward IV's deathbed attempt to reconcile them, the Woodvilles glowered at Hastings and his friends across the council table as they tried to make arrangements for the succession. Each party bid for the support of moderate members of the council: John Russell bishop of Lincoln, John Morton bishop of Ely, Thomas Lord Stanley.

The Woodvilles wanted no protectorate. They feared Richard and could only perpetuate their power through young Edward. They therefore sought to terminate the protectorate by crowning the prince as soon as possible. Gaining the support of the moderates, they scheduled a coronation for early May and directed Rivers to bring Edward to London posthaste. They also strengthened their military position. Dorset was made constable of the Tower; Sir Edward Woodville put to sea with a fleet. Apparently the royal treasure was split up among Dorset, Sir Edward, and the queen. In all this they governed in disregard of the protectorate and over the opposition of Hastings. The best Hastings could do was to persuade them to limit the prince's escort from Ludlow to 2000 men (the Woodvilles wanted Rivers to bring a large army) and to send frantic messages to Richard. It was only through Hastings that Richard learned of his brother's death and his own appointment as protector. No official message came to him from the pro-Woodville chancellor (Thomas Rotherham archbishop of York) or the Woodville-dominated council. Hastings urged Richard to come quickly to London, taking charge of the prince on the way.

Richard, having publicly sworn fealty to his nephew and written to reassure the queen, started south in late April with 300 Yorkshiremen. Simultaneously Buckingham, who had also been in touch with Richard, came from Wales with a small force. The two dukes met at Northampton on 29 April. By this time the Ludlow party had arrived at Stony Stratford, fourteen miles nearer

London, but Rivers rode back to Northampton to greet the dukes and spend the night there. Early the next morning he found himself under arrest. Richard and Buckingham rode hastily to Stony Stratford and offered homage to young Edward. They then disbanded the Ludlow escort and, to Edward's dismay, arrested Sir Thomas Vaughan (the prince's elderly chamberlain) and Richard Grey (the prince's half-brother, who had come out from London the day before). The dukes had neatly severed the prince from the Woodvilles. Accused of plotting to ambush Richard and of dark designs against the prince, Rivers, Vaughan, and Grey were sent as prisoners to Richard's castles in Yorkshire. When news of Richard's coup reached London the next day, the remaining Woodvilles were thrown into confusion. After several lords refused to grant her further military support, the queen, together with her daughters and little York, rushed into sanctuary at Westminster Abbey. Hastings, jubilant, ruled the city until Richard and the prince arrived on 4 May.

During the next month Richard solidified his position as protector. The council recognized his authority and issued writs in the name of Edward V for a parliament in late June. Archbishop Rotherham was replaced in the chancellorship by Bishop Russell. (When the queen fled into sanctuary, Rotherham may have given her the great seal of the realm, to which she had no right whatever. More, at any rate, reports such an incident, and Shakespeare uses it.) Grants of authority were bestowed upon Richard's supporters Buckingham and John Lord Howard. (The latter became duke of Norfolk at the end of June.) Most of Sir Edward Woodville's fleet was induced to return to London, although Sir Edward himself fled to Brittany with several ships. In only one significant action that we know of did the council overrule Richard: they refused to entertain treason charges against Rivers, Vaughan, and Grey on the grounds that, even if the three men had in fact planned any move against Richard at Northampton, Richard at that time held no office that would make an attack upon him treasonable. No new date for the coronation was announced. Although Richard arranged for more oaths of loyalty to be sworn to Edward V, he seems to have planned an indefinite postponement of the coronation and a confirmation of his protectorate by parliament.

Except possibly for the attempt to condemn Rivers, Vaughan, and Grey, Richard's actions in May demonstrate no design on his part to seize the crown. The Woodvilles had attempted to exclude him altogether from power: he had responded with the coup at Northampton and Stony Stratford and then proceeded to shore up his authority. London and the prince were in his hands; he was reasonably popular with the citizens and backed by Buckingham and the council; parliament would meet to seal the status quo. The realm might go comfortably on, ruled by Richard until the prince came of age, by which time Richard might have weaned him away from the influence of his maternal relatives. His failure to crown Edward immediately is no reliable indication that he intended to depose him: the child Henry VI had been king in name for seven years before his council decided to crown him. Unfortunately for Richard, the queen remained hostile. Her refusal to emerge from sanctuary, and especially her refusal to allow little York to join his brother under Richard's care, constituted a loud statement of distrust in Richard and provided a focus for any discontent with his government.

According to the Tudor myth, Richard had long dreamed of the crown and, once Edward IV was dead, deviously and cannily plotted to obtain it. The actual events of April–May 1483 show a less masterful and far less wicked Richard. Thrust into an unexpected situation and openly antagonized by an upstart party he already had reason to distrust, he moved, sometimes skillfully as at Northampton, sometimes awkwardly as with the treason charge, to secure the authority his brother had bequeathed him and to neutralize the threat of Woodville rule. He may have been more the victim of events than their master. Sometime in June, however, whether through ambition or through fear for his own safety, he decided that the protectorate was not enough.

Early in June the council scheduled Edward's coronation for the 22nd. Richard had evidently decided that only under such circumstances would the queen release her younger son. On 10 June, Richard despatched a letter to the city of York, telling his friends there that the Woodvilles were plotting the destruction of Buckingham and himself, and begging them to send troops. Since Richard could hardly have expected these troops to arrive until late in the month, he cannot have foreseen an immediate crisis. Perhaps he wanted them on hand when parliament met. Hastings, however, took fright, perhaps because of Richard's move to reinforce himself. He began to conspire with his former enemies the Woodvilles against his former ally Richard. His plot included the ex-chancellor Rotherham, Bishop Morton, and, oddly enough, Jane Shore. (After her king's death, Jane seems to have become Hastings's mistress or Dorset's, perhaps both. She may have been the go-between in the Hastings plot.) Richard, perhaps equally alarmed, struck hard. On 13 June he suddenly arrested Hastings's fellow conspirators and had Hastings himself executed without trial. On 16 June the queen, persuaded by the arguments of cardinal-archbishop Bourchier of Canterbury that little York should attend his brother's coronation, or perhaps more persuaded by the presence of soldiers around the abbey, at last surrendered York. In the next few days, Richard cancelled both the coronation and the parliament (far too late to prevent people from coming to London for these events) and issued death warrants for Rivers, Vaughan, and Grey. By 22 June he was openly preparing his own accession.

In More and Shakespeare, the order of two crucial events is reversed: the queen releases York before the death of Hastings. This sequence has the merit of making better sense of the queen's behavior: why, unless she was absolutely forced, would she have given York up if Richard had already started high-handedly killing people? Indeed, a historian has recently argued that the Shake-spearean order is correct, but, after a flurry of controversy in the historical journals, it seems that the Hastings plot and execution did in fact come first. Also in More and Shakespeare, the Hastings plot is a mere fabrication designed by Richard to destroy Hastings after Hastings has made it clear that he will not help Richard to the crown. It seems more likely, from Richard's startled response and his hasty illegal procedure, that Richard was gravely frightened by a genuine conspiracy. With Hastings and the moderates on the council joining the Woodvilles, his support was rapidly collapsing. The fate of royal uncles to young kings in the past century (including two previous dukes of Gloucester, Richard II's uncle Woodstock and Henry VI's uncle Humphrey) furnished little hope that he could live to a hale old age. He arrived at the decision to take the crown, I think, after he had dealt with the immediate threat of Hastings and had gotten hold of York. More and Shakespeare, as previously mentioned, suppose that Richard was governed by long-range ambition. It looks much more likely that he was governed by fear, that he was anxiously trying to cut through a difficult and dangerous impasse. Indeed, it looks as if all the persons concerned were governed by fear.

Starting on 22 June, Buckingham and a popular preacher named Ralph Shaa (brother to the lord mayor of London) delivered public addresses claiming that Richard was the true heir to the crown. The reasoning behind the claim was shoddy and inconsistent. Shaa apparently charged that Edward IV was illegitimate. Since that would disinherit the princes, and since Clarence's attainder disqualified his children, Richard was the only available heir of the house of York. Edward's bastardy was an old and feeble story (Warwick and Clarence had both bandied it about) and a peculiarly embarrassing one: the Duchess Cecily, at whose London house Richard had been living in May and early June, cannot have enjoyed a public accusation of adultery. Two days later, it seems, Buckingham charged that it was Edward's children—not Edward himself—who were illegitimate. They were supposedly the fruit of a bigamous union: at the time of his marriage to Elizabeth Woodville, Edward IV had allegedly been contracted to a foreign princess. This story could stand up a little longer, although it too was eventually changed. When circum stances obliged Richard to ask the parliament of the following January for confirmation of his title, Edward's supposed precon- tract turned out to involve, not a foreign lady, but one Eleanor Butler, who had died in 1468. The foreign betrothal could be disproved, but a secret betrothal, to which both parties were now dead, could not be. Even this third story has flaws, however. Edward's marriage to Elizabeth Woodville had long been recog- nized by the clergy and people of England; the secular court of parliament had no authority to pronounce on matters touching the sacraments; and the legitimacy of a prince born in 1470 prob- ably could not be affected by his father's betrothal to a woman who had died two years earlier. In short, Richard had grave trou- ble devising a suitable hereditary claim to the crown. Yet a he- reditary claim was essential. In law, the Yorkist crown was based entirely upon the contention that the Yorkists were the true heirs to Edward III whereas the Lancastrians had been usurpers. More- over, unlike the deposed Edward II and Richard II, the child- king Edward V could not be plausibly charged with bad govern- ment. Richard had to maintain that Edward V had never had any right to the throne. The flimsiness of his declarations was not amended by the peculiar constitutional arrangements he was forced to adopt. Richard was acclaimed king on 26 June by "the lords spiritual and temporal and the commons of this realm." That phrase was intended to suggest parliament, but the persons who had been summoned for parliament under the writs of Ed- ward V could not constitute a legal parliament if the king who had summoned them was no king. That is one of the reasons why Richard needed a further act of parliament the next January. In short, Richard was legally as well as morally the usurper of his nephew's crown. On that point, the Tudor legend is correct.

Richard's usurpation, despite its moments of legal muddle, was in one way the most efficient and least costly of the many irregular seizures of power in medieval England. No lives were lost in battle or riot. Only a handful of men were executed. The dangers of another long minority, with royal relatives squabbling over the government, were averted. A selfish and unpopular faction was removed. An experienced administrator became king, and his proven abilities suggest that, had he ruled longer, England would have enjoyed a reasonably enlightened and strong reign. In another way, however, Richard's usurpation was a startling act of tyranny barely clothed in the rags of legal process. There was no real justification for the execution of Rivers, Vaughan, and Grey. There was no justification for the execution of Hastings without formal trial. The flimsy bastardization of the princes was a flagrant violation of a cherished medieval principle, the right of inheritance. Although Queen Elizabeth Woodville certainly helped to make Richard an enemy and a usurper by behaving as if he already were one, Richard finally acted with no more political finesse or understanding than she had. He certainly alienated many former supporters by his drastic solution to the problem of the minority. Reflecting upon all the experiences of the house of York since the 1450s, he may have thought that taking the crown in one swift and decisive gesture would settle matters, but in his case the cost of the deed was too high. One problem not experienced by earlier Plantagenet princes who had seized the crown dogged him particularly. Although Henry IV and Edward IV almost certainly caused the deaths of the kings they replaced and thus can be held guilty of murder, they replaced adults with a long history of misrule. They could not be accused of slaughtering innocent children.

Did Richard III murder his nephews? It is the master-crime attributed to him in the Tudor legend. More provides the famous account. According to this curious tale, Richard, while on progress through the west country after his coronation, despatched an agent with a letter ordering the constable of the Tower, Sir Robert Brackenbury, to murder the princes. Brackenbury refused. Thereupon Richard, introduced by a "secret page" to the ambitious and unscrupulous Sir James Tyrell, sent Brackenbury orders to surrender his keys to Tyrell for a night. Brackenbury complied. Two ruffians hired by Tyrell smothered the boys and buried them. All this, More claims, Tyrell confessed before he was executed for treason (on a different charge) nineteen years later. Shakespeare dramatizes a large portion of this tale. Its errors and impossibilities have long been exploded, most recently in P. M. Kendall's biography of Richard. Not the least among them concern Tyrell and Brackenbury. Tyrell was hardly unknown to Richard: he had been a Yorkist knight since Tewkesbury, and in the summer of 1483 was Master of the King's Horse. Brackenbury, whose behavior in surrendering the keys after refusing to commit murder appears incredible, neither lost his post for his failure to cooperate nor turned against Richard for a crime he must have known of. Two years later he fought and died for Richard at Bosworth.

Defenders of Richard have passionately argued that Richard was not guilty. Many have pointed out that he had no need to kill the princes since he had already bastardized them. Some have suggested that Buckingham was the culprit. Some have argued that the princes survived Richard only to be killed by Henry VII, who did need to get them out of the way since he had relegitimated them in order to marry their sister. This is also difficult to believe: there is no contemporary accusation of Henry and no evidence that the princes survived the summer of 1483.

The existing historical evidence does not permit a firm conclusion on the fate of the princes. There is really no courtroom evidence upon which to convict anyone. We must rest content with a probability, and the probability points toward Richard. An Italian visitor to London who left England shortly after Richard's coronation in July wrote later that year that many Englishmen (including Edward V himself) feared that they would soon die. In the fall of that year, an alliance against Richard was undertaken by Elizabeth Woodville, Dorset, Bishop Morton, Buckingham, and Henry Tudor. This unlikely quintet sought to place Henry Tudor on the throne. They could hardly have joined in such an aim unless they believed that the princes were dead. Neither of these arguments proves that the princes were indeed dead by late 1483, or if they were that Richard killed them, but they contribute to the likelihood. One overwhelming fact stands out: the princes were not seen after the summer of 1483, when, of course, they were in Richard's hands. Although he was ever after plagued by the rumor of their death, he never produced them to disprove the damaging charge. If he did murder them, it is strange that he did not follow the usual practice in such matters, namely to still the clamor by exhibiting their bodies with some beguiling tale of death from natural causes. Yet the responsibility for their death must touch him most nearly. It was he who had taken their throne. In all other cases of displaced English kings down to the mid-seventeenth century, deposition led to death. To others may belong some of the guilt for the deposition: Edward IV perhaps, for having made no better arrangements for the succession of his son; Elizabeth Woodville perhaps, for treating Richard with such unmitigated hostility; Buckingham perhaps, for urging Richard on. Nonetheless, Richard brought about the deposition, and thereby in some sense signed the princes' death warrant.

3. BOSWORTH AND THE TUDORS

The cat, the rat, and Lovell our dog
Ruleth all England under the hog.

The cat was Sir William Catesby, a lawyer, Hastings's estate-manager, and afterwards councillor and squire of the body to

Richard III. In Shakespeare he serves as a valuable agent for the usurpation. The rat was Sir Richard Ratcliffe, another close advisor, who had fought for Richard at Tewkesbury and against the Scots. Shakespeare accurately depicts him as supervising the execution of Rivers, Vaughan, and Grey. Francis Lovell, whose crest included a dog, was a viscount, Richard's lord chamberlain, and another fellow-soldier against the Scots. The hog was Richard himself, whose personal emblem was a white boar. Hence in Shakespeare Richard is frequently reviled as boar, hog, and hedgehog. The whole scurrilous jingle sums up the disaffection of many Englishmen for their new king. Although the rhyme dates only from 1484, public restiveness under Richard broke into open revolt in the fall of 1483. Dorset appeared with rebel soldiers in Yorkshire; the family of Guilford rose in Kent; the Courtenays (one of whom was bishop of Exeter) did likewise in Devon. Some of these people initially sought to rescue the princes, but, with the rumor of the princes' death, all eventually proclaimed the cause of Henry Tudor. They were ill coordinated and easily crushed, but they represented a widespread threat. The threat was all the greater because the rebels included Richard's most powerful ally, the duke of Buckingham.

Buckingham's motives throughout 1483 remain a matter of conjecture. We do not know why this peer, formerly inactive in politics, suddenly leapt forward and helped Richard to the throne; we do not know why he turned on Richard within three months of the coronation. In June he may have sought vengeance on the Woodvilles, but it is harder to see what he sought in October. Many have supposed that the puzzle of Buckingham's breach with Richard would be solved if we knew more about the princes' death. Perhaps he briefly dreamed of a crown for himself; if so, he soon espoused the Tudor claim. Thomas More has him lured into rebellion by the wily tongue of Bishop Morton, whom Richard had committed to Buckingham's charge. Hall offers several explanations, one of which Shakespeare dramatizes: that Richard welshed on a promise to give Buckingham the earldom of Hereford. This is simply not true. In July Richard signed letters patent giving Buckingham the crown's portion of the earldom (the rest Buckingham had already). Whatever the cause, Buckingham marched from Brecon against Richard. He was hampered by rains and floods until his troops deserted him. He was then captured, denied the favor of a final interview with Richard, and executed at Salisbury on All Souls' Day, 2 November.

The October rebellion made Henry Tudor, hitherto an obscure offshoot of the house of Lancaster, a major figure in English politics. Fifty or more years earlier, his grandfather Owen Tudor, a Welsh squire of no particular standing, had consoled, wooed, and married Queen Catherine, widow of Henry V. This striking misalliance was revealed only at Catherine's death in 1437. The sons of the union, Edmund and Jasper, were acknowledged and made earls of Richmond and Pembroke respectively by their half-brother Henry VI. Edmund died, probably of natural causes, in 1456, a year after marrying Lady Margaret Beaufort. Margaret's ancestry was less obscure. She was the only child of John Beaufort duke of Somerset (d. 1444), who was in turn son to the eldest of John of Gaunt's bastard offspring (later legitimated) by Catherine Swynford. Several months after Edmund's death, Margaret gave birth to Henry Tudor. Since both the main Lancastrian line and all the male Beauforts had been exterminated by 1471, any hope of a Lancastrian revival lay in this hybrid red rose. Henry was reared in Wales by his uncle Jasper, officially losing his father's earldom of Richmond during the Yorkist years, visiting London perhaps once during the re-adeption of Henry VI. (On this occasion, according to Tudor legend and Shakespeare, Henry VI prophesied that the lad would eventually rule England.) After the Yorkist triumph of 1471, Henry fled with Jasper to Brittany. His mother, however, remained in England. She married Thomas Lord Stanley, councillor and steward of the household to both Edward IV and Richard III. (Stanley is a secondary character in *Richard III*, also anachronistically called earl of Derby, a title he received from Henry VII after Richard's death. Margaret Beaufort does not appear in the play, but is alluded to as countess of Richmond.) It seems to have been Margaret and Bishop Morton, assisted by such confidential agents as the priest Christopher Urswick, who spun the plots of October 1483, attempting to bring together the Woodville interest, the Beaufort-Tudor interest, and those simply disaffected with Richard. Margaret won Queen Elizabeth Woodville's support by proposing that, if Henry won, he should marry the queen's eldest daughter. Henry himself attempted to join the October revolt, crossing from Brittany with a small fleet. His ships were scattered by adverse winds and he found the English coast too heavily guarded to risk a landing. He sailed back to Brittany to await a better day.

Shakespeare, compressing the time sequence, converts Henry's return to Brittany into a false report, and arranges for Henry's successful landing of 1485 to follow directly upon the defeat of Buckingham. Thus most of Richard's two-year reign is abolished. During that time parliament confirmed his title as king (supposedly "quieting men's minds") and attainted many persons associated with the October rising. Margaret Beaufort, however, was generously treated. Richard punished her merely by handing her estates over to her husband Stanley. The generosity was not uncharacteristic of the king. He persuaded Elizabeth Woodville and her daughters to emerge from sanctuary and treated them honorably at court. His policies with respect to trade, finance, the administration of justice, and the promotion of learning were beneficent and salutary. Unfortunately, he soon encountered a dynastic problem. His only legitimate son (not mentioned in the play) died in April 1484. For a time he seems to have declared Clarence's son heir presumptive. (He did not, as Shakespeare asserts, imprison the boy, nor did he meanly match Clarence's daughter in marriage. It was left to Henry VII to do both those things and eventually to execute the boy on a trumped-up charge of treason. The daughter lived into her late sixties, becoming the last surviving grandchild of the old duke of York. For this offense Henry VIII chopped off her head in 1541.) Clarence's son, however, may have been feeble-minded; certainly his position was complicated by his father's attainder. Richard eventually designated as his heir another nephew, his sister's son John earl of Lincoln. These arrangements for the succession were the more necessary because Queen Anne was ill and Richard could not expect to have more children by her. She died in March 1485. Upon her death, two damaging rumors circulated: that Richard had poisoned her, and that he intended to marry his niece Elizabeth, sister to the missing princes, in order to secure his tottering throne. There is no reason to believe the first of these exciting stories: in the Middle Ages, suspicions of poison far too commonly accompany the death of the great. The second story presumes a strange streak of illogic in Richard. His claim to the throne hinged on the declared illegitimacy of Edward IV's children: even if he had managed to obtain papal dispensation for an incestuous union, marriage with a bastard could not have strengthened his hereditary right. Nonetheless, the rumor vexed Richard enough to force him into public denials of such an intention, denials that some historians take as evidence of the rumor's truth. Shakespeare uses both stories, suggesting with deliberate murkiness that Richard has done away with Anne, and expanding the marriage project into a striking scene in which Richard woos Queen Elizabeth Woodville for the hand of her daughter.

Meanwhile, refugees from England gathered around Henry Tudor. Bishop Morton fled to the Low Countries, kept in touch with Henry, and helped him escape from Brittany into France at a moment when Richard had persuaded the Bretons to hand Henry over. Dorset joined Henry, although he came to be considered an unreliable ally. Most significantly, Henry gained the services of an experienced general, John de Vere earl of Oxford. Oxford was one of the few surviving unrepentant Lancastrian lords. He had fled after the Lancastrian defeat at Barnet in 1471, led an attack on the southwest coast of England in 1473, and been imprisoned at Hammes Castle near Calais since 1474. In 1484 he escaped and joined Henry, bringing with him the captain of Hammes, James Blunt. Lord Stanley also wrote to assure Henry of his support.

On 7 August 1485 Henry landed at Milford Haven in Wales. As he marched up the Welsh coast and across to Shrewsbury, his following swelled. Sir Walter Herbert of Pembroke, Sir Gilbert Talbot uncle to the earl of Shrewsbury, and Rhys ap Thomas the leading figure in central Wales, joined his cause. Richard called up his nobles. The two armies met on 22 August in the heart of England, near Market Bosworth in Leicestershire.

Among the crucial battles in English history, Bosworth affords a notable peculiarity: the victory was determined, not by those who fought, but by those who delayed fighting until they were sure of being on the winning side. The calculation of his supposed supporters cost Richard the day, the kingdom, and his life. By all military judgment he should have won. Since the age of eighteen (he was now thirty-two) he had been a skillful and successful general. Henry, who was twenty-eight, had never fought in a battle before. Richard also had the larger army. But part of it was under the Percy earl of Northumberland (Richard's only rival as a northern power during Edward IV's reign), who did not strike a blow. Part was under the Stanleys—Henry's stepfather Lord Thomas and the latter's brother Sir William. Richard had tried to secure Lord Stanley's allegiance by holding his son George hostage, but the Stanleys sat on hilltops, awaiting a sign of the outcome. (They may have concerted strategy with Henry beforehand, but this is disputed.)

The main fighting was done by the vans of the two armies, Henry's under Oxford, Richard's under the duke of Norfolk and his son the earl of Surrey. After Norfolk was killed, the royal forces began to waver. Then Richard adopted one last time the strategy of the quick stroke that would, if successful, settle all.

He led his household knights around the main battle in a charge at Henry Tudor on the opposite rise. If Henry fell, his troops would have nothing to fight for. The charge was very nearly successful, Richard himself cutting down Henry's standard and its bearer Sir William Brandon. At this point one Stanley joined the battle: Sir William led his cavalry upon Richard's flank. Richard's knights were killed around him. He himself fought to the last in the thickest press of his enemies: even the most hostile Tudor accounts pay tribute to his courage. His battle crown was found among the spoils and placed on Henry's head by Lord Stanley.

Of Richard's followers, Ratcliffe and Brackenbury as well as Norfolk fell at Bosworth. Catesby was executed during the next few days. Lovell escaped and, together with Richard's designated heir the earl of Lincoln, died in a rising against Henry two years later. Northumberland made his peace with Henry and was murdered while collecting taxes four years later. Tyrell served Henry at the fortress of Guisnes, near Calais, until 1502, when he was called home and executed for treason. Surrey, after a period of disgrace, became a loyal servant of the Tudors and regained his father's duchy of Norfolk.

Henry, of course, became Henry VII, first Tudor monarch. He married Elizabeth of York, ruled for twenty-four years, and founded a dynasty that lasted until 1603. Bishop Morton became his chancellor, archbishop of Canterbury, a cardinal, and the patron of Thomas More. The Tudor myth depicts Henry as a savior figure, an angel rescuing England from the turbulent Plantagenets. In Shakespeare he is God's "minister of chastisement." It is difficult now to see anything angelic about Henry VII. Indeed, he was a man far subtler and craftier than the historical Richard, which is why, with the help of luck, he ruled far longer than Richard did. He had good reason to be a careful, scheming, suspicious man: he had become king of England while having no experience of government and knowing practically no one in the country. He had spent half his life in exile, needing all his wits to stay alive. He again needed all his wits to rule England, maintain the new dynasty, become a respected European power, and amass wealth. (In pursuit of the last aim he gained notoriety for avarice and extortion.) He did not differ greatly from the Yorkist kings in his methods of government. He took over and made even more efficient the techniques developed by the Yorkists: Edward IV's accounting methods and his Welsh council, the council of the north that Richard instituted. The great change from medieval to modern government in England came under Henry VIII, during the Reformation in the 1530s. Before that, the chief difference between Tudor rule and the rule of the later Plantagenets was the success of the Tudor kings in keeping the crown on their heads. In part this difference arose from the relative infertility of the Tudors. Only one of Henry VII's sons survived to adulthood. None of Henry VIII's did. Thus the Tudors were not harrassed by a plethora of royal dukes who might claim the crown. Indeed, their dynastic problem was exactly the opposite: Henry VIII spent the first twenty-eight years of his reign trying to beget a legitimate son who would live more than a few days. In many other respects it made no difference whether England was governed by a Plantagenet or a Tudor.

It did, of course, make a difference to the Plantagenets. Henry VII was for a time pestered by risings in favor of surviving members of the house of York and by pretenders who impersonated them. Henry VIII in turn feared displacement by the last buds of the white rose. Accordingly, the first two Tudors exterminated the remaining Plantagenets. The fates of Lincoln and of Clarence's children have already been noted. Most of Lincoln's younger brothers (that is, the younger sons of Richard III's sister) were hounded to death. Even Buckingham's son, the last representative of the line of Thomas of Woodstock, was executed on a flimsy treason charge in 1521 (see chapter IX). Henry VIII himself was of course half a Plantagenet through his mother, but, aside from that strain, the blood of the Plantagenets, once kings of England and France and lords of Ireland, had become a death sentence to those who carried it in their veins.

ᚦ VIII ᚦ

JOhn
the legitimacy of the king

England now is left
To tug and scamble.

1. THE ANGEVIN EMPIRE

King John is Shakespeare's only play dramatizing English medieval history prior to the fall of Richard II. For once the playwright turned back from the last century of the Plantagenets to deal with one of the first kings of that extraordinary dynasty. The play thus has no narrative connection with the double tetralogy on the houses of Lancaster and York: 161 years intervened between the reign of John (1199–1216) and that of Richard II (1377–1399). Yet the material of *King John* is cut from the same cloth. The later Plantagenets had no monopoly on baronial revolt and disputed dynastic succession, no patent on conspiracy, murder, and war. As the dynasty ended in bloody squabbles over the crown, so also it began. The poet W. H. Auden may have been right when he suggested that history is far too criminal to be a fit subject of study for the young.

John was the third Plantagenet king, but in order to grasp

fully the situation at the start of the play, we must consider the way in which the dynasty itself ascended the throne of England. In 1135 Henry I, the last of William the Conqueror's sons, died, bringing to an end the direct male line of Norman dukes who were also kings of England. Only one legitimate child survived him, his daughter Matilda. First the wife of the Holy Roman Emperor (and thus usually called the Empress Matilda), she was now married to Geoffrey Plantagenet, count of Anjou in northern France. Although Henry had forced his barons to swear allegiance to Matilda, rule by a woman (and an offensively haughty woman at that) was repugnant to many of the English. Another heir stole a march on her. Stephen of Blois, the son of Henry's sister Adela, sped across the Channel, seized the royal treasury, and got himself crowned within a month of his uncle's death. He then tried to rule England for nineteen years.

He did not rule in peace. The Empress and her partisans bitterly contested his kingship, plunging the country into civil war and anarchy. Only in the last year of Stephen's life, when both his eldest son and Geoffrey of Anjou were dead, was a resolution reached: Stephen was to rule for the rest of his life, after which the crown was to descend to the new count of Anjou, Henry, son of Matilda and Geoffrey. Thus in 1154, Henry FitzEmpress became Henry II, first Plantagenet king of England. (Henry and his immediate successors were usually called Angevins, after their ancestral province. The name Plantagenet is an anachronism whose origin is explained in the Appendix.)

The most significant peculiarity of Henry II's realm was that England formed only a part of it. His father's death had made him count of Anjou, the boundaries of which Geoffrey had expanded to include neighboring Maine and Touraine. Geoffrey had also managed to wrest Normandy from Stephen, and along with it Brittany, which the Angevins considered a fief of the Norman duchy. Henry's wife brought him an even greater territory. Two years before becoming king of England, he had married the richest and most remarkable woman of the age, Eleanor, hereditary duchess of Aquitaine and divorced wife of Louis VII of France. Aquitaine, a vast area whose exact borders were ill defined, included the bulk of southwestern France. Thus, at the age of twenty-one, Henry II ruled the greatest empire in western Europe since the time of Charlemagne: it ran from the Scottish border to the Pyrenees. This Angevin empire, however, was a conglomeration rather than a unified state. The French provinces were held in different degrees of feudal tenure from the king of France, who frequently quarrelled with his mighty vassal. The local French barons were restive, often skillfully playing off their allegiance to Henry against their allegiance to his overlord in Paris. The English barons were scarcely more pacific. Henry's own wife and sons occasionally fought against him. Eleanor proved so turbulent that Henry kept her locked up for the last fifteen years of his reign, and his sons waged three civil wars against him, the last of which ended only a few days before his death. For vigor, strength, craft, and quarrelsomeness, the Angevins were a notable family. They made life exciting (and usually uncomfortable) for themselves and for all who dealt with them. But by sheer demonic energy, Henry contrived to keep his ill-assorted empire together. A member of his household recorded of him that "he was impatient of repose, and did not hesitate to disturb half Christendom."

His eldest surviving son, Richard I, succeeded him, ruling from 1189 to 1199. He was equally restless, and did not hesitate to disturb heathendom as well. Richard has become, in romantic legend, the most glamorous of English kings: military genius, embodiment of chivalric knighthood, troubadour, crusader, Coeur-de-Lion. As far as England itself was concerned, he was an absentee king, drawing upon the realm for money but almost never physically present upon English soil or greatly concerned with the governing of England. Within a year of his accession, he departed upon crusade against the great Saracen leader Saladin.

He remained in the east until late 1192. On his way back from the Holy Land, he was captured and held for ransom by Leopold archduke of Austria. He was not released until 1194. For the rest of his reign he fought King Philip Augustus of France, who had taken advantage of Richard's absence to encroach upon the Angevin lands. In April 1199, Richard died of a wound received while attacking the castle of a minor nobleman, Adémar (or Vidomar) viscount of Limoges. His bastard son (of whom more later) avenged his death by killing Limoges later that year.

Richard's death left the succession to the throne in doubt. He had begotten no legitimate children. He had had, however, two younger brothers, Geoffrey and John. As Geoffrey had been trampled to death in a tournament during their father's lifetime, John was, at thirty-two, the only surviving son of Henry II. But before going to his grave, Geoffrey had married Constance, heiress to the duchy of Brittany, and had begot upon her a son, Arthur, aged twelve at the time of his uncle Richard's death. Which was to be considered Richard's heir, the adult youngest brother of the late king or the child-nephew by way of an intermediate brother?

No formal rule existed by which to answer this question. As readers of the previous chapters will have seen, the matter of the royal succession was sufficiently vexatious in the fifteenth century, when primogeniture was a better established custom in England. In the twelfth century, procedures in this matter were almost entirely ad hoc. Before the Norman Conquest, English kingship had been elective, although the candidates usually had to have the royal blood. Of the six kings since the Conquest, only one (Richard I himself) had gained the throne without dispute. The real or supposed wishes of the dying king, the preferences of the leading magnates, the strength and celerity of the various heirs, and sheer luck were all potentially powerful elements in the highly fluid situation created by a demise of the crown. The situation was all the more fluid because the crown governed a conglomerate empire whose various provinces maintained different feudal customs. Finally, a disputed English succession offered Philip Augustus a splendid opportunity to stir up trouble and hasten the dissolution of the Angevin empire.

On his deathbed, Richard seems to have named John as his heir, and in the event, for a brief time at least, John won most of the empire. Its richest province, Aquitaine, was technically the property of Queen Eleanor, still a formidable personage despite her nearly eighty years. She gave it to John, retaining only a life-interest. John's speed assured him of the remaining chief prizes. Within two months of Richard's death, he seized Richard's treasury, secured investiture as duke of Normandy, and had himself crowned king of England. During this period, certain lords upon whom Richard had relied to govern England provided John with crucial support. These were Hubert Walter archbishop of Canterbury, the chief ecclesiastic of England; Geoffrey FitzPeter the justiciar, the leading secular officer of government; and William FitzJohn, usually known as William Marshal because of his post as master marshal of the court. (The title, as it was hereditary, came to be treated as a surname.) These three magnates inclined to John largely for practical reasons. He was an adult. He had lived in England for some years, though hardly in consistent loyalty to his father or his brother. He was known to be vigorous. Arthur, on the other hand, was a child dominated by the Bretons (especially by his mother Constance), a stranger who had never crossed the Channel, and a likely tool for Philip Augustus. John was equally practical in his response to the lords' support. After the coronation, he bestowed upon Archbishop Walter the chancellorship of the kingdom, and he made Geoffrey FitzPeter and William Marshal earls of Essex and Pembroke respectively. These two secular lords had long been married to the heiresses of the earldoms in question, and thereby claimed the lands concerned, but it was John who formally invested them with their titles. (The archbishop does not appear in *King John*. Essex and Pembroke do, but Shakespeare gives little indication of their historical importance. Essex appears in but one scene and is never addressed by name. Pembroke appears in seven scenes, but his name occurs only once outside of stage directions. For all practical purposes, they are as anonymous as the lords in *Henry V.*)

Meanwhile, Constance and the lords of Brittany sought to escape the domination of John. To that end, they enlisted the aid of Philip Augustus and placed Arthur under his protection in Paris. The lords of the central Angevin provinces (Anjou, Maine, Touraine) also declared for Arthur. The empire appeared to be split in two: Eleanor's Aquitaine in the south was severed from John's England and Normandy in the north by a band of territories loyal to Arthur and allied with Philip.

War was inevitable. In Shakespeare, this war is a major conflict occupying four consecutive scenes and focusing upon the city of Angiers (Angers, in Anjou). In fact, it was a sporadic affair, waged, dropped, and taken up again for a period of five years, with battles in various French provinces. Both sides had suffered severe depredations in the recent conflicts between Philip and Richard, and neither could count upon alliances contracted during those conflicts. Alternating forays and truces during 1199–1200 led to an agreement at Le Goulet in May 1200. As was characteristic of the time, the agreement hinged on a dynastic marriage. John offered his niece Blanche, daughter of his sister Eleanor and King Alphonso of Castile, as a wife for Philip's son, the dauphin Louis (later Louis VIII). As a dowry for Blanche, he gave Louis various French lordships. (These were neither as numerous or as extensive as they appear to be in the play, where John foolishly gives away most of France.) He also gave directly to Philip a large sum of money and certain territories Philip particularly wanted, notably a portion of Normandy called the Vexin (in Shakespeare, the Volquessen). In return, Philip acknowledged John's rule over the remainder of the Angevin empire. Arthur got only Brittany, and that merely as John's vassal.

During the following year, his disappointed mother Constance died.

The solution at Le Goulet was temporary. Hostilities began again in 1202, again for dynastic reasons. The northern part of Aquitaine, the provinces of Poitou, Angoulême, and La Marche, had long posed problems to the Angevins. The barons living in this area were notably independent of their Angevin overlords. John tried to strengthen his grip upon them by marrying Isabella, the heiress of Angoulême, thereby disrupting dynastic plans that the local lords had concerted in their own interests. The disappointed lords naturally quarrelled with John and eventually appealed to Philip Augustus, whose court of peers found John to be a contumacious vassal and declared his French lands forfeit. Thus Philip gained the legal justification for attacking John once again. The most spectacular engagement of the ensuing war, a battle to which Shakespeare is indebted for some details of his battle of Angiers, occurred in August 1202 at Mirebeau, in southern Anjou. There the Poitevin lords and the fifteen-year-old Arthur besieged the aged Queen Eleanor, who gallantly held out in the keep of the castle. Speedily marching down from the north, John arrived at Mirebeau in time to defeat the Poitevins, rescue his mother, and capture Arthur. John's chief rival, and Philip's major weapon against him, was now in John's hands.

Arthur was kept prisoner at Falaise under the supervision of John's chamberlain, Hubert de Burgh. Later he was transferred to the castle at Rouen, the Norman capital. There, sometime around April 1203, Arthur died. As is usual in these cases, it is not certain how he came to his end. According to one chronicle, John ordered that Arthur be blinded and castrated, in order to incapacitate him for kingship without incurring the guilt of killing him. (One can only marvel at the scrupulosity of a conscience that will consent to such mutilation but baulk at murder.) Hubert de Burgh supposedly saved Arthur from this fate. In an effort to convince Arthur's partisans that their cause was lost, Hubert falsely gave out that Arthur was dead. The rumor only further incensed Arthur's lords, whereupon Hubert told the truth and was not believed. Another account is simpler: Arthur, in attempting to escape from Rouen, fell into the Seine and was drowned. Shakespeare uses a combination of these two tales, setting the episode in England and changing Arthur's Breton and Poitevin supporters into English lords. A third story, recorded in the abbey chronicle of Margam in southern Wales and considered probable by several recent biographers of John, stresses the fits of wrath for which all the Angevin kings were famous. In this version, John, "after dinner . . . when he was drunk and possessed with the devil, slew Arthur with his own hand, and tying a heavy stone to the body cast it into the Seine." This seems like sheer melodrama, but melodrama is to be encountered along many of history's corridors. John was at Rouen at the date mentioned by the story, and he was certainly capable on other occasions of raging cruelty. As in the case of Richard III's nephews, the disappearance of a rival for the throne while in the king's prison must leave the king under grave suspicion of murder.

After 1203, events went badly for John in France. He contrived to alienate one of his best generals. His treatment of his prisoners (the Poitevin lords captured at Mirebeau as well as Arthur) led to desertions. Norman restiveness encouraged the further attacks of Philip Augustus, and John's indomitable mother Eleanor died in April 1204. (Pairing Eleanor and Constance as rival mothers, Shakespeare unhistorically has them die at the same time.) By June 1204, Philip had overrun Normandy. All of John's northern provinces in France were now in the hands of the French king and his allies. During the later years of his reign, John made repeated expeditions into France, but despite some excellent strategy and occasional local victories, he never regained much. After 1204, then, the question of the succession was settled: John was the undisputed ruler of the "Angevin empire," but that empire now consisted only of England and of Aquitaine far to the south.

2. THE LIMITS OF ROYAL AUTHORITY

John was a man of mixed and variable personality, by turns ingratiating, terrifying, clever, greedy, intelligent, cruel—above all, vigorous. He enjoyed considerable success: few medieval kings dealt as well as he with the Irish, Welsh, and Scots. But as well as losing much of the Angevin empire, he failed to bring to a conclusion satisfactory to himself the two major struggles that occupied his reign after 1204. From 1205 to 1213 he locked horns with Rome, drawing excommunication upon himself and a papal interdict upon England. He was finally obliged to submit altogether to the pope's wishes. In 1214 he was beset by a baronial revolt that produced Magna Carta (1215) and culminated in an invasion of England by the dauphin Louis (1216). These two struggles loom large in medieval history, the former being an important episode in the contest for supremacy between the Holy See and the secular crowns of Europe, and the latter proving vital for the development of the English constitution. My account of both struggles, however, will be brief: they are less important to Shakespeare than they have become to subsequent historical writers.

The death of Archbishop Walter of Canterbury precipitated the conflict with Rome. Three parties strove to influence the choice of his successor. The monks of the cathedral church at Canterbury claimed the right to elect their leader. The bishops of southern England, who fell under Canterbury's authority, also claimed an interest. Finally, the king himself wished to pick the chief English ecclesiastic. The church so permeated medieval life, in its temporal as well as spiritual aspects, that the archbishop was automatically a magnate greater than most lay lords, frequently an official of the secular government, and always a power to be reckoned with. In 1205, the quarrels of Henry II with Thomas Becket were still recent history. Of course, the power actually to consecrate the archbishop lay with the pope. In 1205 the pope was Innocent III, distinguished lawyer and theologian, possibly the greatest ruler of the Middle Ages, and a man indefatigable in his efforts to assert the authority of the papacy over all the affairs of mankind. "The Lord left to St. Peter," wrote Innocent, "the governance not of the church only but of the whole world."

The monks of Canterbury elected one of their own number and sent him off to Rome. When John heard of this, he obliged them to elect another man and duly despatched him to Rome as well. The bishops also sent representatives to the Holy See. Eventually Innocent summoned proctors from all three parties, quashed both elections, declared that only the monks had the canonical right to make the choice, and contrived that they elect his own candidate, Stephen Langton, whom he consecrated archbishop in July 1207. Langton was in many ways an excellent choice, an Englishman, a highly reputed theologian, a capable diplomat; but he was not John's choice, and he had pursued so much of his theological career at the University of Paris that some Englishmen regarded him as a foreigner. John refused to accept him, dispossessed the monks, and seized the Canterbury revenues. After a quarrel with the archbishop of York, he took the York revenues as well.

In 1208 the pope imposed an interdict upon England: administration of the sacraments and performance of other ecclesiastical rites were forbidden until John should give way. This constituted a heavy blow to the devout. Many of the remaining English bishops fled the country, whereupon John confiscated their property. In the next year, Innocent excommunicated John, an even more serious move as it threatened John's sovereignty and the fealty of his lords. Increasingly angry, John extorted tremendous sums from the English dioceses and churches, pillaging the

Cistercian abbeys with particular vigor. (Shakespeare hints at these actions when he has John order the abbeys plundered to pay for the wars.) The struggle dragged on until 1213, when John was threatened with formal deposition by the pope and by invasion from France. In these straits, he yielded. In May of that year, he agreed to accept Archbishop Langton, to reinstate the bishops who had fled, and to compensate the church for his depredations. He did something even more striking, the one deed in this struggle upon which Shakespeare lays considerable emphasis. Apparently of his own choice, he surrendered his crown to Pandulph, the papal legate who negotiated his submission, and received it back again from him.* Thus he made himself the vassal of the pope; England was thenceforth to be considered as a fief held by the king from the Holy See. Although Englishmen of later ages, both before and after the Reformation, came to regard this subordination of the English crown to the papal tiara as an extraordinary and humiliating act, it was probably not so considered at the time. Henry II had once acknowledged the pope's feudal supremacy, and other European crowns stood in a similar relation to Rome. Furthermore, now that John was the pope's formal vassal, he had gained the advantage of having the church on his side during his subsequent struggle with the barons.

Because the civil war that occupied the last two years of John's reign produced (among other things) Magna Carta, and because Magna Carta has subsequently been enshrined as a founding document asserting the liberties of Englishmen, an enduring popular myth surrounds the events of 1214–1216. According to the myth, a wicked and tyrannical John is brought to book by a united and patriotic peerage. At Runnymede he is obliged to seal a charter granting all sorts of freedoms and enabling the English-

---

* One Peter of Pomfret (or of Wakefield) had prophesied that John would lose his kingdom at this time. John hanged the man. Holinshed, while labelling Peter a fraud, points out that in a way his prophecy came true. Shakespeare uses the incident.

speaking peoples to set splendidly forth on the path that led to parliament, limited monarchy, the Glorious Revolution of 1688, the American Constitution, and the resignation of Richard Nixon. That is, at any rate, the simplified version of events that most of us remember. More than a few qualifications are in order. John was no more wicked or tyrannical than any other strong king of his time. The barons objected, not to anything uniquely dreadful about John, but to practices also pursued by both his predecessors. Only a portion of the baronage revolted: many lords were on John's side at Runnymede. Magna Carta did not settle the revolt, which continued two years after its signing. It was not even called Magna Carta in 1215: it gained that title when it was reissued a decade later by John's son. (Upon reissue, it was accompanied by a shorter document dealing with forest law. The Magna of the title does not mean distinguished, merely large, the big charter as compared with the small forest charter.) The provisions of the document are in fact more reactionary than progressive: the barons desired to regain privileges they claimed had been theirs before the coming of the Angevins, and its truly libertarian clauses were probably inserted by Archbishop Langton, who mediated between the king and the rebels. Finally, although it was reissued and cited in the later Middle Ages, it gained its hallowed place in English thought only in the seventeenth century, during the struggle between the Stuart kings and their parliaments. Shakespeare makes no reference to it whatever. To us, a play about John that omitted the Charter might appear as invalid historically as, say, a play about Edward VIII that failed to mention Mrs. Simpson. In the Elizabethan view, Magna Carta was a detail (mentioned by Holinshed, but without particular emphasis) that Shakespeare could skip without seriously undermining the historical authenticity of his play.

It was chiefly barons of the northern and eastern counties who rebelled, and their grievances were largely financial. The Angevin kings taxed heavily. Richard had exacted great levies to pay first for his crusade and then for his ransom. John's needs for his French wars were equally large. In particular, to finance an invasion of France in 1214, he imposed an enormous scutage (literally, shield-money: a tax paid by men not serving in the war, to compensate for their absence). Had John won his wars, as Richard had, he might have gotten away with the taxes. But when his allies lost the crucial battle of Bouvines in 1214 to Philip Augustus, and thus lost any chance of reestablishing Angevin power on the continent, defeat was coupled with expense to produce rebellion.

About forty barons defied the king in spring 1215. They thereby also defied the pope, who had ordered them not to conspire against John. The northern rebels included Eustace de Vesci and William de Mowbray, the eastern ones Geoffrey de Mandeville earl of Essex and Roger Bigod earl of Norfolk. (Of these, only Norfolk appears in Shakespeare, as Lord Bigot. Mandeville was the son of the Geoffrey FitzPeter previously mentioned as justiciar and earl of Essex: the latter had died in 1213.) Those loyal to John included his chamberlain Hubert de Burgh, soon to become justiciar, William Marshal earl of Pembroke; and William Longsword earl of Salisbury. (All three appear in Shakespeare, although Hubert is much altered in a way that will be discussed below. Although Holinshed mentions the fact, Shakespeare omits to note that Salisbury was a bastard son of Henry II and thus John's half-brother.) Fighting broke out in May. After a vain attempt to take Northampton, the rebels gained possession of London. Although John was probably strong enough to crush them by force, he sought reconciliation, using Archbishop Langton as an emissary. Negotiations resulted in the Charter, sealed at Runnymede in June. According to A. L. Poole, this document "was a practical assertion of existing law and custom, and it imposed limitations on the arbitrary power of the crown." It further provided that twenty-five barons should constitute an enforcement committee entitled to rebel if the king broke the provisions. John thereupon obediently took steps to carry out the Charter. Some of the rebel barons, however, did not trust him, further fortified their castles, and refused to surrender London. Informed of their continued contumacy, the pope annulled the Charter and excommunicated some of the barons. Civil war broke out again in September, and in November John took the important castle of Rochester in Kent.

At this point, the barons felt in need of allies. They therefore invited the dauphin Louis to claim the crown of England in right of his wife, John's niece Blanche. Louis did not immediately act, however, and John took prompt steps to secure his kingdom. Leaving Salisbury to watch the rebels in London, he marched north in early 1216 to the Scottish border, then back to the eastern counties. Castles fell to him everywhere. At the end of this successful foray, he ordered his fleet to guard Dover from the French, and himself retired to await developments at Winchester.

In late May, after a storm had dispersed John's fleet, Louis landed unopposed on the Kentish coast. The events of this summer are somewhat obscure. The king seems to have stayed mostly in the west country. Louis and the rebels held London and the southeast, and, for a time, John's half-brother Salisbury joined them. In September John marched east to resume the offensive. He broke the rebel siege of Lincoln and then proceeded to King's Lynn in Norfolk. There, however, he fell ill with dysentery. He nonetheless moved on, arriving at Swineshead Abbey on 12 October. While crossing the River Ouse on the way to the abbey, he lost his baggage train, including his treasure and jewels. Later accounts, followed by Shakespeare, report that John was poisoned at Swineshead (or Swinestead, as Shakespeare calls it). A monk, outraged by John's actions against the church, gave him poisoned wine, first drinking it himself in order to persuade the king that the wine was harmless, and thus himself perishing while assassinating the king. This is not true, but John did make himself more ill by voraciously dining on peaches and new cider. In the next few days he staggered on to the bishop of Lincoln's castle at Newark, where he died on 18 October.

The war went on into the new year. John's elder son, Henry III, was but a youth of nine. But in his march from the west to Lincoln, John had at least severed the northern rebels from Louis and the eastern barons. He also left able men to carry on the defense of the kingdom, notably William Marshal, who became protector. In early summer 1217, the royalists defeated the rebels soundly, again at Lincoln, and Hubert de Burgh destroyed a French fleet coming to reinforce the dauphin. In September, peace was concluded at Lambeth and the dauphin returned to France, leaving young Henry to rule his own kingdom for one of the longest reigns in English history.

3. USURPED RIGHTS

As we have seen, John's seventeen years on the English throne encompassed three major conflicts: the struggle over the succession, the dispute with Rome, and the civil war. All three conflicts appear in Shakespeare's play, but they are compressed so that the ecclesiastical and baronial struggles are subordinated to the dynastic rivalry between John and Arthur. The first three acts depict the challenges and battles that result from that rivalry. In this sequence, the marriage of Louis and Blanche furnishes a mere breathing space in the middle of a single campaign that begins with the first confrontation between John and Arthur's supporters and ends with the capture of Arthur. John's difficulties with Rome, although correctly ascribed to his rejection of Archbishop Langton, anachronistically become a mere eddy in this sequence. Shortly after the marriage is arranged, Pandulph arrives to excommunicate John and to spur the French into renewed hostility on Arthur's behalf. Once Arthur is taken, the scene returns permanently to England: the later conquest of Normandy by Philip

Augustus is omitted. Act IV is devoted almost wholly to the death of Arthur. Outrage at his supposed murder (rather than taxation or other grievances) prompts the revolt of the barons in Act V. Louis's invasion of England, from the start connected with the baronial revolt, also relates to Arthur: Louis has earlier been persuaded by Pandulph to hope that John will kill Arthur, so that horror at the crime will assist him to dethrone John. The claims and the ultimate fate of Arthur have become the mainspring of the plot, the hinge upon which the whole of John's reign is made to turn. The only significant rearrangement in the historical sequence of events that does not bear upon Arthur comes at the very end of the play: for the sake of a neater close, Shakespeare arranges that the conclusion of the civil war should coincide with John's death rather than follow after.

In thus reshaping history, Shakespeare may have been borrowing from an earlier playwright, the anonymous author of *The Troublesome Reign of King John.* * Even so, Shakespeare is unique (at least among late sixteenth-century writers dealing with John) in his interpretation of the reign. In the contest with Arthur, Shakespeare's John is flatly a usurper. Eleanor of Aquitaine is made to remark that he holds the crown "by strong possession much more than . . . right." As we have seen, this notion entails stricter views of royal inheritance than were in fact current in 1199. It implies a firm legitimist rule of dynastic descent that was to develop only in much later times. The notion is also at variance with Tudor accounts of John. Most Tudor historians do not question the legitimacy of John's crown. In Holinshed there is no serious doubt about his right: Richard I wills all his dominions to

---

* Although *King John* far surpasses *The Troublesome Reign* in poetic power, thematic depth, and solidity of characterization, the two plays resemble each other very strongly in their handling of historical facts, in the selection, omission, and compression of the events reported by Holinshed and other Tudor chroniclers. Clearly one playwright borrowed from the other. Shakespearean scholars are currently debating which playwright was the debtor.

John, the English lords swear fealty accordingly, and only a few French towns consider that Arthur has a better claim. Only if we go back to Polydore Vergil, a Catholic historian who reflects medieval monastic chroniclers hostile to John because of his defiance of the pope, do we find charges of usurpation. Even *The Troublesome Reign*, while manifesting the same pattern of events, does not harp on this string.

Illegitimacy, indeed, is a central idea in *King John*. Not only does it appear in the form of illegitimate rule (usurpation), but also as illegitimate birth (bastardy), and illegitimate honor (boastful pretensions). We may conveniently marshal most of the differences between the characters of the play and their originals in history under this heading.

Arthur, for example, died at sixteen, an age at which most medieval princes were considered mature, an age, for instance, at which the future Henry V was busily trying to govern Wales. The historical Arthur, moreover, seems to have been an active person, and Holinshed describes him as willful and presumptuous. Shakespeare, however, makes Arthur an innocent and unambitious child in order to increase the pathos of his situation and sharpen the effect of John's raw, illegal seizure of power. Shakespeare also ignores the fact that Constance was married twice after the death of Arthur's father. Thus her energy can be focused altogether on the abused rights of her son. Eleanor too is handled so as to enforce the theme of legitimacy. Disregarding Holinshed's remark that Eleanor backed John on the reasonable (and, for 1199, quite satisfactory) ground that an adult makes a better king, Shakespeare exploits Holinshed's second suggestion that she was motivated by jealousy of Constance, to whom she would have to yield place if Arthur were king.

Historical changes in characters standing on the fringe of the central dynastic quarrel also bear on the issue of legitimacy. The personalities and individual interests of the English lords (Salisbury, Pembroke, Bigot) are neglected. These men serve as a nearly anonymous chorus, responding to the struggle between might and right, measuring by their shifts of allegiance how far John can go without forfeiting their loyalty. A fantastic kind of pretension is embodied in a character who is both an anachronism and a conflation: Limoges duke of Austria. This sovereign, who is allied with Philip and Arthur in the play, is based on two historical persons who were both enemies of Richard Coeur-de-Lion and were both dead at the time of the action. Leopold archduke of Austria, who had captured Richard in Germany, died in 1194; Adémar viscount of Limoges, in the siege of whose castle Richard had died in 1199, himself perished later that year. In the play, this boastful man wears a lionskin to celebrate his victory over the heroic Coeur-de-Lion. He proves, however, to be rather sheepish when directly challenged, and is easily slaughtered in battle.

A pretension far more important to Elizabethans is embodied in the papal legate Pandulph, also by means of historical changes. Although in most subsequent centuries King John has had a very bad press, many Protestant Englishman of the sixteenth century considered him a hero because of his defiance of Rome. He is no hero in Shakespeare, but he does express heroic resistance to Pandulph. The speeches in which he does so are couched in specifically Reformation terms: he condemns the pope's "usurped supremacy," a common Protestant phrase for the pretensions of the bishop of Rome, and he describes himself as "supreme head" of the English Church, the very title devised for Henry VIII during the English break with Rome. Pandulph himself displays a quantity of chicanery, chop-logic, and underhanded scheming thought by Protestants to be characteristic of Rome. He is also unhistorically made a cardinal. Some Shakespearean scholars have suggested that this elevation of a mere subdeacon results from a confusion with an earlier Pandulph who was in fact a cardinal. It is true that some earlier writers (not otherwise known to have been read by Shakespeare) do call our Pandulph a cardinal, but there is perhaps a much more obvious explanation. Most Elizabethan playwrights whose plots touch the church of Rome (to keen Protestants, the scarlet whore of *Revelations*) exploit the theatrical and symbolic effects of the red robes worn by cardinals.

The most literal embodiment of the notion of legitimacy in *King John* is an almost wholly unhistorical character with a major role in the play: Philip Faulconbridge, bastard son of Coeur-de-Lion. Richard I did have an illegitimate son, but very little is known of him. He was given a French castle, and drew a pension from John, and he avenged his father's death, as abovementioned, upon the viscount of Limoges. But unlike Shakespeare's Bastard, this man played no role in great events. Shakespeare's Bastard does indeed kill Limoges/Austria, but some of his other actions are drawn from accounts of famous bastards Shakespeare found elsewhere: one Faukes de Breauté, a soldier who led a royalist army during the baronial revolt; a Faulconbridge bastard of the Neville family who was active in the Wars of the Roses and receives passing mention in *3 Henry VI;* Dunois, the bastard of Orléans, one of the great French generals of the Hundred Years War and a character in *1 Henry VI.* It was recounted of Dunois in particular that he preferred to be the bastard of a great man rather than the lawful son of a humble one. Likewise Philip, when introduced in Act I of *King John* with his erring mother and his ugly half-brother (both invented characters), chooses to be an illegitimate Plantagenet instead of a legitimate Faulconbridge. Like Falstaff in *Henry IV,* the Bastard of *King John* is a strikingly vivid fictional person based remotely on various historical figures. Like Falstaff, he exists partly to utter views and perform actions that help to amplify the historical facts into a coherent and complex work of art.

The Bastard is a man of questionable social status who proves to be nobler than the bluebloods who surround him. One other major person in the play, Hubert, has a somewhat similar status as a result of Shakespeare's alterations of history. Although not illegitimate, Hubert is a bourgeois among aristocrats. The spokesman for the citizens of Angiers during the confrontation between John and Arthur's partisans, he becomes John's servant and makes the crucial decision not to blind Arthur. This character resembles the historical Hubert de Burgh in only two respects: his first name and his position as Arthur's jailer and near-murderer. Although the historical de Burgh's parentage is uncertainly known, he was a great man, holding many high official posts in John's time and receiving the earldom of Kent during the next reign. The low social status of Shakespeare's Hubert is vividly clear when one of the lords addresses him as "dunghill."

The exploration in *King John* of legitimacy, right, and honor deserves (and has in part received) more attention than the scope of this book allows. I am concerned here simply with the differences between John's reign and Shakespeare's version of it. As constitutional historians have seen more significance than contemporaries saw in the barons' challenge to John's authority at the end of the reign, so Shakespeare sees more significance than contemporaries saw in the contested succession with which the reign began. Although the Angevins were capable of invoking legitimism as a principle when it suited them, strength and energy in hanging on to their dominions were more valuable to them. In this respect, despite his efforts, John's reign was a failure. Under him, England's continental empire broke up. Aside from Aquitaine (and a diminished Aquitaine at that), England was an island nation again. Mirebeau was England's last significant victory on French soil until Edward III won at Crécy 130 years after John's death. But although John died in the middle of a civil war, with his inheritance in ruins, the events of his reign had a beneficial effect entirely unintended by him. It was as an island nation that England was to grow into a great power. England was left to tug and scamble, but in doing so she developed that insular confidence and patriotism that Shakespeare's Bastard anachronistically voices at the end of the play:

> Come the three corners of the world in arms
> And we shall shock them.

After Holbein: *Henry VIII* (National Portrait Gallery).

ֆ IX ֆ

ḣeṅʀᴙ VIII
the supreme head

The will of Heaven be done, and the king's pleasure.

1. HENRY VIII AND HENRY VIII

We must begin with two negative statements. First, Shakespeare's *Henry VIII* may not be entirely the work of William
Shakespeare. Written probably in 1613, at the close of Shakespeare's career and more than a dozen years after he had completed his other histories, the play may also contain the hand of
his successor in the post of principal dramatist for the King's
Men, John Fletcher. Second, and much more important for the
purposes of the present book, *Henry VIII* is not about Henry
VIII. True, the play dramatizes certain events in the reign of that
king, and the longest role is assigned to a character called Henry
VIII. But the historical king whose egocentricity is perhaps un-
matched elsewhere in the records of human personality, who
changed from a splendid young athlete into a gross and diseased
hulk, who destroyed the English monasteries and wasted the
money he gained from their dissolution, who married six wives
and executed two of them, who struck down saints like Thomas
More and statesmen like Cardinal Wolsey and Thomas Cromwell,

who was once described by Charles Dickens as "a most intolerable ruffian, a disgrace to human nature, and a blot of blood and grease upon the history of England," is not here. Instead Shakespeare gives us an embodiment of benevolence, wisdom, virtue, and majesty, a dream of a semidivine king. The historical Henry certainly had virtues as well as vices, but Shakespeare's Henry is a character out of romance, at times more like Prospero or Mozart's Sarastro or Tolkien's Elrond Halfelven than he is like any man who ever ruled England. He is not quite perfect; he is sometimes testy (as is Prospero); he is sometimes crucially ignorant of the designs of evil men; but he becomes a numinous center of righteous power, eventually and effortlessly seeing that the good will triumph.

Two circumstances principally account for the wide divergence between Shakespeare's treatment of Henry and his handling of earlier kings. A bare decade intervened between the end of the Tudor dynasty and the composition of the play. Protestant Englishmen genuinely revered the king who had severed England from Rome and had begotten the great Elizabeth. A searching or ironic portrayal of Henry Tudor would have been unwelcome, probably dangerous. This circumstance alone, however, does not explain the comparative mildness of Shakespeare's Henry: another playwright, Samuel Rowley, had depicted Henry as a more splenetic person. Greater significance lies in the difference in kind between this play and Shakespeare's other histories. *Henry VIII* is not a chronicle of foreign or civil conflict dramatizing the issues of legitimacy and power, exploring the sources of weakness and strength in monarchs, dealing at length with the realities of politics. It is a historical pageant, perhaps composed to celebrate a specific diplomatic occasion, the wedding of James I's daughter to the Elector Palatine. This pageant moves majestically to a moment seen (with hindsight) as magical in the history of England: the birth of the princess who was to become Queen Elizabeth. In this pageant, plots are laid and people rise and fall, but all events are bathed in a lofty compassion and a lively sense of active providence that are characteristic of Shakespeare's other late plays, *The Winter's Tale* and *The Tempest*. When great ones fall in *Henry VIII*, they do not rage and curse like the weeping queens of *Richard III*. Rather, they swiftly arrive at steadfastness, an exalted patience, a firm belief in the ultimate justice of heaven and heaven's ways. The play is less a dramatic chronicle about a monarch than a dramatic myth about monarchy.

Henry VIII succeeded to his father Henry VII's crown in April 1509, two months short of his eighteenth birthday. He ruled until his death in January 1547. Some of the most profound changes in English history occurred during his reign. To put it bluntly, England ceased to be a medieval kingdom governed essentially by the king's household and forming part of Catholic Europe; it became a modern kingdom with an independent and omnicompetent national sovereignty and a developed bureaucratic administration. The play, however, deals with only thirteen years, from the French peace treaty celebrated on the Field of the Cloth of Gold in 1520 to the christening of Elizabeth in 1533. This period includes the most important event of the reign, the break with Rome, but Shakespeare touches only lightly the great issues of foreign policy, papal authority, canon law, parliamentary statute, religious reform, and governmental structure that arose from the break. The action consists rather of a series of personal falls and rises. The duke of Buckingham, Cardinal Wolsey, and Queen Katharine fall; Queen Anne Boleyn, Archbishop Cranmer, and Thomas Cromwell rise; the king grows in authority and active wisdom until, after the glories of Elizabeth's reign are prophesied, he concludes that his greatest act was the begetting of "this happy child."

2. HENRY'S REIGN TO 1529

England greeted Henry's accession with enthusiasm. Young, handsome, an indefatigable sportsman, a patron of learning and the arts, a welcome contrast to his withdrawn and rather avaricious father, he appeared to promise an enlightened and exciting reign. But in significant ways, the new king was a throwback to the old Plantagenets. Although moderately interested in the new humanism, he was even more interested in the old chivalry. His models were kings like Edward III and Henry V. He wished to strut large on the stage of Europe, to win the glory associated with successful war. He yearned for the role of a conquering hero: wars against France (1512–1513 and 1544–1545) frame his reign. The crucial events of his middle years were in large part the result of accidental and unforeseen circumstances.

Unfortunately for Henry's martial ambitions, the European stage had changed since Plantagenet times. France was no longer the sprawling, disunited kingdom that had been so vulnerable to Henry V, but a unified, wealthy, populous power governed (from 1515) by a young king who was Henry's equal in vigor and ambition, Francis I. The Low Countries, the kingdoms of the Spanish peninsula, and (from 1519) the German states were gathered under the rule of a single man, the Hapsburg emperor Charles V. European politics were dominated by the rivalry between Francis and Charles, and in that league Henry of England was a lightweight. Significantly, the major English military triumph in Henry's time involved no continental power: it was a victory over Scotland, and Henry himself did not win it. In 1513, when Henry was trying to conquer a piece of northern France, Thomas Howard earl of Surrey destroyed James IV and his army at Flodden. Surrey really did belong to the earlier age: he was seventy, he had fought for Richard III at Bosworth, he had slowly worked his way back to favor under Henry VII, and by virtue of his success at Flodden he finally regained the duchy of Norfolk that Richard III had given to his father.

It was the occasional continental warfare, and perpetual continental diplomacy, that produced such events as the Field of the Cloth of Gold, description of which occupies much of the first scene of *Henry VIII*. This famous display of pageantry in June 1520 constituted the formal end to the hostilities between England and France of 1512–1513. Henry and Francis met in the Vale of Andren, midway between the French town of Ardres and the English town of Guisnes (near Calais), for a magnificent reconciliation and celebration that included two weeks of tilting, jousting, wrestling, dancing, banquets, and high masses. A party of some five thousand people, including most of the nobility of England, accompanied Henry. The French turned out in matching display, and everyone was dressed to the teeth, hung with jewelry and cloth of gold. (Although the duke of Buckingham was certainly present, in Shakespeare he is too ill to attend. Thus Norfolk can open the play by describing the occasion to him.) But this sort of elaborate ceremony was only a part of the tortuous diplomacy of the time. Although the Field of the Cloth of Gold might appear to indicate firm friendship between Henry and Francis, Henry in fact met Charles V both immediately before and immediately after going to Andren, and by the end of the next year had signed a pact with the emperor against the French.

The Englishman chiefly responsible for organizing these events and conducting the diplomacy was not the king himself. For the first eighteen years or so of his reign, Henry's attention to business was sporadic. He was intelligent and politically shrewd, and could be energetic when he chose, but, unlike his father or Henry V, he did not like work. He preferred his hunting, his tilting, his music, and his women. He never retreated altogether from public business—his was always the final decisive voice in England—but the daily work and most of the real shaping of policy he left to others. In particular, down to 1529, he left them to one other, the last great medieval ecclesiastical statesman of England, Cardinal Wolsey.

The son of an Ipswich butcher and cattledealer, Thomas Wolsey was in his middle thirties at Henry's accession. His skillful administrative work, demonstrated when he raised, supplied, and maintained Henry's army in France in 1512–1513, showed his capacities. Henry, although lazy himself, had a sharp eye for the talents of others. By 1515 Wolsey was lord chancellor and had taken over almost all the powers of the king's council: the council met at his bidding on an agenda that he set. He gained an ascendancy over the English church similar to his control over the state, becoming archbishop of York and a cardinal, and securing from the pope permanent designation as papal legate to England. Subject only to the occasional intervening voice of the king, Wolsey governed England for nearly fifteen years.

Unquestionably Wolsey had extraordinary ability. In judicial administration, he had a lasting effect on English history, greatly expanding the work of the crown in law enforcement and equity cases. In raising money he was less skillful. Here he was partly the victim of circumstance: a fierce inflation, understood by no one at the time, bedevilled all Europe during the first half of the sixteenth century. Wolsey's taxation policies ignited a crisis in 1524, when the ironically named Amicable Grant (calling for a sixth of the income of laymen, a third from the clergy) provoked near-rebellion in several counties. Henry stepped in to cancel the grant and pardon those who had resisted it. Wolsey disingenuously put it about that his own intercession had prompted the king's mercy. (This episode occurs in the second scene of *Henry VIII,* where Shakespeare gives Queen Katharine the intercessory function.) But Wolsey's great interest was foreign policy. He saw himself as a protector of the papacy (impossibly, he wished to become pope himself) and as the astute diplomat who would preside over the fate of Europe. Here he was guilty of some self-delusion: great as his talents were, they were no match for the practical impact of the troops of Charles V, who defeated and captured Francis I at Pavia in 1525 and, two years later, sacked Rome, capturing the pope himself. Wolsey's foreign policies ultimately failed. But he certainly enjoyed a number of successes before the full strength of the Hapsburg emperor was exerted.

Wolsey's primacy in England inspired jealousy. His wealth and pomp increased the ill-feeling: he was greedy and arrogant as well as clever and hardworking. He derived a large income from his various posts, from bribes (a common practice at the time), and by diverting to himself the revenues of vacant bishoprics and ab-bacies. He was fond of display: he dressed, built, and entertained on a lavish scale. (This side of his character appears in the banquet he gives in *Henry VIII, I.iv.*) He also kept mistresses. The aristocracy in particular detested this butcher's son for his power and extravagance: they considered themselves to be the natural advisors of the king, and he elbowed them aside.

Among Wolsey's noble enemies we may number the aged duke of Norfolk and his son, also named Thomas Howard, earl of Surrey after his father gained the ducal title. (Norfolk died in 1524; his son thereby became the third duke of Norfolk in the Howard line; and the grandson became that earl of Surrey who is remembered as a sonneteer and early experimenter with blank verse. Thus the Norfolk who was the senior English aristocrat for the bulk of Henry's reign was the third duke. Shakespeare, however, ignores the second duke's death. Although the events of the play run well beyond 1524, the Norfolk and Surrey of the play are consistently the Flodden hero and his son.) Another prominent lord was Charles Brandon duke of Suffolk. This man was the son of Sir William Brandon, Henry VII's standard-bearer who was slain by Richard III at Bosworth. Suffolk became a boon companion to Henry VIII and married the king's younger sister in 1515. He appears in the play not only under his ducal title but also, apparently, as the mere "Brandon" of the first scene. Another lord was the descendant of the great fifteenth-century families of Neville and Beauchamp: George Lord Abergavenny. Yet another was a very recent creation: Sir William Sands or Sandys, made Lord Sandys in 1523 and given the post of lord chamberlain three years later. (Because the play includes events both before and after the date of Sandys's ennoblement, and alters the chronological order of those events, Sandys appears inconsistently under both his knightly and baronial titles. Because Shakespeare also makes use of a quite anonymous lord chamberlain, there are several scenes in which both Sandys and the chamberlain appear when in fact the two were the same person.) *

The bluebloodedness of some of these lords was rather recent: the Howards' noble titles went back only to Richard III, and Henry VIII himself had created the peerages of Suffolk and Sandys. Although all these men had enjoyed knightly status before ennoblement, their snobbery about Wolsey strikes one as faintly ironic. But there was one peer of unquestionably exalted position: Edward Stafford duke of Buckingham, son to Richard III's Buckingham and direct descendant of Edward III's youngest son, Thomas of Woodstock.† Buckingham was a magnate in the old style, with lands across England and particularly extensive holdings in Wales. His relatives included most of the great: his mother had been Edward IV's sister-in-law, his wife was a Percy of Northumberland, and his sons-in-law were Surrey and Abergavenny. (Surrey, as Shakespeare accurately reports, was posted in Ireland at the time of his father-in-law's fall.) Open hatred lay between the powerful cardinal and this duke in whose veins flowed the old royal blood. Their antagonism is the chief cause of the downfall of Buckingham in the first two acts of *Henry VIII*. ✔ In the spring of 1521, Buckingham was suddenly arrested,

---

* The lesser courtiers of *Henry VIII*—Sir Nicholas Vaux, Sir Henry Guilford, Sir Anthony Denny, and Sir Thomas Lovell—are also historical persons. Denny, a lifelong favorite of the king, was bold enough in January 1547 to tell the dying king that it was time for him to think upon God.

† Shakespeare gets Buckingham's surname wrong, calling him Edward Bohun rather than Edward Stafford. Thomas of Woodstock's wife was Eleanor Bohun, and through her the dukes of Buckingham claimed to inherit the earldom of Hereford and the lord high constableship of England.

tried, and executed for treason. Following the Tudor historians, Shakespeare attributes his fate entirely to Wolsey's malevolence and chicanery. Wolsey certainly had a hand in the matter, but he was acting on Henry's orders. Otherwise Shakespeare's account is reasonably accurate. Buckingham was beheaded because he was a dynastic threat to the Tudors. According to evidence from his recently dismissed surveyor and the other servants, Buckingham had listened to the prophecy of a friar, one Nicholas Hopkins, that Henry would die without heirs and that Buckingham himself would thereupon become king. He had also supposedly plotted usurpation and announced his readiness to stab Henry. It is not at all clear that Buckingham was really so foolish as to do these things, but the evidence was accepted as sufficient to condemn him. His mere existence as a potential Plantagenet claimant to the throne was dangerous, especially since Henry had so far failed to beget a surviving legitimate son.

Henry VII had disposed of several of the Plantagenets who survived Bosworth. Henry VIII carried out the same policy with greater ruthlessness, judicially murdering the last descendants of the old royal house at various times throughout his reign. Buckingham was merely the most distinguished of those who suffered But killing off potential rivals was only a preventive move. Henry needed an heir.

A month after Henry had mounted the throne, he had married Katharine of Aragon, daughter to the great Ferdinand and Isabella. Katharine was a distinguished person, learned, energetic, upright, popular, noble in character as well as descent. (The warmth and majesty of this queen appears strongly enough in the speeches reported of her by Holinshed that in some passages Shakespeare merely versifies Holinshed's prose.) Unfortunately, after many years of wedlock and many pregnancies, she had produced only one child surviving infancy, the princess Mary. As few thought that a woman could rule England, Katharine had failed in her one essential duty. By the mid-1520s, she had also lost her husband's interest. Sometime around 1526, Henry fell in love with one of her ladies in waiting, Anne Bullen or Boleyn, a much younger, livelier, more beautiful woman. Anne has been much romanticized and much slandered over the past four centuries: it is difficult to ascertain her real character now. Shakespeare makes her charming and humble: remarkably, he allows us to like both Katharine and Anne, whereas many writers have felt compelled to defend one at the expense of the other. Charming she certainly must have been. Humble she was not: she contrived both to captivate Henry and to resist his desires until he could make her his lawful queen. Out of virtue, or out of ambition to take advantage of Katharine's failure, she managed to keep Henry out of her bed for at least six years.

Exactly when Henry met and fell in love with Anne we do not know. (Shakespeare places the episode at a banquet given by Wolsey, a banquet we know Anne did not attend.) By 1527 desire for her and the need for an heir had led Henry to seek dissolution of his marriage to Katharine. He did not announce his motives in this way, however. Rather he claimed that he was impelled by conscience to set his first wife aside. Upon an occasion in 1528 when a crowd cheered the popular Katharine, Henry publicly explained that he loved her dearly and would choose to live with her over all other women were it not sinful. (This statement deserves no more credit than any other set of pacifying remarks made by a politician to those hostile to his intentions. In the lofty world of Shakespeare's play, however, Henry's speech to this effect is evidently intended as truth.)

The supposed sinfulness of Henry's marriage lay in the fact that Katharine had been his brother's widow. In 1501, Henry VII had secured a diplomatic triumph by arranging the marriage of the princess of Spain to his eldest son Arthur. Five months later, Arthur died. Anxious to keep both the Spanish alliance and Katharine's dowry, Henry VII proposed that Katharine should marry his second son. A papal dispensation was necessary for this arrangement, since the affinity created between Katharine and the younger Henry by her first marriage constituted an impediment to lawful union. Pope Julius II duly granted the dispensation, although for a variety of political reasons the wedding did not take place until after Henry VII died. Henry VIII now argued that the union of a man with his brother's widow was wholly forbidden by the law of God, specifically by two passages in Leviticus, and therefore not subject to dispensation. The failure of the marriage to produce male heirs revealed a divine judgment upon it. How Henry happened upon this view of the matter is not certain. At one point he claimed that a French bishop, while negotiating for the hand of the princess Mary, asked about her legitimacy in view of the possible invalidity of her parents' marriage. (This story seems most unlikely. What ambassador would so defeat the purpose of his embassy?) Several Tudor historians report that John Longland, Henry's personal confessor and bishop of Lincoln, suggested the problem to Henry. Shakespeare combines these two accounts. Henry's latest biographer, J. J. Scarisbrick, believes that Henry himself thought of applying Leviticus to his situation. Henry was a considerable theologian in his own right: in 1521 he had written a book against Luther, for which service the pope had named him defender of the faith. Under pressure of the succession problem and moved by desire for Anne, Henry needed no one else to tell him of the possible utility of Leviticus.

Unfortunately, Henry did need the pope—now Clement VII—to grant the divorce. (Technically Henry sought a nullity, a declaration that the marriage was void from the beginning. Divorce, however, has always been the term used.) Two obstacles stood in the way. The first was theological. The Leviticus argument appeared to be undermined by a text in Deuteronomy that positively commands a man to marry his brother's widow if the brother has died childless, which was exactly Henry's case. The theological problem thus posed by Henry's divorce suit became an intellectual *cause célèbre* generating volumes of commentary from the learned of Europe, volumes in which Henry generally got the worst of the argument. The second obstacle was political. Clement was under the thumb of Charles V. As well as being the most powerful man in Europe, Charles was Katharine's nephew, and naturally had no wish to see his aunt thrust aside. Had the pope been independent, and benevolently inclined toward Henry, he might have acted favorably. Popes had granted stranger requests for such urgent political reasons as Henry could offer, although Clement might have jibbed at the implicit denial of his predecessor Julius's right to issue the original dispensation. As matters stood, however, the posture of European affairs could not have been less favorable to Henry's cause.

Henry was nonetheless determined. When determined, and when convinced of his own righteousness (a conviction he frequently arrived at), Henry was not to be gainsaid. Wolsey therefore set to work to obtain the divorce. He found the task unwelcome, not only because of the theological and political obstacles, but also because he did not favor Anne Boleyn, who personally disliked him and was related to his enemies, the Howards. Nonetheless, with Henry driving him on, Wolsey had no real choice. Katharine made the matter no easier for him, resisting the divorce with a steadfastness that demonstrated as much steel in her character as there was in her husband's. (Katharine seems to have believed that Wolsey was her enemy and the source of her troubles, and so Shakespeare represents her. Here the servant is taking the blame for the master.) In April 1528, Wolsey managed to wrest from Clement a commission to hold a formal trial in England upon the validity of the marriage. In issuing the commission, however, Clement insured himself against an outcome displeasing to the emperor: the commission was made out, not to Wolsey alone, but to Wolsey and another papal legate, Lorenzo Campeggio or Campeius, an Italian cardinal distinguished as a canon lawyer. Campeggio was instructed to delay the trial, empowered to adjourn it should it actually take place, and in general told to do anything he could to prevent Henry from carrying out his intentions. Accordingly, Campeggio occupied the rest of 1528 and the beginning of 1529 by discussing alternative solutions with the English. (He suggested, for example, that Katharine enter a convent, which she refused to do.) In summer 1529, when Campeggio could finally delay matters no longer, the court at last sat at the Blackfriars monastery in London. At this trial, which provides the material for the major scene of Shakespeare's second act, Katharine made an impassioned plea not to be dishonored and appealed the case to Rome. She then left the court, disregarding the crier's call to return. Henry made a less dignified impression, arguing violently with Katharine's counsel and endeavoring to prove by the gossip of elderly ladies in waiting that Katharine's first marriage had been consummated. (This point, which made a legal difference in the case, had been stoutly denied by Katharine.) Eventually the trial gained Henry nothing. Campeggio used his authority to adjourn the court before any decision was reached, and Clement revoked the case to Rome.

Like Katharine, Wolsey had failed his king in a crucial matter. Hence, like Katharine, Wolsey could go. It was easier to get rid of Wolsey. Surrounded by jealousies, he was sustained in his great post only by the king he served. Once the king ceased to support him, he fell headlong. In Shakespeare, Wolsey's fall results from an ironic episode directly reflecting his greed and ambition: he inadvertently includes in a packet of papers sent to the king an inventory of the wealth he has amassed in order to buy the next papal election. The substance of this anecdote Shakespeare found in Holinshed, where a bishop of Durham is reported to have undone himself by similar carelessness during the previous reign. In history, Henry brought charges against Wolsey based on the statutes of *praemunire*, fourteenth-century laws that forbade certain kinds of papal interference in English affairs. The choice of such a weapon indicates Henry's legal subtlety and hypocrisy. Wolsey, with his papal legateship, had been governing the English church despotically for more than a decade; only when Wolsey had failed him did Henry choose to notice the fact. Wolsey was obliged to confess his guilt, resign the chancellorship, and surrender his property. With unaccustomed mercy, Henry spared his life. Wolsey survived his fall, however, by only a year. Incurably ambitious, he kept in touch with Rome and other foreign courts, seeking a way to regain power. When evidence of these activities fell into the hands of his enemies, the aristocrats around Henry, his fate was sealed. He was arrested for treason in November 1530. Nearly sixty and ill, he died on the way to London for his trial. The deathbed at Leicester Abbey was widely reported, and his final remarks became the germ for the great speeches Shakespeare gives him in the scene of his fall.

3. THE ENGLISH REFORMATION

In Shakespeare, Wolsey falls even more rapidly than in history. In a single long scene, Wolsey enters believing himself wholly secure, is rejected by the king (1529), is accused of various crimes by the lords (these come from the treason charges of 1530), and then utters his final speeches to his secretary Thomas Cromwell. In the same scene, by an even more drastic compression, we are informed that the king has married Anne Boleyn (in Holinshed, November 1532; actually January 1533). The play then proceeds directly to Anne's coronation (June 1533). This dramatic reshaping of history omits the most crucial events of the English Reformation, the decisive actions that severed England from Rome.

Between the close of the Blackfriars trial in 1529 and early 1532, Henry tried a variety of devices to secure his divorce. Chiefly he brought hostile pressure upon Pope Clement, quite without success. At the suggestion of an obscure Cambridge don, Thomas Cranmer, Henry's agents solicited the views of the European universities on his marital problem. This tactic secured a number of learned opinions favorable to his cause, but also a number of adverse arguments. Clement paid no attention. Henry had more success in stifling opposition among his own clergy. He cowed them with threats of wholesale indictment of the entire English ecclesiastical establishment on charges of *praemunire,* mulcted them of large sums as a fine for their supposed offenses, and even induced them to declare him Supreme Head of the English church. The new title was meaningless, however, since it was accompanied by a qualification. The bishops were persuaded to approve the title only after Archbishop Warham of Canterbury had amended the wording: Henry was Supreme Head "as far as the law of Christ allows," a perfect escape-hatch clause since no one required the bishops to say how far that was. In any case, Henry's real difficulties lay, not with the English bishops who had sided with Katharine, but with Rome. No policy seemed to move Rome.

During this period, no one in the English government seemed to have the capacity really to grasp Henry's problem and find a way to solve it. The talents of Henry himself, although great, did not include intellectual originality. His chief councillors after Wolsey's fall—Norfolk, Suffolk, the earl of Wiltshire (Anne's father)—were much less accomplished men than Wolsey. Henry's only really distinguished minister during this period, the new lord chancellor Thomas More, accepted his post only under the condition that he have nothing to do with the divorce, to which he was opposed. According to the arguments of the eminent historian G. R. Elton, it was not until Henry recognized the talents of Thomas Cromwell that his cause began to prosper.

Cromwell was the son of a London tradesman, a soldier of fortune in his youth, and an agent of Wolsey's in the 1520s. He was appointed to the council in 1530, had gained the king's confidence by 1532, and for the rest of the decade was Henry's chief minister, holding the posts of principal secretary and lord privy seal. (Unlike most earlier chief ministers of the crown, he was neither a cleric nor an aristocrat, although he was eventually created earl of Essex in 1540.) Apparently it was Cromwell who saw the way to secure the divorce. Henry's difficulties really arose from Rome's jurisdiction over much of England. English ecclesiastics owed allegiance to Rome as well as to Henry. Ecclesiastical courts were responsible to Rome, and cases heard in them could be appealed to Rome. Since these courts sat on all matters touching the sacraments as well as all cases involving the clergy themselves, they penetrated deeply into ordinary life. Cromwell's solution was essentially simple: he used parliament to abolish Rome's jurisdiction in England.

In March 1532, the commons presented to the king a "Supplication against the Ordinaries," an attack on ecclesiastical legislation and the ecclesiastical courts. After some resistance, the bishops gave way. (At this point, Thomas More, unable to go along with this submission of the church to the king's authority, resigned his chancellorship.) Next, the act of annates was passed, a bill abolishing the large fees paid to the pope by bishops upon appointment to their sees. Finally, in March 1533, Cromwell got the decisive bill through parliament: the act of appeals, which prohibited litigants in cases concerning wills and marriages from appealing to Rome. Thus, two months later, with full legal justification as far as England was concerned, the new archbishop of Canterbury, Thomas Cranmer, could hold a trial on Henry's marriage and pronounce it void. Just in time, too. The previous fall, Anne Boleyn had finally yielded to Henry's desires. By January she was pregnant, and the king secretly married her at the end of the month. In June she was crowned queen in ceremonies of especial magnificence, and on 7 September the princess Elizabeth was born.

The whole story is fraught with irony. In search of a male heir, the defender of the faith defied the power that had bestowed that title upon him, destroyed the capable Wolsey and the regal Katharine (and was yet to destroy the witty and saintly More), only to produce another daughter. Daughters, in Henry's view, were useless (except as pawns in the international chess game of dynastic marriages) The joy that Shakespeare's Henry displays over Elizabeth, and the prophecy that Shakespeare's Cranmer utters of her greatness, are of course entirely unhistorical. Henry continued on his course. After Anne miscarried of her second pregnancy in 1536, Henry had her beheaded on a charge (probably trumped up) of adultery with five different men, one of them her own brother. Her execution, together with Katharine's death of cancer some months before, wiped the marital slate clean for him.* His third wife, Jane Seymour, finally gave him a son. She died in doing so, and the son, the future Edward VI, was a sickly lad who perished of tuberculosis at the age of fifteen. After Jane's death, Henry took to himself three more wives: Anne of Cleves, who proved so unattractive to him that he never consummated the union; Katharine Howard, who was beheaded on charges of adultery, this time certainly justified; and Katharine Parr, who proved a stable companion for him in his old age and managed to survive him.

Meanwhile, the English Reformation rolled on. The work of the parliamentary statutes of 1532–1533 described above was confirmed by six acts passed in 1534 that variously assigned to the king or the archbishop of Canterbury powers formerly exerted by the pope. These culminated in an act of supremacy that unconditionally declared the king to be Supreme Head on earth of the English church. (Perjured evidence that the resolutely silent More had denied the validity of this act brought him to the block.) It is crucial to recognize that the revolution effected by these acts was a political one, not a doctrinal one. The statutes altered jurisdiction—they did not deviate from Catholic orthodoxy on transubstantiation, faith and works, or other matters of belief.

---

* Shakespeare moves Katharine's death back in time, placing it before Anne's coronation. The visit to Katharine of Charles V's ambassador Capuchius (Eustace Chapuys) is historical. Her maid Patience is an invented character.

Many Englishmen were critical of clerical power without being in the least hostile to traditional dogma or ritual. They sought to destroy papal authority in England. (In so doing, they gave the king more power, both over their lives and over their purses, than the popes had ever dared to exert in England.) The all-important preamble to the act of appeals asserted that: "This realm of England is an empire . . . governed by one Supreme Head and King." The crucial word is "empire": as G. R. Elton observes, the term means, not a conglomeration of several countries (like the old Angevin empire of Henry II), but a wholly self-sufficient and self-governing state, a sovereign state owing no outside allegiance. No religious doctrine (save of course the authority of the pope) is here denied. England was schismatic but as yet not heretic. Even the abolition of the monasteries, which Cromwell carried out in 1535–1540 in spite of a major rebellion, was not really a doctrinal matter. The motives for destroying the monasteries were partly political (some owed allegiance only to their own orders), largely economic (they owned approximately a quarter of the land in England). Monasticism was no longer the flourishing medieval institution it had been, and there was much sentiment against monks, but the houses were destroyed, not in the name of new doctrine, but upon charges (often false) that they practiced the old doctrine corruptly.

At Henry's death, England was officially still Catholic in belief, although Henry himself, that old theologian, occasionally flirted with heretic notions. With England severed from Rome, however, and with a real doctrinal revolution proceeding on the continent under Luther, Calvin, Zwingli, and others, Protestant doctrine was bound to emerge in England. A growing tussle between conservatives and reformers marks Henry's last decade. It was, for example, a false charge of extreme heresy, together with the failure of the Cleves marriage, that toppled Cromwell in 1540. Two months after being made earl of Essex, Cromwell was attainted of treason, and a month later he was executed. (Cromwell's death falls outside the scope of Shakespeare's play, but Shakespeare has Wolsey half-prophesy the event in one of his great farewell speeches.) This struggle between conservatives and reformers provides the only episode in Shakespeare's play that really touches upon religious doctrine, Gardiner's attack on Cranmer.

Stephen Gardiner, bishop of Winchester after 1531, had been Wolsey's agent in Rome. Indeed, it was he who secured the papal commission authorizing the Blackfriars trial. He went along with the political Reformation, carrying Anne Boleyn's train at her coronation (as in the play) and writing a book supporting Henry's Supreme Headship with arguments that were to become standard. He remained firmly Catholic in doctrine, however. (Indeed, he seems to have played a double game, easily returning to the Roman obedience during the reign of the Catholic Queen Mary and serving as her chancellor.) He and the Howards led the conservatives late in Henry's reign. The gentle, scholarly Archbishop Cranmer, on the other hand, moved slowly toward Protestantism. Gardiner saw Cranmer as his enemy, and tried to bring him low with a charge of heresy in the 1540s. Henry, who considered Gardiner willful and troublesome, supported his archbishop, thus saving him for the great work he was to do in the next reign: the definition of the Anglican faith and the writing of the Book of Common Prayer. This one episode of doctrinal strife Shakespeare picks out of the 1540s and moves prior to the christening of Elizabeth. Thus he can cap the trial of Buckingham (in which his Henry is deceived), the trial of Katharine (in which he is honest, troubled, and conscience-driven), and the informal trial of Wolsey (in which he asserts his power over a scheming minister), with a trial of Cranmer in which Henry can providentially rescue his good and faithful servant from the wolves.

The English Reformation only started in Henry's reign. It was doctrinally carried out under his son Edward VI, reversed under his daughter Mary, and reestablished under his daughter Elizabeth. But the political break enacted in the statutes of the 1530s made it possible, giving the English king (in parliament) the authority to determine the course of England. Thus the reign of Henry VIII initiated the most profound changes in English life between the Norman Conquest and the Industrial Revolution. Although the accomplishments of the reign were the work of many people, although Cromwell in particular appears to have been the effective genius of the period, although Henry's own mind excelled not in invention but in quickness at absorbing and using other men's ideas, the whole reign bears testimony to the mightiness of this king. The majestic and intimidating figure in Holbein's portraits of Henry well depicts the man who, by his deeds and his drive, dominated his half-century of English history. Shakespeare clothes that figure in gorgeous majesty and omits or blurs Henry's more appalling acts. His Henry is the agent of a divine providence that is wholly benevolent. Luther, on the other hand, suggested a relationship between Henry and the deity that, in my opinion, more closely approximates the real king: "Junker Heintz," Luther remarked, "will be God, and does whatever he lusts."

appendix on names and titles

*You should study the Peerage, Gerald . . . it is
the best thing in fiction the English have ever done.*
—WILDE, *A Woman of No Importance*

The history of English noble titles is long and at times tortuous:
witness the busy activity from the Middle Ages to the present of
herald offices, genealogists, family historians, inquiring ama-
teurs, and just plain snobs. This appendix is intended primarily
for American students, who are sometimes puzzled by the array of
names borne by the persons in Shakespeare's history plays. Those
desiring fuller treatment may consult such works as J. Enoch
Powell and Keith Wallis, *The House of Lords in the Middle Ages*
(London, 1968), and *The Complete Peerage*, rev. ed. Vicary Gibbs,
13 volumes (London, 1910–1959).

The gradations of the nobility and the composition of the
house of lords were subject to variation, refinement, and development during the period covered by this book. Generally these exalted persons come in five ranks: in descending order, duke,
marquess, earl, viscount, baron. Their wives (and the occasional
women holding titles in their own right) are, respectively,
duchess, marchioness, countess, viscountess, and baroness. "No-

bles," "peers," and "lords" are collective terms referring to all of the above ranks. "Barons" may also be used as a collective term referring to the whole nobility as well as a specific term referring to the members of the lowest rank: a parallel term is "angels," which may generally refer to all the celestial beings waiting upon the throne of God (seraphim, cherubim, archangels, etc.) or may specifically designate the lowest of the nine ranks of the celestial hierarchy.

The term "magnate," frequently used in these pages, is not a specific title but a general class designation. It is simply the Latin *magnates,* great ones. It was a usual and convenient term to indicate, not only prominent secular lords, but also influential bishops and other men of great wealth and power.

Knighthood is a chivalric distinction, not a noble title. It was customarily bestowed upon a noble youth by the king or another great lord, usually in connection with military service. A commoner in the service of the king might also win a knighthood. Unless a knight happened to be a noble as well, he is known as *sir* (as with Sir Thomas Erpingham, long a servant of the Lancasters). The title does not raise him to the nobility, nor is it hereditary. It is today conferred as an honor upon persons of particular achievement in various fields. The term "baronet," meaning lesser baron, was only occasionally used in the Middle Ages and is not employed in this book. Early in the seventeenth century, during the reign of James I, baronets were formally instituted as a rank taking precedence over knights. Like knights, baronets are commoners whose given names are prefixed by *sir;* unlike knights, their titles are hereditary.

In the Middle Ages a particular man may become a peer in various ways. He may have been personally summoned, as Lord Soandso, to parliament, in which case he held a barony by writ; his dignity may have been specifically created by the king; or he may have inherited a barony by writ or a creation from his father. Inheritance usually required formal recognition. Generally honors were heritable by heirs male of the body. In the failure of male heirs, a daughter might carry to her husband the lands to which she was heiress, in which case the husband sometimes took her father's title "in right of his wife." Where there were several daughters, they were usually considered coheiresses. Dignities became extinct either through the failure of all heirs or through the parliamentary process of attainder consequent upon conviction for treason. Often, however, attainders were reversed after the lapse of time, so that the heir of a convicted and executed noble traitor might eventually regain the family title. Reversals of attainder were particularly frequent during the Wars of the Roses: a Lancastrian nobleman executed or killed in battle by victorious Yorkists might be attainted, and his son secure reversal of the attainder when the Lancastrians returned to power or when the Yorkists decided to be conciliatory.

Of the five ranks of the peerage, only earls and barons existed in England at the beginning of the fourteenth century. The titles of duke, marquess, and viscount were imported from France by the later Plantagenets themselves. The first English duke (other than the king himself, who was duke of the French province of Aquitaine) was the Black Prince, created duke of Cornwall by his father Edward III in 1337. This duchy was thereafter regularly granted, like the principality of Wales, to the heir apparent to the crown. Edward III subsequently granted ducal titles sparingly to other members of the royal family. He raised his cousin Henry earl of Lancaster to duke of Lancaster in 1351, and sustained the title after Henry's death by granting it to Henry's son-in-law (his own third son) John of Gaunt in 1362. He also gave the duchy of Clarence to his second son Lionel. The two younger surviving sons of Edward III had to wait until the reign of their nephew Richard II for their duchies, those of York and Gloucester respectively. But Richard II went farther: by a more lavish creation of dukes he brought the title into some disrepute. When he rewarded five of his friends, three of them only indirectly related to the royal house, with ducal titles for helping him to destroy the senior Lords Appellant in 1397, the honored men came to be contemptuously known as *duketti,* or dukelings. Henry IV and Henry V returned to the practice of restricting ducal titles to close royal relations. Henry VI, weak and extravagant like Richard II, once again spread the honor more widely.

Richard II also created the first English marquess, making his friend Robert de Vere marquess of Dublin. (De Vere was already hereditary earl of Oxford; by granting the new title, Richard gave him precedence over the other earls.) The unfortunate history of de Vere seems to have tainted the title of marquess, which was used only once again before the middle of the fifteenth century and even now remains the rarest of English titles. The title of viscount came into English use in 1440, during the reign of Henry VI. As its first two holders both held *comtés* in the English dominions in France, the title was evidently designed to give them a status in the English peerage superior to ordinary barons.

The geographical names associated with peerages (earl of Suchandsuch) were usually drawn from the names of counties (e.g. Norfolk) or important county towns (e.g. Cambridge). The first English earldom not so named was that of March, bestowed on Roger Mortimer in 1328. March is not a specific place but the general term for a border area: the Mortimers held extensive lands in Wales and western England, the so-called Welsh marches. Originally there was a correspondence between the name chosen for a peer and the place where his chief lands were located, but this becomes less reliable as English history proceeds. A lord may, by inheritance, marriage, purchase, or crown grants, acquire lands far from the original holding that gave rise to his title. The enormous patrimony of Lancaster, for example, came to include not only the county palatine of Lancaster but also properties in all but seven of the other English counties. Titles granted to members of the royal family are particularly likely to diverge from any geographical justification. When Edward earl of Rutland was made duke of Aumale by his first cousin Richard II, an ancient title was being revived: a sister of William the Conqueror had been called countess of Aumale or Albemarle, but the Norman town providing the title had long been taken back by the French. During our period the names Clarence and Gloucester were thrice used as ducal titles for the younger sons or younger brothers of kings: Lionel and Thomas the sons of Edward III, Thomas and Humphrey the brothers of Henry V, and George and Richard the brothers of Edward IV. The second Thomas was duke of Clarence despite the fact that the ancient honor of Clare was still in the hands of Lionel's descendants the earls of March, and Richard of Gloucester's chief lands and interests were in Yorkshire and other northern regions, not in the western county of Gloucestershire. Clarence and Gloucester had apparently come to be regarded simply as appropriate titles for royal dukes. The eccentricity of this arrangement occasionally misled foreign visitors to England: Dominic Mancini, for example, who wrote an account of Richard III's usurpation, naturally but mistakenly supposed that the duke of Gloucester lived in Gloucester.

Many lords and princes, as well as having Christian names and official titles, had added territorial names. Richard II was sometimes called Richard of Bordeaux, the great duke of Lancaster was John of Gaunt (an anglicized form of Ghent). These extra geographical names are not formal titles nor do they indicate possession of land: rather they are birthplaces, tacked on to the Christian names as a convenient way of identifying particular persons in families where the same Christian name was frequently repeated. Since medieval kings and lords were always on the move, going about from one castle to another, one battlefield to another, a whole family of brothers could easily be born at different places in England and France. Among the seven sons of Edward III, a birthplace is repeated only once: Edward the Black Prince and Thomas duke of Gloucester were both "of Woodstock." In some cases, notably with Thomas of Woodstock, John of Gaunt, and Henry of Bolingbroke, the chroniclers and playwrights have made these soubriquets the most well-known names of the persons concerned. I have not used these geographical nicknames, however, in cases where they are not well remembered. For the student who is already struggling hard to keep straight the ramifications of the Plantagenet dynasty, life would only become more burdensome were he told that the Richard earl of Cambridge who conspired against Henry V in 1415 was also sometimes called Richard of Conisburgh.

The name Plantagenet presents a particular oddity. Most writers, including Shakespeare, treat it as the surname of all the kings of England from Henry II to Richard III. It is indeed a convenient name by which to refer to all the branches of this family: the original Angevins Henry II, Richard I, and John; John's direct descendants Henry III, the first three Edwards, and Richard II; and the two houses of Lancaster and York. Although the succession was occasionally diverted to a brother or a cousin, all these kings were descended in the male line from Henry II; they should all have the same surname; and if Plantagenet is not that surname, they have none at all. But the application of this particular name to them is unhistorical and retrospective. Plantagenet was originally a nickname applied to Henry II's father, Geoffrey count of Anjou. It derived from an emblem he wore, a sprig (*planta*) of broom (*genesta,* a white or yellow-flowered shrub). The name was in fact not used by any of Geoffrey's descendants until about 1450. At that time Richard duke of York, desiring to emphasize his descent from the long line of English kings, started calling himself Richard Plantagenet, and the use was carried on by his sons. Thus only in the last three decades of their 330 years of rule over England did this remarkable family establish in popular awareness the name by which they would be known to history.

Genealogical Charts

1. The later Plantagenets (York and Mortimer lines).
2. The later Plantagenets (Lancaster and Beaufort lines).
3. The Tudors.
4. The earlier Plantagenets and the last Capetian kings of France.
4. The Nevilles.
5. The Mowbray and Howard dukes of Norfolk.

These charts are selective. They show the relationships of principal historical figures, omitting less significant spouses and offspring. The dates appearing under the names of monarchs are the dates of their reigns, not of their lives.

Symbols used:

        =   married
        d. died of natural causes
        †   murdered, executed, or died in battle
        da. daughter
        §   illegitimate descent

1. the later plantagenets [york and mortimer lines]

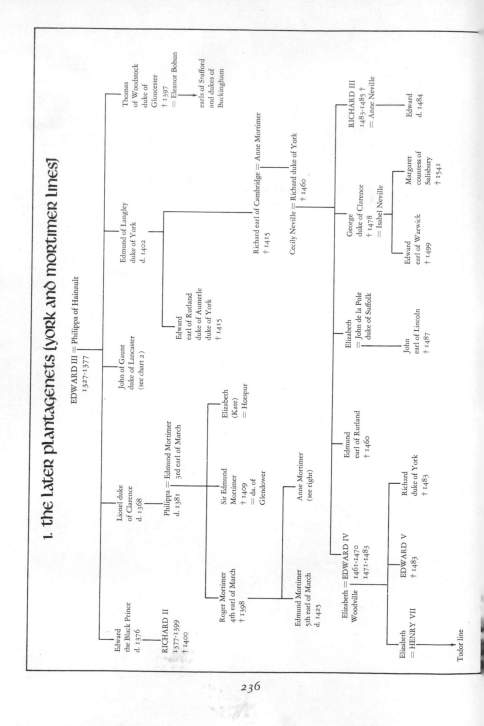

EDWARD III == Philippa of Hainault
1327-1377

Edward
the Black Prince
d. 1376

RICHARD II
1377-1399
† 1400

Lionel duke
of Clarence
d. 1368

Philippa == Edmund Mortimer
d. 1381   3rd earl of March

Roger Mortimer
4th earl of March
† 1398

Sir Edmund
Mortimer
† 1409
= da. of
Glendower

Elizabeth
(Kate)
= Hotspur

Anne Mortimer
(see right)

Edmund Mortimer
5th earl of March
d. 1425

John of Gaunt
duke of Lancaster
(see chart 2)

Edmund of Langley
duke of York
d. 1402

Edward
earl of Rutland
duke of Aumerle
duke of York
† 1415

Edmund
earl of Rutland
† 1460

Richard earl of Cambridge == Anne Mortimer
† 1415

Cecily Neville == Richard duke of York
† 1460

Elizabeth == EDWARD IV
Woodville   1461-1470
            1471-1483

EDWARD V
† 1483

Richard
duke of York
† 1483

Thomas
of Woodstock
duke of
Gloucester
† 1397
= Eleanor Bohun

→ earls of Stafford
and dukes of
Buckingham

RICHARD III
1483-1485 †
= Anne Neville

Edward
d. 1484

George
duke of Clarence
† 1478
= Isabel Neville

Edward
earl of Warwick
† 1499

Margaret
countess of
Salisbury
† 1541

Elizabeth
= John de la Pole
duke of Suffolk

John
earl of Lincoln
† 1487

Elizabeth
= HENRY VII

Tudor line

236

2. the later plantagenets [lancaster and beaufort lines]

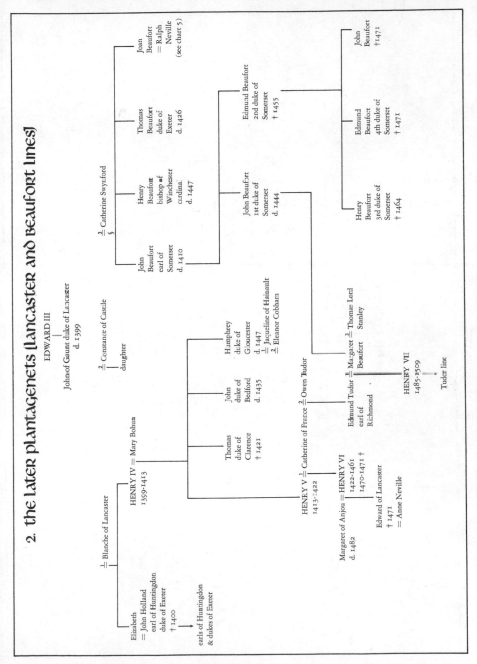

EDWARD III
|
John of Gaunt duke of Lancaster
d. 1399

$\underline{1}$ Blanche of Lancaster

$\underline{2}$ Constance of Castile
|
daughter

$\underline{3}$ Catherine Swynford
§

Elizabeth
= John Holland
earl of Huntingdon
duke of Exeter
† 1400

earls of Huntingdon
& dukes of Exeter

HENRY IV = Mary Bohun
1399-1413

Thomas
duke of
Clarence
† 1421

John
duke of
Bedford
d. 1435

Humphrey
duke of
Gloucester
d. 1447
$\underline{1}$ Jacqueline of Hainault
$\underline{2}$ Eleanor Cobham

John
Beaufort
earl of
Somerset
d. 1410

Henry
Beaufort
bishop of
Winchester
cardinal
d. 1447

Thomas
Beaufort
duke of
Exeter
d. 1426

Joan
Beaufort
= Ralph
Neville
(see chart 5)

HENRY V $\underline{1}$ Catherine of France $\underline{2}$ Owen Tudor
1413-1422

Edmund Tudor $\underline{1}$ Margaret $\underline{3}$ Thomas Lord
earl of   Beaufort   Stanley
Richmond

HENRY VII
1485-1509

Tudor line

Margaret of Anjou = HENRY VI
d. 1482   1422-1461
1470-1471 †

Edward of Lancaster
† 1471
= Anne Neville

John Beaufort
1st duke of
Somerset
d. 1444

Edmund Beaufort
2nd duke of
Somerset
† 1455

Henry
Beaufort
3rd duke of
Somerset
† 1464

Edmund
Beaufort
4th duke of
Somerset
† 1471

John
Beaufort
† 1471

237

3. the tudors

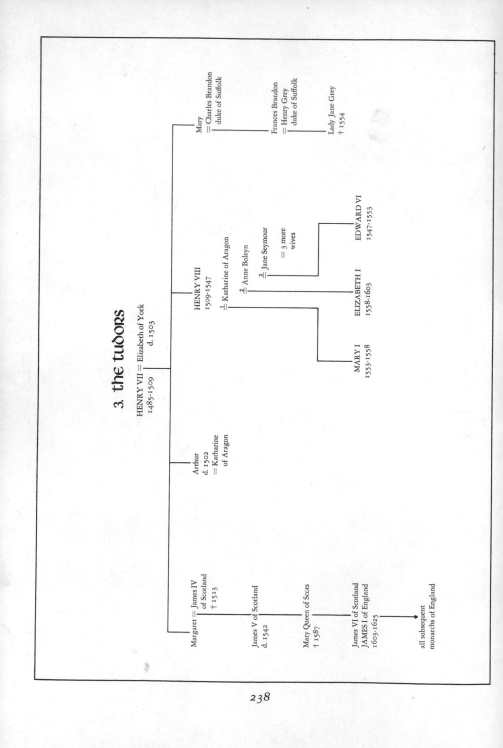

HENRY VII = Elizabeth of York
1485-1509   d. 1503

Arthur
d. 1502
= Katharine
of Aragon

HENRY VIII
1509-1547

$\frac{1}{=}$ Katharine of Aragon

$\frac{2}{=}$ Anne Boleyn

$\frac{3}{=}$ Jane Seymour
= 3 more
wives

MARY I
1553-1558

ELIZABETH I
1558-1603

EDWARD VI
1547-1553

Margaret = James IV
of Scotland
† 1513

James V of Scotland
d. 1542

Mary Queen of Scots
† 1587

James VI of Scotland
JAMES I of England
1603-1625

→ all subsequent
monarchs of England

Mary
= Charles Brandon
duke of Suffolk

Frances Brandon
= Henry Grey
duke of Suffolk

Lady Jane Grey
† 1554

238

4. the earlier plantagenets and the last capetian kings of france

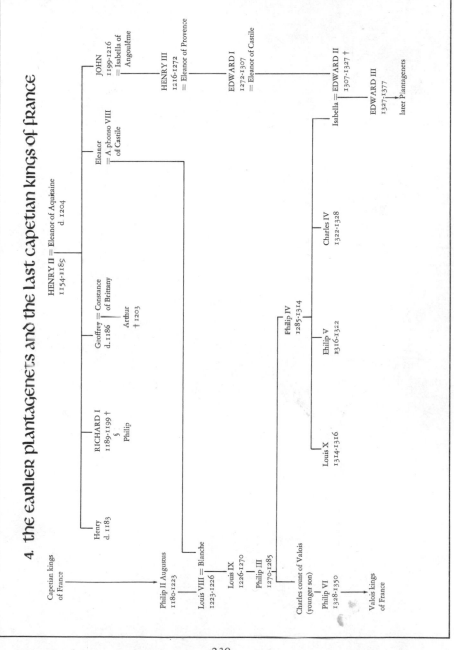

Capetian kings
of France
→

HENRY II = Eleanor of Aquitaine
1154-1185   d. 1204

Henry
d. 1183

RICHARD I
1189-1199 †
§
Philip

Geoffrey = Constance
d. 1186 | of Brittany

Arthur
† 1203

Eleanor
= Alphonso VIII
of Castile

JOHN
1199-1216
= Isabella of
Angoulême

HENRY III
1216-1272
= Eleanor of Provence

EDWARD I
1272-1307
= Eleanor of Castile

Isabella = **EDWARD II**
1307-1327 †

EDWARD III
1327-1377
→ later Plantagenets

Philip II Augustus
1180-1223

Louis VIII = Blanche
1223-1226

Louis IX
1226-1270

Philip III
1270-1285

Charles count of Valois
(younger son)

Philip VI
1328-1350
→ Valois kings
of France

Philip IV
1285-1314

Louis X
1314-1316

Philip V
1316-1322

Charles IV
1322-1328

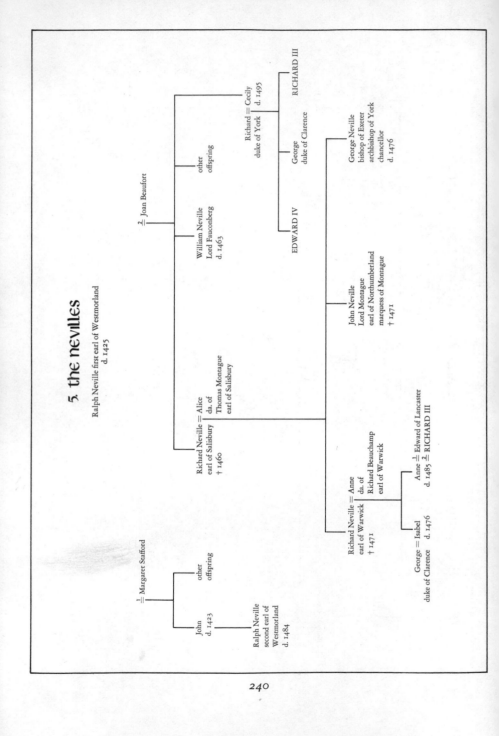

5. the nevilles

Ralph Neville first earl of Westmorland
d. 1425

=¹ Margaret Stafford

John
d. 1423

other
offspring

Ralph Neville
second earl of
Westmorland
d. 1484

=² Joan Beaufort

Richard Neville = Alice
earl of Salisbury   da. of
† 1460   Thomas Montague
earl of Salisbury

William Neville
Lord Fauconberg
d. 1463

other
offspring

Richard = Cecily
duke of York   d. 1495

RICHARD III

EDWARD IV   George
duke of Clarence

Richard Neville = Anne
earl of Warwick   da. of
† 1471   Richard Beauchamp
earl of Warwick

John Neville
Lord Montague
earl of Northumberland
marquess of Montague
† 1471

George Neville
bishop of Exeter
archbishop of York
chancellor
d. 1476

George = Isabel   d. 1476
duke of Clarence

Anne =¹ Edward of Lancaster
d. 1485 =² RICHARD III

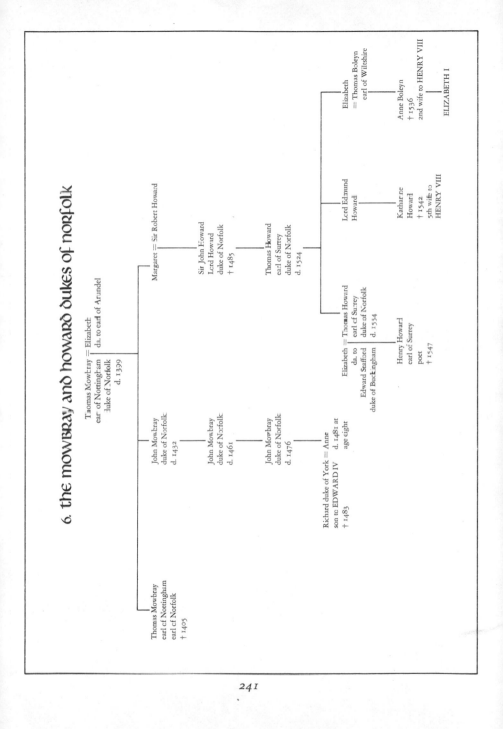

6. the mowbray and howard dukes of norfolk

Thomas Mowbray = Elizabeth
earl of Nottingham   da. to earl of Arundel
duke of Norfolk
d. 1399

Thomas Mowbray
earl of Nottingham
earl of Norfolk
† 1405

Margaret = Sir Robert Howard

John Mowbray
duke of Norfolk
d. 1432

John Mowbray
duke of Norfolk
d. 1461

Sir John Howard
Lord Howard
duke of Norfolk
† 1485

John Mowbray
duke of Norfolk
d. 1476

Thomas Howard
earl of Surrey
duke of Norfolk
d. 1524

Richard duke of York = Anne
son to EDWARD IV   d. 1481 at
† 1483   age eight

Elizabeth = Thomas Howard
da. to   earl of Surrey
Edward Stafford duke of Norfolk
duke of Buckingham d. 1554

Lord Edmund
Howard

Elizabeth
= Thomas Boleyn
earl of Wiltshire

Henry Howard
earl of Surrey
poet
† 1547

Katharine
Howard
† 1542
5th wife to
HENRY VIII

Anne Boleyn
† 1536
2nd wife to HENRY VIII

ELIZABETH I

241

chronological chart

Note: The dates at which Shakespeare composed his history plays, as given at the end of this chart, are the product of scrappy evidence and inference, and are subject to scholarly dispute.

1066–1087	Reign of William the Conqueror.
1087–1100	Reign of William II.
1100–1135	Reign of Henry I.
1135–1154	Reign of Stephen (contested by Empress Matilda).
1152	Henry FitzEmpress count of Anjou marries Eleanor of Aquitaine.
1154	Henry of Anjou becomes Henry II, first Plantagenot king of England.
1180	Louis VII of France dies. Philip II Augustus becomes king.
1186	Death of Geoffrey, son to Henry II, father of Arthur.
1189	Death of Henry II, accession of Richard I Coeur-de-Lion.
1189–1192	Third Crusade.
1199	Death of Richard I, accession of John.
1200	Blanche of Castile marries the dauphin Louis.
1203	Death of Arthur.
1204	Death of Eleanor of Aquitaine; Normandy lost to Philip Augustus.

1208	Innocent III places England under interdict.
1213	John reconciled with Innocent.
1215	Magna Carta.
1216	John dies in middle of civil war.
1216–1272	Reign of Henry III.
1272–1307	Reign of Edward I.
1307–1327	Reign of Edward II, ending in Edward's deposition and murder.
1327	Accession of Edward III.
1337	Start of the Hundred Years War.
1340	Edward III proclaims himelf king of France.
1346	Edward III's victory at Crécy.
1356	Edward the Black Prince's victory at Poitiers.
1360	Treaty of Brétigny.
1376	Death of the Black Prince.
1377	Death of Edward III, accession of Richard II.
1381	Peasants' Revolt.
1387–1388	Lords Appellant destroy Richard's favorites.
1394	Richard in Ireland.
1397	Death of Thomas of Woodstock.
1398	Quarrel between Norfolk and Bolingbroke.
1399	Death of John of Gaunt; deposition of Richard; Bolingbroke becomes Henry IV.
1400	Earls' rebellion, death of Richard.
1403	Battle of Shrewsbury.
1405	Rebellion of Archbishop Scrope.
1408	End of the Percy and Glendower opposition to Henry IV.
1413	Death of Henry IV, accession of Henry V.
1415	Cambridge plot; Henry victorious at Harfleur and Agincourt.
1417	Start of Henry's Norman campaign.
1419	Fall of Rouen; murder of John the Fearless.
1420	Treaty of Troyes; Henry marries Catherine of France.

1422	Death of Henry V and Charles VI; Henry VI inherits England and France.
1424	English victory at Verneuil.
1429	Joan of Arc raises siege of Orléans; coronation of Charles VII.
1431	Joan burnt.
1435	Congress of Arras; death of Bedford; defection of Burgundy.
1444	Truce of Tours.
1445	Henry VI marries Margaret of Anjou.
1447	Deaths of Gloucester and Cardinal Beaufort.
1449–1450	French retake Normandy.
1450	Fall and death of Suffolk; Cade's rebellion.
1453	Death of Talbot near Bordeaux (end of Hundred Years War). Henry VI mad.
1455	Yorkist victory at St. Albans.
1459	Lancastrian victory at Ludlow.
1460	Yorkist victory at Northampton; Richard duke of York claims the crown; defeat and death of York at Wakefield.
1461	Yorkist victory at Mortimer's Cross; Margaret marches south and defeats Warwick at St. Albans; Edward IV proclaimed king and defeats Lancastrians at Towton.
1464	Edward IV marries Elizabeth Woodville.
1469	Warwick briefly captures Edward.
1470	Warwick invades from France; Edward flees; Henry VI restored.
1471	Edward IV defeats Warwick at Barnet and Margaret at Tewkesbury. Death of Henry VI.
1478	Execution of Clarence.
1483	Death of Edward IV; Richard III usurps after brief reign of Edward V. Buckingham's revolt fails.
1485	Plantagenet line ends with death of Richard III at Bosworth. Henry VII becomes first Tudor king.

1501	Henry's son Arthur marries Katharine of Aragon.
1502	Death of Arthur.
1509	Death of Henry VII; accession of Henry VIII; Henry marries Katharine.
1516	Birth of princess Mary.
1520	Field of the Cloth of Gold.
1521	Execution of Buckingham.
1527	Henry begins divorce proceedings.
1529	Blackfriars trial; fall of Wolsey.
1532–1533	First Reformation statutes passed.
1533	Anne Boleyn marries Henry, is crowned, and bears Elizabeth.
1537	Birth of prince Edward.
1540	Fall of Cromwell.
1547	Death of Henry VIII.
1547–1553	Reign of Edward VI.
1553–1558	Reign of Mary I.
1558	Accession of Elizabeth I.
1564	Birth of Shakespeare.
1590–1593	*1, 2, and 3 Henry VI, Richard III.*
1594–1595	*King John.*
1595	*Richard II.*
1596–1598	*1 and 2 Henry IV.*
1599	*Henry V.*
1603	Death of Elizabeth; accession of James I, first Stuart king of England.
1613	*Henry VIII.*
1616	Death of Shakespeare.

BIBLIOGRAPHY

The following list is meant not only to provide interested students with suggestions for further reading, but also to constitute acknowledgment of the books and articles I have used. Works to which I am particularly beholden, including all that I have actually quoted from in the text, are starred. Asterisks, I know, express very inadequately my indebtedness to the achievements of scholars such as Chrimes, Elton, Lander, McFarlane, Perroy, Scarisbrick, Storey, the compilers of *The Complete Peerage*, and the authors of the Oxford History of England. I have supplemented the asterisks with occasional annotation.

The list consists almost exclusively of historical rather than literary scholarship. Since my purpose has been to narrate history rather than to interpret drama, I have not swelled this bibliography by including commentaries devoted to the history plays, many of which naturally touch upon the alterations wrought by Shakespeare on his sources. Students seeking criticism of the plays should consult the easily accessible bibliography of Ronald Berman, *A Reader's Guide to Shakespeare's Plays,* revised edition (Glenview, Ill., 1973). Readers interested in general discussion of the complex relationships between historical fact and history plays should consult Herbert Lindenberger's thoughtful new book, *Historical Drama: The Relation of Literature and Reality* (Chicago, 1975).

For books, the place of publication is London unless otherwise indicated. For articles, the following abbreviations have been used for journal titles:

BIHR	*Bulletin of the Institute of Historical Research*
BJRL	*Bulletin of the John Rylands Library*
EHR	*English Historical Review*
TRHS	*Transactions of the Royal Historical Society*

A. PRIMARY HISTORICAL AND LITERARY SOURCES

*Bullough, Geoffrey. *Narrative and Dramatic Sources of Shakespeare.* Vols. III & IV. 1960–62. The standard work reprinting generous selections from the sources and analogues of Shakespeare's plays, with long analytical essays discussing Shakespeare's handling of the sources. Volumes III and IV cover the ten history plays.

English Historical Documents. A series of thirteen volumes reprinting "a wide selection of the fundamental sources of English history." Gen. ed. David C. Douglas.

Vol. III, 1189–1327. Ed. Harry Rothwell. 1975.

Vol. IV, 1327–1485. Ed. A. R. Myers. 1969.

Vol. V, 1485–1558. Ed. C. H. Williams. 1967.

*Hall, Edward. *The Union of the Two Noble and Illustre Families of Lancaster and York.* 1550. Rpt. Menston, Eng.: Scolar Press, 1970.

*Holinshed, Raphael, *et al. Chronicles of England, Scotland, and Ireland.* 2nd ed., 1587. Ed H. Ellis in 6 vols., 1807–1808.

*Mancini, Dominic. *The Usurpation of Richard III.* Tr. and Ed. C. A. J. Armstrong. 2nd ed. Oxford, 1969.

*More, Thomas, *The History of King Richard III.* Ed. Richard S. Sylvester. New Haven, 1963. Vol. II of *The Yale Edition of the Complete Works of St. Thomas More.*

*Shakespeare, William. The New Arden Edition of the Works of William Shakespeare. Gen. eds. H. F. Brooks and Harold Jenkins.

Richard II, ed. Peter Ure, 1956.

1 Henry IV, ed. A. R. Humphreys, 1960.

2 Henry IV, ed. A. R. Humphreys, 1966.

Henry V, ed. J. H. Walter, 1954.
1 Henry VI, ed. A. S. Cairncross, 1962.
2 Henry VI, ed. A. S. Cairncross, 1957.
3 Henry VI, ed. A. S. Cairncross, 1964.
King John, ed. E. A. J. Honigmann, 1954.
Henry VIII, ed. R. A. Foakes, 1957.
(The New Arden *Richard III* has not yet been published.)
The introductions and annotations in the New Arden Shakespeare
contain, among other things, much useful historical information. The
notes of Cairncross on the Henry VI plays are especially valuable. I
have also consulted other editions of Shakespeare, particularly the
New Cambridge Shakespeare (gen. ed. John Dover Wilson) and the
Riverside Shakespeare (notes on history plays by Herschel Baker).
Vergil, Polydore. *Anglicae Historiae Libri Vigintiseptem*. Basel, 1555.
Rpt. Menston, Eng.: Scolar Press, 1972.
Vergil, Polydore. *The Anglia Historia of Polydore Vergil*. Tr. and ed.
Denys Hays. Royal Historical Society, 1950. Camden Series, vol. 74.

B. GENERAL HISTORICAL WORKS

Anselme, Père. *Histoire de la Maison Royale de France*. Paris, 1726–1733.
9 vols. Rep. 1967.
Bean, J. M. W. *The Decline of English Feudalism, 1215–1540* Manches-
ter and New York, 1968.
Chrimes, S. B. *Constitutional Ideas in the Fifteenth Century*. Cambridge,
1936.
*Chrimes, S. B. *Lancastrians, Yorkists, and Henry VII*. 1964. The best
brief account of English political history in the fifteenth century.
Does not touch upon Shakespeare's version of events.
*Chrimes, S. B., C. D. Ross, and R. A. Griffiths. *Fifteenth-century En-
gland. 1399–1509: Studies in Politics and Society*. Manchester and New
York, 1972. Useful essays by Ross on Edward IV, Chrimes on Henry
VII, A. L. Brown on Henry IV, R. L. Storey on the north, and Griffiths on Wales. The essay by B. F. Wolffe, "The Personal Rule of
Henry VI," interestingly challenges the conventional view that Henry
did little ruling.
The Complete Peerage. Ed. G. E. C., rev. ed. Vicary Gibbs *et al*.
1910–1959. 13 vols. Exhaustive, documented compilation of information on all holders of noble titles.

Dictionary of National Biography. Ed. Leslie Stephen. 1885–1900. 63 vols. with supplements.

Dictionnaire de Biographie Française. Ed. J. Balteau, M. Barroux, M. Prevost, Roman D'Amat, *et al.* Paris, 1933– . 13 vols. to date.

Dunham, W. H., Jr., and Charles T. Wood. "The Right to Rule in England: Depositions and the Kingdom's Authority, 1327–1485." *American Historical Review,* 81 (1976), 738–61.

French, G. R. *Shakespeareana Genealogica.* 1869. Information on Shakespeare's historical characters. Largely superseded by W. H. Thomson.

Furber, E. C. *Changing Views on British History: Essays on Historical Writing since 1939.* Cambridge, Mass., 1966.

Green, V. H. H. *The Later Plantagenets: A Survey of English History between 1307 and 1485.* 1955. Contains many useful genealogical tables.

Holmes, G. A. *The Estates of the Higher Nobility in Fourteenth Century England.* Cambridge, Eng., 1957.

Holmes, George. *The Later Middle Ages, 1272–1485.* 1962.

*Keen, M. H. *England in the Later Middle Ages.* 1973. A recent and excellent textbook survey of English political history from 1290 to 1485, with useful bibliography.

Kingsford, C. L. *Prejudice and Promise in Fifteenth Century England.* Oxford, 1925. Notable for the ardent defense of William de la Pole duke of Suffolk.

*Lander, J. R. *Conflict and Stability in Fifteenth Century England.* 1969. An overview of the century by a scholar who has done much specialized work (see section F).

Lander, J. R. *The War of the Roses.* New York, 1966. An account told largely through extracts from contemporary chronicles.

Lyon, Bryce. *A Constitutional and Legal History of Medieval England.* New York, 1960.

McFarlane, K. B. *The Nobility of Later Medieval England.* Oxford, 1973. Originally delivered as lectures in the 1950s, these essays contain some of the best work available on the position, activities, and interests of the aristocracy.

Myers, A. R. *England in the Late Middle Ages.* 8th ed. Baltimore, 1971. Vol. 4 of the Pelican *History of England.*

The Oxford History of England. Oxford.
A. L. Poole, *From Domesday Book to Magna Carta, 1087–1216.* 1951. 2nd ed. 1955.
May McKisack, *The Fourteenth Century, 1307–1399.* 1959.

E. F. Jacob, *The Fifteenth Century, 1399–1485*. 1961. Corr. ed. 1969.

J. D. Mackie, *The Earlier Tudors, 1485–1558*. 1952.

Petit-Dutaillis, Ch. *The Feudal Monarchy in France and England from the Tenth to the Thirteenth Century*. Tr. E. D. Hunt. 1936.

Powell, J. Enoch and Keith Wallis. *The House of Lords in the Middle Ages*. 1968.

*Powicke, F. M. and E. B. Fryde, eds. *Handbook of British Chronology*. 2nd ed. 1961.

Ramsay, James H. *The Angevin Empire*. 1903.

Ramsay, James H. *The Genesis of Lancaster*. Oxford, 1913. 2 vols.

Ramsay, James H. *Lancaster and York*. Oxford, 1892. 2 vols.

*Thomson, W. H. *Shakespeare's Characters: A Historical Dictionary*. Altrincham, 1951. A helpful dictionary of all historical persons appearing or mentioned in the ten history plays and *Macbeth*. Unfortunately, Thomson mentions few of his sources, and his occasional errors have led others (e.g., J. H. Walter in the New Arden *Henry V*) astray.

Vale, M. G. A. *English Gascony, 1399–1453*. 1970.

Vickers, Kenneth H. *England in the Later Middle Ages*. 7th ed. 1950.

Wilkinson, Bertie. *Constitutional History of England in the Fifteenth Century*. 1964.

C. KING JOHN

Butterfield, Sir Herbert. "Magna Carta in the Historiography of the Sixteenth and Seventeenth Centuries." The Stenton Lecture. University of Reading, 1969.

Cheney, C. R. "King John and the Papal Interdict." *BJRL*, 31 (1948), 295–317.

Cheney, C. R. "King John's Reaction to the Interdict in England." *TRHS*, 4th ser., 31 (1949), 129–50.

Davis, H. W. C. *England under the Normans and Angevins, 1066–1272*. 3rd ed. New York, 1912.

Holt, J. C. *Magna Carta*. Cambridge, Eng., 1965.

*Painter, Sidney. *The Reign of King John*. Baltimore, 1949. A detailed discussion of the political problems of the reign rather than a biography of the king.

Painter, Sidney, William Marshal. Baltimore, 1933.
Richardson, H. G. "The Marriage and Coronation of Isabelle of Angoulême." EHR, 61 (1946), 287–314. Response by Fred A. Cazel, Jr., and Sidney Painter in EHR, 63 (1948), 83–89; riposte by Richardson, EHR, 65 (1950), 360–71.
Warren, W. L. Henry II. Berkeley and Los Angeles, 1973. A magisterial biography of the first Plantagenet king and a thorough study of his reign.
Warren, W. L. King John. New York, 1961. The best recent biography of John, but not on the scale of Warren's Henry II.

D. RICHARD II

Armitage-Smith, Sydney. John of Gaunt. Westminster, 1904.
*Aston, Margaret. "Richard II and the Wars of the Roses," in The Reign of Richard II: Essays in Honor of May McKisack, ed. F. R. H. DuBoulay and C. M. Barron. 1971. A significant revaluation of Richard's position in late medieval history.
*Barron, Caroline M. "The Tyranny of Richard II." BIHR, 41 (1968), 1–18.
Clarke, M. V. Fourteenth Century Studies. Ed. L. S. Sutherland and M. McKisack. Oxford, 1937.
Edwards, J. G. "The Parliamentary Committee of 1398." EHR, 40 (1925), 321–33.
Goodman, Antony. The Loyal Conspiracy: The Lords Appellant under Richard II. Coral Gables, Fla., 1971.
Hutchison, H. F. The Hollow Crown: A Life of Richard II. New York, 1961.
Jones, R. H. The Royal Policy of Richard II: Absolutism in the Later Middle Ages. Oxford, 1968.
Lapsley, Gaillard. "The Parliamentary Title of Henry IV." EHR, 49 (1934), 423–49, 577–606.
Lapsley, Gaillard. "Richard II's 'Last Parliament.' " EHR, 53 (1938), 53–78.
Mathew, Gervase. The Court of Richard II. 1968.
*Steel, Anthony. Richard II. Cambridge, Eng., 1941. An influential and controversial biography of the king, suggesting that he was mad in his final years.
Tuck, Anthony. Richard II and the English Nobility. New York, 1974.

E. THE LANCASTRIAN KINGS AND THE 100 YEARS WAR
(Henry IV, Henry V, and foreign affairs under Henry VI)

*Bean, J. M. W. "Henry IV and the Percies." *History*, 44 (1959), 212–27. Valuable analysis of the Percy revolts and their causes.

Bennett, H. S. *Six Medieval Men and Women*. Cambridge, Eng., 1955. Essays on Humphrey duke of Gloucester, Sir John Fastolfe, and others.

*Burne, Alfred H. *The Agincourt War*. 1956. The standard military history of the latter part of the Hundred Years War (1369–1453).

Chrimes, S. B. "The Pretensions of the Duke of Gloucester in 1422." *EHR*, 45 (1930), 101–3.

D'Avout, Jacques. *La Querelle des Armagnacs et des Bourguignons*. 4th ed. Dijon, 1943.

Dickinson, J. G. *The Congress of Arras, 1435*. Oxford, 1955.

Fowler, Kenneth, ed. *The Hundred Years War*. 1971. Essays by various hands.

*Harriss, G. L. "Cardinal Beaufort—Patriot or Usurer?" *TRHS*, 5th ser., 20 (1970), 129–48.

Hutchison, H. F. *King Henry V*. New York, 1967.

Jacob, E. F. *Archbishop Henry Chichele*. 1967.

Jacob, E. F. *Henry V and the Invasion of France*. 1947. A good brief account of the reign, stressing the war.

Kirby, J. L. *Henry IV of England*. 1970. The latest biography of the king.

McFarlane, K. B. "Henry V, Bishop Beaufort, and the Red Hat." *EHR*, 60 (1945), 316–48.

*McFarlane, K. B. *Lancastrian Kings and Lollard Knights*. Oxford, 1972. Essays on Henry IV (his career before the usurpation, the usurpation, his government) and Henry V.

McKenna, J. W. "Henry VI of England and the Dual Monarchy: Aspects of Royal Political Propaganda, 1422–1432." *Journal of the Warburg and Courtauld Institutes*, 28 (1965), 145–62. A fascinating specialized study in political iconography.

*Perroy, Edouard. *The Hundred Years War*. Tr. W. B. Wells. New York, 1961. (Original French version published in 1945.) A good standard history of the war.

Vickers, Kenneth H. *Humphrey Duke of Gloucester*. 1907.

Williams, E. Carleton. *My Lord of Bedford, 1389–1435*. 1963. Biography of John of Lancaster duke of Bedford.

Wylie, J. H. *History of England under Henry IV*. 4 vols. 1884–1898.

Wylie, J. H. and W. T. Waugh. *The Reign of Henry V*. 3 vols. Cambridge, Eng., 1914–1929.

F. THE WARS OF THE ROSES AND THE YORKIST KINGS
(Domestic affairs under Henry VI, and the reigns of Edward IV and Richard III)

Armstrong, C. A. J. "The Inauguration Ceremonies of the Yorkist Kings and their Title to the Throne." *TRHS*, 4th ser., 30 (1948), 51–73.

*Armstrong, C. A. J. "Politics and the Battle of St. Albans, 1455." *BIHR*, 33 (1960), 1–72. A richly detailed account of the first battle of the Wars of the Roses and the events immediately leading to it.

Bellamy, J. G. "Justice under the Yorkists Kings." *American Journal of Legal History*, 9 (1965), 135–55.

Griffiths, Ralph A. "Local Rivalries and National Politics: The Percies, the Nevilles, and the Duke of Exeter, 1452–1455." *Speculum*, 43 (1968), 589–632.

Griffiths, Ralph A. "The Trial of Eleanor Cobham: An Episode in the Fall of Duke Humphrey of Gloucester." *BJRL*, 51 (1968–1969), 381–99.

*Hanham, Alison. *Richard III and his Early Historians, 1483–1535*. Oxford, 1975.

Hanham, Alison. "Richard III, Lord Hastings, and the Historians." *EHR*, 87 (1972), 233–48.

*Kendall, P. M. *Richard III*. New York, 1956. The most recent full biography of the king. The extensive and useful detail provided by this book, however, is unfortunately mingled with much novelistic speculation about people's feelings and motives, speculation asserted as fact. The forthcoming biography by Charles Ross is expected to supersede Kendall.

Lander, J. R. "Attainder and Forfeiture, 1453 to 1509." *The Historical Journal*, 4 (1961), 119–51.

Lander, J. R. "Edward IV: The Modern Legend and a Revision." *History*, 41 (1956), 38–52.

Bibliography

Lander, J. R. "Henry VI and the Duke of York's Second Protectorate, 1455 to 1456." *BJRL*, 43 (1960-1961), 46–69.

Lander, J. R. "The Hundred Years War and Edward IV's 1475 Campaign in France," in *Tudor Men and Institutions: Studies in Low and Government*, ed. Arthur J. Slavin. Baton Rouge, La., 1972.

*Lander, J. R. "Marriage and Politics in the Fifteenth Century: The Nevilles and the Wydevilles." *BIHR*, 36 (1963), 119–52.

*Lander, J. R. "The Treason and Death of the Duke of Clarence: A Reinterpretation." *Canadian Journal of History*, 2 (1967), 1-28.

Lander, J. R. "The Yorkist Council and Administration, 1461 to 1485." *EHR*, 73 (1958), 27–46. Lander's articles form an excellent series of specialized studies.

*Levine, Mortimer. "Richard III—Usurper or Lawful King?" *Speculum*, 34 (1959), 391–401. A careful examination of the "precontract" story, disputing the conclusions of P. M. Kendall and arguing that Richard was indeed a usurper.

*McFarlane, K. B. "The Wars of the Roses." *Proceedings of the British Academy*, 50 (1964), 87–119. Examination of the causes of the wars, which McFarlane places in the inability of the lords to "rescue the kingdom from the consequences of Henry VI's inanity by any other means."

Myers, A. R. "The Character of Richard III." *History Today*. 4 (1954), 511–21. With subsequent correspondence by Audrey Williamson, J. M. Wigram, and Myers on pp. 706–10.

Myers, A. R. "Richard III and the Historical Tradition." In *The Tudors*, ed. Joel Hurstfield. New York, 1973.

*Ross, Charles. *Edward IV*. Berkeley and Los Angeles, 1974. The new standard biography of the king.

Scofield, C. L. *The Life and Reign of Edward IV*. 2 vols. 1923. Although partly superseded by Ross, Scofield has much useful detail, especially on Edward's foreign diplomacy.

*Storey, R. L. *The End of the House of Lancaster*. New York, 1967. The best discussion to date of the events leadings to the Wars of the Roses, especially those of 1450–1455.

Thomson, J. A. F. "Richard III and Lord Hastings—A Problematical Case Reviewed." *BIHR*, 48 (1975), 22–30.

Virgoe, R. "The Composition of the King's Council, 1437–1461." *BIHR*, 43 (1970), 134–60.

Virgoe, R. "The Death of William de la Pole Duke of Suffolk." *BJRL*, 47 (1964–1965), 489–502.

Wolffe, B. P. "When and Why Did Hastings Lose his Head?" *EHR*, 89 (1974), 835–44.
*Wood, Charles T. "The Deposition of Edward V." *Traditio*, 31 (1975), 247–86. A careful reconstruction of the events from April to July 1483, and a discussion of the constitutional significance of Richard III's claim to his nephew's throne.

G. THE TUDORS

*Chrimes, S. B. *Henry VII*. Berkeley and Los Angeles, 1972. The new standard biography of the king.
*Elton, G. R. *England under the Tudors*. 1955. An excellent textbook survey of the Tudor century.
Elton, G. R. "Henry VIII." In *The Tudors*, ed. Joel Hurstfield. New York, 1973.
Elton, G. R. *Reform and Renewal: Thomas Cromwell and the Common Weal*. Cambridge, Eng., 1973.
*Elton, G. R. *Studies in Tudor and Stuart Politics and Government*. 2 vols. Cambridge, Eng.,1974. A collection of the papers and reviews of one of the leading historians of the period, including useful essays on Henry VII, Henry VIII, Wolsey, More, and Cromwell.
Levine, Mortimer. "The Fall of Edward, Duke of Buckingham," in *Tudor Men and Institutions: Studies in Law and Government*, ed. Arthur J. Slavin. Baton Rouge, La., 1972.
Levine, Mortimer, *Tudor Dynastic Problems, 1460–1571*. 1973.
Mathew, David. *The Courtiers of Henry VIII*. 1970.
Mattingly, Garrett, *Catherine of Aragon*. Boston, 1941.
Morris, Christopher. *The Tudors*. 1955. A revaluating essay on each of the Tudor monarchs.
*Scarisbrick, J. J. *Henry VIII*. Berkeley and Los Angeles, 1968. A magnificent book superseding previous biographies of the king. Contains an especially fine chapter on the legal issues entailed in Henry's quest for a divorce.
Smith, L. B. *Henry VIII: The Mask of Royalty*. Boston, 1971. Not a chronological biography but a portrait of Henry in a series of interrelated essays. The chapter, "The Conscience of a King," offers a striking discussion of the way in which Henry may have convinced

himself of his own righteousness in seeking to divorce his first wife.

Storey, R. L. *The Reign of Henry VII.* New York, 1968.

Tucker, Melvin J. *The Life of Thomas Howard Earl of Surrey and Second Duke of Norfolk, 1443–1524.* The Hague, 1964.

index of persons

This index is intended to facilitate reference to persons mentioned in the text. Accordingly, it lists all historical figures, Shakespearean characters, and early chroniclers named in Chapters I–IX and in the Appendix. Modern scholars are not included, as they are fully listed in the Bibliography. In a work of this sort, an index entry for Shakespeare himself would be ridiculously long, and pointless.

Royal persons are entered under their Christian names or their ducal titles. Nobles outside the royal house appear under their family surnames. Since many persons have several names and titles, any one of which may be uppermost in the reader's mind, I have provided cross-references and tried to include all the relevant titles in the main entry.

Persons appearing as characters in Shakespeare's plays, whether or not they are also historical figures, are indicated by the parenthetical inclusion of abbreviated play-titles. Persons who are merely mentioned in Shakespeare's dialogue without appearing on stage are not so marked. Thus, Hotspur is parenthetically marked as appearing in *Richard II* and *1 Henry IV*, but not (despite allusions to him there) in *2 Henry IV*. I have used the following standard abbreviations:

Jn	*King John*	*1 H6*	*1 Henry VI*
R2	*Richard II*	*2H6*	*2 Henry VI*
1 H4	*1 Henry IV*	*3 H6*	*3 Henry VI*
2H4	*2 Henry IV*	*R3*	*Richard III*
H5	*Henry V*	*H8*	*Henry VIII*

The titles king, queen, prince, duke, marquess, earl, viscount, bishop, and archbishop are abbreviated to their initial letters (thus, p. of Wales, a. of Canterbury). A number following the letter G at the end of an entry indicates that the person in question appears on the Genealogical Chart so numbered.